# Challenging
# Newt Gingrich

## *Chapter*
## *by Chapter*

*An In-Depth Analysis of America's Options
at its Economic, Political, and Military
Crossroads*

**PART I:** *A Chapter-by-Chapter, Section-by-Section
Critique of Gingrich's Book, "To Renew America"*

**PART II:** *Economic and Political Structures Which
Would Assure "Justice for All," Local to Global*

Alfred F. Andersen

Published by Tom Paine Institute
Eugene, Oregon

CHALLENGING NEWT GINGRICH, CHAPTER BY CHAPTER. Copyright ©
1996 by Alfred F. Andersen. All rights reserved.

Printed and bound in the United States of America. Regarding reproduction or
transmission, the author asks only that care be taken to represent accurately and in
fairness the author's views as conveyed, in context, within the following pages.

For information of all kinds, address Tom Paine Institute, 467 River Rd., Eugene,
OR 97404-3210.

FIRST EDITION

---

Library of Congress Cataloging-in-Publication Data

Andersen, Alfred F., 1919-
    Challenging Newt Gingrich, chapter by chapter: an in-depth analysis of
America's options at its economic, political, and military crossroads ... /
Alfred F. Andersen.
        p.   cm.
    Part I: a chapter-by-chapter, section-by-section critique of Gingrich's
book, "*To Renew America*." Part II: Economic and political structures which
would assure "justice for all" local to global.
    Includes biographical references and index.
    ISBN 0-931803-05-5 (alk. paper)
    1. United States—Politics and government.  2. United States—Economic
policy.  3. United States—Social policy.  4. Constitutional History  5. Gingrich,
Newt.  To renew America.  I.  Title.
JK424.A54  1996
973.929—dc20                          95-51201
                                          CIP

# Acknowledgments

In thinking of those to whom I am indebted for contributions to the contents of this book my mind keeps moving back in time over about three quarters of a century. Surely, my parents must be mentioned — my father especially for his example in moral integrity and his many fatherly lessons; and my mother especially for selfless love and purity of soul. My teachers, formal and informal, who showed faith in me, from first grade through those on my PhD committee, cannot be left out. William Ernest Hocking, my mentor in philosophy, was central in my adult intellectual development, and especially in inspiring my commitment to truth and intellectual integrity generally.

Those precious five years our young family spent in that very special place called Yellow Springs, Ohio, stand out in my mind. Indeed, a dear friend of a half century, then Mimi Stroop and now Mildred Luschinsky, whom I met there and who has edited and inspired my writings since then — including this work — remains a reminder of the many who in that small town influenced my life during my formative, young-adult years. Nor can I neglect to mention the hundreds of kindred spirits in and around the cooperative community my children grew up in and still return to with affection — Tanguy Homesteads, near Westtown, Pennsylvania — and in that other special small town, Ukiah, California, in which Dorothy and I still have many precious friends.

The hundreds and thousands of kindred spirits who have influenced my life for the better during my half-century affiliation with the Religious Society of Friends (Quakers) move across the stage in my mind as a write. My first wife of thirty-five years, Connie Manende Andersen, and the three "children," now with children of their own, we helped bring into this earthly life — Dick Andersen, Janet McBeen, and Laurie Brook — have surely incalculably enriched and inspired the life which made this book possible.

And surely, also, it is understandable that the person to whom I have been most deeply committed for almost two decades now, Dorothy Norvell Andersen, and whose support and inspiration has been "the miracle of my life" since we met, is the person in this world to whom I feel most deeply indebted, and who has most inspired and contributed to the contents of this volume.

* * * * * * *

Appreciation is also hereby extended to the authors and publishers of the following books, from which excerpts have been quoted in keeping with "fair use" practices. In the order of their employment, they are as follows:

*The Uses of the University,* by Clark Kerr, Harper and Row, New York, 1963. *Land in America, Its Value, Use and Control,* by Paul M. Wolf, Pantheon Books, New York, 1981. *The Power of the People,* edited by Robert Cooney and Helen Michalowski, New Society Publishers, Philadelphia, 1987. *The Tyranny of the Majority,* by Lani Guinier, The Free Press, New York, 1994. *The Making of A Counterculture,* by Theodore Roszak, Anchor Books, New York, 1969. *A People's History of the United States,* by Howard Zinn, Harpers & Row, New York, 1980. *On the medieval Origins of the Modern State,* by Joseph P. Strayer, Princeton University Press, 1970. *The Power Game; How Washington Works,* by Hedrick Smith, Random House, 1988. *Main Currents in American Thought,* by Vernon Louis Parrington, Harcourt, Brace, and World, 1927 & 1958. *The Encyclopedia of the American Constitution,* edited by Leonard Levy, Macmillan Co., New York, 1986. *Papers of the Continental Congress,* National Archives, Washington, DC, 1971. *An Economic Interpretation of the Constitution,* by Charles Beard, The Macmillan Co., 1913 & 1935. *Records of the Federal Constitution of 1787,* edited by Max Ferrard, Yale U. Press, New Haven, 1911. *Pennsylvania and the Federal Constitution,* by Bach McMaster and Frederick Stone, Historical Society of Pennsylvania, 1970. *The Federalist Papers,* by Alexander Hamilton, James Madison, and John Jay, vol. 43 of *Great Books of the Western World,* Encyclopaedia Britannica Inc., Chicago, 1952. *The Writings of John Quincy Adams,* edited by W. C. Ford, Greenwood Press, Westport, CT, 1917 & 1968. *The Writings of Thomas Paine,* edited by Moncure D. Conway, AMS Press, New York, 1967. *Liberating the Early American Dream,* by Alfred F. Andersen, Transaction Books, Rutgers University, 1985. *The Politics of Nonviolent Action,* by Gene Sharp, Porter Sargent, Boston, 1973. *The Directory of Intentional Communities,* published by The Fellowship for Intentional Communities, Rt. 1, Box 151-C, Rutledge, MO. *The Small Community,* by Arthur E. Morgan, Community Service Inc., Yellow Springs, OH, 1942 & 1984. *The Uses of the University,* by Clark Kerr, Harper & Row, New York, 1963. Physics and Philosophy, by Werner Heisenberg, Harper & Row, NY, 1958. *Statistical Abstracts,* compiled by the U.S. Department of Commerce, 1995. The Work of Nations, by Robert Reich, Random House, NY, 1991. *Census of Governments,* U.S. Chamber of Commerce, 1992.

Finally, to those many persons who have influenced my life and this work, both mentioned and not mentioned, I hereby extend not only acknowledgment but sincere thanks. And to each one I invite your comments and criticisms, in order that my next effort at addressing this world's injustices may be more effectively presented and the goal of "justice for all" more surely achieved.

# Contents

# *Preface*

## P-1: *Why Am I Writing This Book?*

I agree with Newt Gingrich[1] that America is in crisis. Indeed, after reading his book I am more persuaded than ever — but not, I hasten to add, because I agree with his description of it, or with his proposed "solution." Rather, I hope to show that the ominous agenda which he sets forth in the twenty-nine chapters of that book would feed the actual crisis we face rather than address it.

But even more ominous is the realization that this isn't merely the agenda of one more would-be intellectual. This is the agenda of a person who has so mastered the political nuances of the written and unwritten[2] U.S. Constitution that we now find ourselves, our lives, and the lives of our loved ones in danger of having that agenda implemented before our eyes!

Yes, I am implying that our problem is deeper than Newt Gingrich. Our problem goes to the very structure of the U.S. Constitution itself. We shall see (Chapters XI, XII, and XIII) that it was designed to encourage power brokers like Gingrich. So we need not be surprised that someone as clever as Gingrich has prepared himself, since a teenager, to take full advantage of the power-seeking opportunities inherent in this most empowering of all political documents.

Nor has Gingrich been the first to seize such opportunities. We will see that Alexander Hamilton, as Washington's Treasury Secretary, lost no time in doing just that as soon as he took office. And the practice has continued up to the present day. We need only survey in our minds some of the power

---

1. *To Renew America*, by Newt Gingrich, Harper Collins, pub., 1995
2. See *America's Unwritten Constitution*, by Don K. Price, Louisiana State University Press, Baton Rouge, 1983, 202 pp

brokers who have traversed the U.S. political stage during the latter part of this century, all under the protection of the U.S. Constitution.

Consider those who presently are offering themselves as candidates for the world's most powerful office. Are they offering a plan for helping to make this a more humane and equitable world, a world in which its residents feel good about each other because they can count on being treated by others with simple fairness and human compassion? Are they even offering a plan for reducing poverty and economic injustice in America?

The answers I must give are in the negative. What we mostly see are men who are able to raise the millions of dollars needed to put themselves "in the running" in *the* biggest power-seeking game in the world. And what they are appealing to isn't "justice for all" in this troubled world, but voter self-interest and "America's self-interests."

But we will get to the constitutional issues in Part II of this volume after we have become sufficiently alarmed by the agenda of perhaps the most skillful constitutional craftsman of our day. Newt Gingrich and his agenda "to renew America" is our immediate problem. That is, he is a problem for those of us who are committed to strive for a *truly just* world order, rather than one in which the most aggressive and acquisitive are constantly urged to achieve #1 status of some kind — whether in the world, or in one's own country, city, town, social group, or family. He is a problem for those of us who are committed to see what simple *fairness* can do in today's complex world of confused, justifiably anxious, suspicious, and, above all, politically manipulated inhabitants.

In the short run, there is a sense in which Newt Gingrich is a virtual personification of the crisis we face. As we explore the intricacies of his manipulative thinking, chapter by chapter, we get a *feeling* for the Constitutional bias upon which he draws for his power. And because of America's economic and military power-position in today's world, and especially because of the way Gingrich would have us build that power to the point of dominating all life on earth, no individual or group anywhere on this earth is beyond the reach of that constitutional bias.

Turning, then to Gingrich and his 29 chapters, I agree with him that "we will create a better future and renew America only if enough people decide

there is a problem, and go on to decide that we can do something about it."
I agree that it's *crucial* that we decide that this is so.

Why so crucial? Because, otherwise, evasion and denial is too easy. The
word, "crisis" will not one day appear on each of our foreheads. The evidence for it, though clear some days, will be all but drowned out by
distractions on other days. But, if we *decide*, and especially if we *commit* to
some action from which we cannot pull out, then the drowning out cannot
be complete on *any* day.

Gingrich doesn't make as big a thing of it — of deciding and committing,
that is — as I do. But he does make the point. And knowing how pro-
crastinating, comfort-seeking, channel-switching, and easily distracted we
TV-watching, Mall-addicted, Information-Age Americans are, he's right,
isn't he? He's right thus far. Let's admit it. We admit it, Newt. We admit
that you are right thus far. America is at a crossroads. America is in crisis.
And we must *decide* to do something about it.

I'm grateful for Gingrich's book, because it makes the job of showing
what really is America's crisis, and what must be done about it, very much
easier. That's why I'm using a critique of it as a kind of launching pad for
my own analysis of the crisis.

Still another way Gingrich has made our task easier is by setting forth
his agenda for America with such forthrightness, even courage. He has
indeed set before us a challenge. In this *To Renew America* book of his, he
doesn't pussyfoot around. He puts himself on record, just as in his Contract
with America. I give him credit for that. He's put his analysis, his proposed
agenda for America, and himself as a person front and center.

To be sure, there is a degree of hedging in at least one chapter. And his
final chapter backs off on bringing into a single focus the disparate, energetic lunges which comprise the preceding twenty-eight chapters. But, on the
whole, no hedging. On the whole, he has put something substantive and
challenging out there for all to see. And that makes it incalculably easier to
address his challenge with the same amount of courage and forthrightness
that he himself has displayed. It makes it easier for me to call arrogant what
I feel to be so, to charge "confusion" when he displays it, and to express
*outrage* that nowhere in his entire book does he include in his evidence for

"crisis" the mounting economic and other *injustices* in America and the world.

In fact, that last point suggests the main reason, Newt Gingrich, I can go along with you just so far. You enticed me into reading your book. I have said I agree with you that America really is in crisis, and that it's important for us to decide and commit. But now that I've read just how you would have us "renew America," my rational self, my intellectual integrity, my sense of justice, my conscience, my very American soul calls a halt! In a resounding chorus they cry out in concert:

> *Hold it Newt. What you are calling "the solution" is really the problem. In your excitement you've jumped on the wrong bandwagon. The one you're on is heading deeper into the crisis, not out of it!*

So, while acknowledging that America (indeed, the whole world) really is in a serious crisis, I profoundly disagree with Gingrich about what *constitutes* the crisis, and what's to be done about it. Nor has it been very difficult to demonstrate wherein our differences lie. In page after page and chapter after chapter of *To Renew America,* his conception of the crisis shows its selective bias and its narrowness of focus. In chapter after chapter he sets the stage for my being able to direct my reader's attention to the actual crisis and to what might be done about it.

What I'm suggesting is that Gingrich may have helped to get us out of the true crisis in ways none of us could have predicted. Not only has he helped us to think in terms of crisis, not only has he encouraged us to decide and commit, but the energy with which he has sprung into action *in the wrong direction* has also added so much to the *actual* crisis, that it has been much easier for me to point to it.

*All I had to do, all anyone has to do, is to point out a few of the most devastating implications of the proposals set forth in the pages and chapters of Gingrich's book. This is because the crisis we actually face consists largely of the values and proposals he there sets forth and of the amazing political power he has mounted — again, in the wrong direction — to further their implementation. All in all, that adds up to a daunting crisis!*

Therefore, though he hasn't written *crisis* on our foreheads, it's written into almost every page and every chapter of his book for all to see. Again, all I had to do was to point this out as, time and time again, he attempts to make his patron saint, corporate America, the knight in shining armor who, he says, will "Renew America" by again making us #1 in the world, as we were at the end of World War II — #1 militarily and #1 economically, with each part of the resulting military-industrial complex feeding the other, and with corporate America funding the joint operation.

The truth is, as I hope to show, that the practical result of implementing Gingrich's proposals would be not only to fail to remedy the existing scope and level of injustices among us, but to spread and deepen them. The resulting winners would benefit far more than they do now and the victimized losers would suffer far more. The continued encouragement of bald-faced economic and military aggressiveness and acquisitiveness which his agenda entails would widen still more the gap — financially and other-wise — between the beneficiaries of the present economic and political *systems* and their human cast-asides. Indeed, I hope to persuade readers that the moral outrage which already exists in the land among the marginalized would mount to such a crescendo that only a major salvaging effort would prevent the resulting rioting from spreading into a second American civil war, a war which would then likely spread worldwide.

The logic behind this prediction is simple. In a *system* in which the rules of the game permit unfairness, whether in sports, business, or politics, those who are willing to be unfair have an advantage over those who aren't. In an economic, political, or social *system* which rewards aggressive and acquisi-tive maneuvers designed to win over and dominate others, survival instincts tend to make all but the most morally courageous and sacrificing do what-ever is necessary (to use one of Gingrich's favorite phrases) "in order to compete."

Thus, in a political-economic *system* which, as at present, permits multi-national corporations to subcontract to or trade with exploiters of child labor or violators of the human rights of workers in any of countless ways, those who are willing to stoop to this disreputable level are the ones who "compete." They are the ones who tend to survive and to dominate. This is what is happening in today's global marketplace, and this is what would happen still more if we were to adopt the Gingrich proposal "to renew America."

Nor would the resulting tragedy be limited to the territory over which the government of the United States claims sovereignty. Given the role of the U.S. government in today's global civilization, given its military might, the increasingly "global reach" of its multinational corporations and conglomerates, this widening gap between winners and losers would continue to extend throughout the world, and not only for us humans but for all of this earth's sentient beings. Gingrich calls himself "an Eisenhower Republican," but he shows no concern for the undue influence of the military-industrial complex that former President Eisenhower warned us of in his farewell address.[3]

Again, I do not limit myself to pointing out the ways in which his proposals would mislead us. Nor is my only offering an alternative conception of the nature of America's crisis. I also suggest a way to meet that *actual* crisis using the pages and chapters of his book as a springboard and launching pad. The actual launching takes place in the last three chapters, in which I suggest how a commitment to "justice for all" would renew America in ways of which we can truly be proud. In the balance of this Preface I will give a peek here and there into the contents of those three chapters. I will do so just enough to indicate the moral, ethical, and rational standards on which they are based, because these are the same standards on which my critique of Gingrich's proposals is based.

## P-2: *An Alternative to Both Gingrich and Clinton Agendas*

A major problem with Gingrich's agenda is that despite his advocacy of extreme forms of competition in the economic realm it seems that he would want to greatly restrict competition in the marketplace of ideas. A large part of his agenda to renew America includes a return to what is not unfair to

---

3. In his final radio and television address to the American people, January 17th, 1961 Eisenhower said the following: "This conjunction of an immense military establishment and a large arms industry is new in the American experience. We must guard against the acquisition of unwarranted influence, whether sought or unsought, by the military-industrial complex. The potential for the disastrous rise of misplaced power exists and will persist."

describe as brainwashing the young. They are to be taught American history in the old fashioned way, presumably complete with the myth about George Washington's "I cannot tell a lie." It is as if Gingrich pictures our "Founding Fathers" (especially George Washington) as moral giants only slightly below the angels. In the pages to follow we shall see how much of this myth can stand up to the light of American history as it really happened.

It is true that Gingrich advocates giving youth a great deal of freedom (I would say too much) to pursue skills in computers, technology generally, in mathematics and the sciences, and in literacy *in these fields* — because these skills are called for by corporate America in its competition with corporate Japan, corporate Germany, etc. But in the political arena they are to be taught "what it means to be an American." This is to include certain myths about American history, and about America as some kind of God's chosen people destined to be the #1 world leader economically, politically, militarily, and culturally. Indeed, it amounts to advocating the establishment of a kind of global American empire!

What is suggested here, in contrast to the Gingrich agenda, is that in the area of politics and political theory we should encourage younger generations to turn to their own consciences for guidance — and to do so in the light of the most complete *and most honest* historical picture we can offer them. Let us have faith that thereby they will help us to perfect an American system of considerable, but not absolute, moral merit into one which truly does reward the fair-minded and thereby truly does promote "liberty and justice for all" rather than, as now, one which primarily promotes and rewards the most aggressive and acquisitive among us.

Thus, in the following pages major departures from what Gingrich advocates will take the form of radically different economic and political structures. In the area of economic structure, those who are concerned about the deterioration of family and community life, or about poverty and homelessness, generally tend to look for ways to generate more *jobs*; or, what is presumed better, higher paying jobs "in high-tech."

*Such efforts are important, but in this volume it will become increasingly clear that the problem of increasing poverty within 80% of the population, while those in the upper 20% move from rich to super-rich at an unprecedented rate, will not be solved until we turn our attention to what constitutes a just distribution of income from capital as distinct from labor.*

One can argue, as Robert Reich does,[4] that the only cure for poverty and the many social ills that spring from it is more jobs at higher pay. But he and his fellow advocates seem to be fighting a losing battle with downsizing and with the practice of exporting jobs to countries offering labor which is not unfairly described as "dirt cheap."

This is why Reich, a genuinely compassionate man, is in agreement with Gingrich, at least to the extent of pushing hard for American workers to become ever more skilled in high-tech through a form of "lifelong learning" which promotes math, science, and the technology built on it.

This is why, in order to replace those jobs lost, Reich and the Clinton administration are also working with corporate America toward making the United States the major supplier of high-tech, and technological skills generally, in the mushrooming global marketplace. Only high-tech can generate a substantial number of high-paying jobs, and only among the wealthy elite in other countries is there a sufficient market for its most exotic products. It is called "technology transfer." It is the method whereby the wealthy elite in other countries pay corporate America for both their high-tech consumer products and for the wherewithal to develop a near-monopoly of production facilities in their countries much as corporate American has done in America.

Corporate America hopes to maintain a dependency, however. In some countries they may. In others it will likely slip away from them, as it did some time ago in regard to Japan. Thus, as we uncover the moral flaws in the Gingrich agenda we remember that the Clinton-Reich agenda is significantly different only in the amount of safety-net the latter would provide. What I offer here is an alternative to both.

## P-3: *Income from Capital Goes to Its Owners*

With every step higher up the high-tech ladder (in order to generate more high-tech "jobs") the *major* beneficiaries are the *owners of the production*

---

4. Reich, Robert. *The Work of Nations*, Vintage Books. NY. 1992

*facilities* to which the labor-saving high-tech is inevitably applied. They are the ones who then will save ever more on labor costs, because each advance in high-tech permits still more down-sizing. Co-beneficiaries are the owners of the land upon which factories and infrastructures are built. Co-beneficiaries, also, are the owners of the land's oil and other energy resources.

Those who are legal owners of these various facilities and resources, to which even the most high-tech must be applied if it is to produce anything, don't have to worry about developing their high-tech skills through lifelong learning. Whether what they own is land in urban centers (often more valuable than the buildings upon it); oil wells in Texas or Arabia; factories in Detroit; railroads with surrounding lands once deeded them by the U.S. Government; airlines with their thousands of planes; newspapers; radio and TV stations; entertainment complexes; or patents on certain kinds of computer software, they are free to go vacationing in the Bahamas. There they can live on the income from, in effect, renting out these facilities and the natural resources on which they stand and from which they are built.

To be sure, those who put their own labor into what they own add to their income as owners per se. But it is not necessary for them to do so. Income from all forms of capital, whether in material form (of land or factory), or in the form of invested money, accrues to its owners without those owners having to do anything more than let their brokers know where to send the money.

And the more technological an economy becomes the greater is the portion of its income coming from capital and the less from human labor. Visualize the case where all production of goods and services in this country is completely automated, using the latest in high-tech. There would then be no income from labor except for personal services, and this primarily to the owners of the automated facilities. And that is precisely the direction in which we are headed.

The more technological capital goods become, the more income they generate for their owners. And the farther we go in this labor-saving direction, *under the present economic-political structure,*[5] the more those who

---

5. Under the alternative system I am suggesting in Chapter XIII, everyone will benefit from labor-saving equipment, because each such advance will increase

must get all their income from labor will be competing with each other for fewer and fewer "jobs," and thus pushing lower and lower the wages offered for the jobs which remain. This method of replacing jobs lost to high-tech by going even more high-tech will eventually result in either serious environmental breakdown or a further deterioration of individual, family, and community sanity — or, what is most likely, all of this at once.

In the next Section we shall see how applying the principle of "justice for all" solves this high-tech dilemma beautifully.

## P-4: *Distinguishing Two Kinds of Income-Producing Capital*

If we really want to solve the poverty and social deterioration problem now becoming an epidemic all over the world, we must shift our attention from job-creation as such to considering the fairness or unfairness of the distribution of income from *capital* in its various forms. The first step in doing so is to recognize that there exist in all the economies of the world two quite distinct kinds of capital:

(A) that productive capital which will be called *our common heritage capital,* and

(B) that capital which someone generates over and beyond this most basic of all capital, while standing on its shoulders.

Included in our common heritage capital, obviously, is all the earth's land and its resources. The injustice of having this basic natural capital monopolized by those who were strong enough to simply seize it, or by those who simply inherited it from those who seized it, is most obvious in agrarian economies. But the same injustice exists in the most technological economies, *because these are also based on the natural capital of land and its resources.* The most complex automated machinery is fabricated out of, and energized by, materials mined from the land. In industrialized societies, the most aggressive have distracted the rest of the population from insisting on a fair share of the benefits of this common heritage by offering "jobs" working for those who have seized it or inherited it. *That's why, if we would have a truly just economic system, we must give our primary atten-*

---

the amount of the fair share each receives from income generated by our common heritage (See Section P-4 to follow).

*tion to income from capital, especially nature's basic capital, and only secondarily to income from jobs.*

Clearly, then, all the land of the earth, and its resources, must be included in our common heritage. What is not so obvious (and which was overlooked in an earlier book of mine[6]) is that a large part of modern technology is also rightly included in our common heritage. My undergraduate education was in mathematics and science, and this has gradually made me aware of how much of modern high-tech is dependent on the centuries-long technical foundation painstakingly laid down for us by previous generations. Its most obvious manifestation is in the form of urban infrastructure.

But any practitioner of modern high-tech must constantly draw on the basic mathematics and scientific principles upon which our entire high-tech superstructure is built — from the Hindu-Arabic system of simple numbers to basic formulas like $f = ma$ in physics, to $q = ir$ in electricity, to $e = mc^2$ in modern physics. Without these and countless other building blocks from our common heritage of capital in technology we would be far less technologically advanced than we are today.

Therefore, with advance in technology the main determiner of economic superiority in today's world, it is absolutely essential that we identify that part of such technology which is rightly considered our common heritage of capital. Having done so, governments must see to it that those who make use of it pay a kind of rental charge, or royalty, for such use to a Common Heritage Trust Fund. Doing so will yield a steady flow of income to that Fund.

Governments must then assure that the income to that Fund is distributed *in a truly fair manner* to the earth's inhabitants as a Common Heritage Right. *In the case of the U.S. Government, it must assure, as a crucial part of assuring justice, that existing social programs be continued <u>in lieu of</u> income from this economic Right — until, and except as, this basic Right is acknowledged and honored.*

---

6. *Liberating the Early American Dream,* pub. by Tom Paine Institute, Eugene, Oregon 97404, 1985, 272 pp

In the course of evaluating Gingrich's proposal it will be argued, therefore, that our common heritage of capital should not be privately owned. But it will be as strongly argued that private ownership should be permitted of any capital (and of the income from it) generated over and beyond this basic capital — *provided only that both are generated within the moral bounds of justice.*

There may have to be time limits on such private gain in capital and its profits. For instance, at present, in the U.S., patent rights, and royalties from them, are held by inventors as private property for only 17 years. Thereafter they can be used by anyone, which turns out to be those who are rich enough to make use of them.

On the other hand, if, after 17 years, patents became part of Our Common Heritage Trust Fund, then further royalties would be paid to that Fund and the income distributed to everyone as part of the Common Heritage Right. Since such distribution would be to rich and poor alike, there would be no prying into a person's "needs," no humiliating pleading, such as takes place in the welfare programs so much under attack at the present time. In this regard, Gingrich and I have the same goal (See Chapter XIII).

## P-5: *Free Enterprise, Yes — But Within Moral Bounds*

Though this position constitutes a partial agreement with Gingrich's view that the role of government should be severely limited, we disagree as to the manner and extent of limitation — because our goals are radically different. I see his goal as promoting corporate America in the world as the main means of making "America #1" in the world. My goal is "justice for all" all over the world. And this calls for keeping all forms of "free enterprise" within appropriate moral bounds at all times.

Again, the most basic requirement of such moral bounds would be the assurance to everyone of a fair share of the financial and other benefits of our common heritage capital. Gingrich speaks passionately in favor of moral bounds in our personal lives; and I agree. But he fails to transfer this concern to appropriate moral bounds for our economic lives.

So long as the private enterprises that Gingrich champions <u>are</u> kept within these moral bounds, they are an important part of giving meaning to life. Such individual and corporate enterprises are not only exciting and invigorating for those who undertake them, but they also help more timid souls see what they also might do, and encourage them to try.

But such private enterprise becomes a menace, as it so often is today, when it is permitted to go *beyond* the bounds of justice, such as when near-monopoly by an elite few is legally permitted. This happens when governments fail to perform the only task which justifies their tremendous coercive power — that is, when they fail to prevent the most serious forms of injustice in the first place, and fail to provide remedy (in the form of compensation) to the victims of those injustices which are not prevented.

Indeed, the governments which fail the most in this regard are those which come under the control of those very corporate interests most in need, themselves, of being controlled — that is, most in need of being governed. In fact, the major reason we today have a civilization crisis is that, all over the world, governments are controlled by the very private enterprises most in need of governing, most in need of being restrained to remain within the moral bounds of justice.

On the other hand, we dare not give too much power to governments themselves. Political, as well as economic, power tends to corrupt. So, as history has clearly demonstrated, governments are capable of inflicting much more injustice than they prevent or remedy. Granted, governments need power sufficient to prevent and remedy injustices of great variety, but we dare not give them power beyond that. We dare not give them power over those aspects of our lives which fall *within* the bounds of justice. *All activities within those bounds must be out-of-bounds for governments.*

In summary, since power tends to corrupt, it is crucially important that we reduce to the absolute minimum the coercive power we yield to the institutions designed to "govern" (i.e., to coerce if necessary). Yet, we must give them power sufficient to effectively assure that the free-enterprising of all those gung-ho individuals and corporate bodies increasingly operating the global as well as national marketplaces will at all times be forced, by governments, to remain *well within the moral bounds of justice for all.*

*Thus, the central political challenge of all time is that of envisioning and establishing governments which, by their very structure, give us sufficient (though never absolute) assurance that the power conveyed to them will effectively be used to keep themselves, as well as individuals and corporate bodies, within the moral bounds of justice.*

This analysis makes it clear that we must not give governments power to control the education of our children (or ourselves), *except in regard to informing us (1) about the way the government operates and (2) about what the laws are and how they will be enforced — in short, where, according to the government, the bounds of justice are located.*

If governments provide *economic* justice in the fullest sense — including assuring to all a fair share of income from our common heritage — then each family will have sufficient income for joining with others in funding not only the entire family's educational needs, but in countless other voluntary activities also. These could include providing health care, emergency relief, recreation, religious ceremonies, and a great variety of cultural events.[7]

Where will the funds for such joint, voluntary associations come from? First, each family will have its basic, common heritage income. This is estimated to average, in the United States, about $36,000 per year in 1995 dollars for a family of four (See Appendix A). Add to this common heritage income the wages and salaries of family members, and it becomes clear that each family will have very substantial funds for investing in a great variety of culturally enriching activities, while still being able to save and invest for retirement.[8] *Again, the role of governments will continue to be that of assuring that the activities of all such voluntary associations — both cultural and economic — remain at all times within the moral bounds of justice.*

---

7. In the Danish community in which I was raised in the 1920s there was both a Danish Brotherhood and a Danish Sisterhood which provided these things as part of a self-supporting community.

8. Add to this common-heritage income that from wages and salaries, which would be much fairer than they are today because common-heritage income would give each of us economic leverage to bargain for truly fair wages.

But, so long as governments fail in their duty to assure each and every person of every family a fair share of the income from *our common-heritage capital,* such voluntary associations designed to meet personal and cultural needs are reserved for an elite few. And so long as governments permit the most aggressive and acquisitive among us to have, as now (and as Gingrich's agenda would intensify), a near-monopoly of this common heritage capital, *and of the income from it,* this ever-more-wealthy elite will continue to have an insurmountable advantage over the rest of us.

## P-6: *Who Should Pay for the Cost of Governing?*

It remains to speak briefly in this Preface to the matter of a fair distribution of the cost of governing.

The basic principle is simple to state but not so simple to apply. *It is this: persons and corporate bodies are justly charged for governing to the extent to which they behave in ways which require governing.*

Since "power tends to corrupt," the more economic, political, or other power a person or corporate body controls the more s/he or it will require governing, and thus the more such a power source is justly required to cover the cost of governing it — and, in some cases, of absolutely preventing it from employing power in certain ways.

Also, entirely apart from the *amount* of such power, the more hazardous or threatening the behavior of an individual or corporate body, the more s/he or it requires governing, and the more coercive measures can with justice be applied (in the form of taxes) to recover the costs of such governing. On the other hand, the more benign or socially and ecologically wholesome the behavior in question, the less the justification for coercive charges or other measures. Indeed, in some cases reward rather than charges may be in order.

These, then, are the moral standards in terms of which, in the following pages, I will be *Challenging Newt Gingrich, Chapter by Chapter.* In the course of evaluating Gingrich's agenda, I will also be critiquing the U.S. Government and the Constitution on which it is founded. Both are found to be structured to favor the most aggressive and acquisitive among us.

However, because of the saving grace of the Bill of Rights, the Constitution of the United States provides a means to build alternative and redeeming economic and political structures which are truly federated.

It will be shown that the existing Constitution was established by means of a maneuver which is not unfairly described as a coup. I say this because its promoters manipulated the imposition of a strictly top-down, entrapping governmental structure on the already federated states, and on the unsuspecting residents of those states. Evidence in support of these statements will be provided in great detail in Chapters XI and XII.

Then, in Chapter XIII, quite specific suggestions will be offered regarding how to proceed from here in a nonviolent fashion in order to rescue the people of these United States, and thereby, to a considerable extent, of the world, from the resulting, and mounting, world-wide crisis. Again, it is a crisis which the economic and political structures presently dominating life on this earth have largely brought about, and to which Gingrich's plan "to renew America" would add fuel to the fire.


Moral standards,
and accepting responsibility to adhere to them,
must,
in this complex Third Wave Age,
extend far beyond
the personal
to include the economic,
political,
and cultural aspects
of our increasingly intricately interrelated lives.

# Part I

A
Chapter-by-Chapter
Section-by-Section
Critique
of
Gingrich's Book
"To Renew America"

# Chapter I

# *Evaluating Gingrich's "Six Challenges Facing America"*

### I-0: *Introducing the Chapter*

Gingrich doesn't immediately state the "six major changes" that he is seeking to bring about. Rather, he begins with a more general statement:

> While we as a people were winning our battles around the world, here at home our elites were deserting us. For the past thirty years, we have been influenced to abandon our culture and seem to have lost faith in the core values, traditions, and institutions of our civilization. The intellectual nonsense propagated since 1965 — in the media, on university campuses, even among our religious and political leaders — *now threatens to cripple our ability to teach the next generation to be Americans* [emphasis added]. We have placed men on the moon, led the world in molecular medicine, and entered the age of computers and telecommunications. Yet we have simultaneously allowed our schools to decay to the point where our children regularly score below all others of the industrialized world in math and science. We risk not being able to understand the very world we have invented.

Here, then, we have the basic clues needed to understand why Gingrich feels that America needs to be "renewed," and how that is to be brought about. It remains to clarify more precisely answers to the following five questions:

**A.** Which "elites" is he referring to "in the media, on university campuses, even among our religious and political leaders"?

**B.** In what ways have these "elites" been "deserting us" and been influencing us to "abandon our culture"?

**C.** What are the "core values, traditions, and institutions of our civilization" in which we "seem to have lost faith," and which presumably constitute the "culture" which is being abandoned as the result of said "elite" influence?

**D.** What is the substantive nature of "the intellectual nonsense propagated since 1965" which constitutes "desertion" by these notorious "elites," which has influenced "us" to abandon the traditional American culture, and which "now threatens to cripple our ability to teach the next generation to be Americans" ?

**E.** Finally, *what is it that he would have us teach this next generation,* and presumably ourselves also, as the way to regain America's culture and American dominance in the world?

We keep these questions in the backs of our minds as we proceed with our evaluation of Gingrich's complete proposal in this and subsequent chapters. Our next step in this journey is to go on to the main topic of this chapter: what Gingrich calls "The Six Challenges Facing America," and which he introduces as "six major changes that I believe are necessary to leave our children with an America which is prosperous, free, and safe." So, I will consider them in the form of six Challenges to Change.

## I-1: *Change #1: How Gingrich Would "Renew America"*

Gingrich begins by stating "We must reassert and renew American civilization. From the arrival of English-speaking colonists in 1607 until 1965, there was one continuous civilization built around a set of commonly accepted legal and cultural principles."

This simply is not true. Until the Declaration of Independence in 1776 the "legal and cultural principles" which prevailed in *all* parts of English-speaking America were those laid down under various charters granted by the King of England and containing provisions favorable to that monarch. Even the independent-minded William Penn set foot on this continent only after having in hand such a charter from the King of England. And even the more independent-minded Roger Williams, who lacked such a charter at first, eventually returned to England to secure it.

In fact, it was precisely in order to escape these "legal and cultural principles" that Tom Paine's *Common Sense* pamphlet and Jefferson's *Declaration of Independence* urged a radical change in such legal and cultural principles. Furthermore, the major point of Gordon Wood's *The Radicalism of the American Revolution*, to which Gingrich refers with such approval (pages 32-33), is the "radical" nature of the change that took place at the time of the American Revolution — and with special emphasis on the radical nature of the cultural as well as the political change. In view of Gingrich's acceptance of Wood's authoritative status it is incredible that Gingrich should argue as he does for the historical *continuity* he claims to exist.

What, then, does Gingrich claim to have been "commonly accepted" for these several centuries? He goes on to say that "our civilization is based on a spiritual and moral dimension. It emphasizes personal responsibility as well as individual rights." It is true that the kings of England would have accepted this statement. But Paine and Jefferson differed radically with English royalty regarding what such responsibilities are, and to whom, and what these rights are, and with what restrictions.

Then, in the next sentence he again lays vague charges against "a cultural elite," but this time with the significant additional charge that there has been "a *calculated* [emphasis added] effort by cultural elites to discredit this civilization and replace it with a culture of irresponsibility that is incompatible with American freedoms as we have known them." This is especially serious, because it implies something bordering on treason. Making such a charge would seem to place on him a special responsibility to back it up in an unmistakable way. Yet this he doesn't do.

We note, also, that he claims this "irresponsibility" to be incompatible "with American freedoms as we have known them," presumably from the time of the first royal charters. This is quite a sweep, considering that the first American colonists had their charters on the condition of pledging "responsibility" to the king of England, and generally accepted those *limitations* on human rights laid down by royal mandate.

In fact, if we read the statements of the most articulate of those who opposed American independence at the time, they sound very much like the complaints about irresponsibility voiced by Gingrich in our day. At that time it was the "legal and cultural principles" traditional in the kingdom of England which were being held sacred and the American rebels who were being charged with being irresponsible. So, if Gingrich expects reasonable, fair-minded people to take seriously his charges, then he will have to make a far better case than he as yet has done.

Let's also take a close look at "American freedoms as we have known them." Gingrich doesn't here say what freedoms he is referring to. Because of his criticisms of the freedoms which have been exercised by critics of some of America's recent foreign and domestic policies, it seems unlikely that he has freedom of expression in mind, especially since he is advocating a rather strict educational program regarding what he considers to be the true American values. No, the freedom he would advocate — and this becomes clearer as his book proceeds — is connected with "free enterprise," especially for American multinational corporations. He wants them to be "free" to pursue the kind of economic and military power that has made America #1 in the world in the past, a "freedom" which he feels is presently in jeopardy.

It is interesting to compare this desire on Gingrich's part to the concern expressed by Dwight D. Eisenhower in his farewell address upon leaving office (see the footnote, Section P-1). Eisenhower evidently had a genuine concern about the tendency for power to corrupt. But that doesn't seem to be a Gingrich concern. And, as our evaluation of his book continues we shall see that over and over again he advocates power-building as such. He advocates it primarily for the very military-industrial complex which former President Dwight Eisenhower — supposedly one of his heroes — warned us against.

Repeatedly, as our evaluation proceeds we shall see that his advocacy of power-building is in almost complete disregard of the tendency for power to corrupt. Accordingly, we shall see that the amount of power which he advocates for American industry would require much more governing than he advocates. Nor need this surprise us, considering his power-seeking agenda.

We shall see that a large part of this additional governing will be needed in order to assure that corporate America not only obeys environmental and social safeguards, but also in order to assure what was referred to in the *Preface*: namely, that each person born into this earthly life gets a fair share of the financial and other benefits of our common heritage. And we shall see that to the extent that this basic right becomes a reality, there will be no need for governmental welfare programs or for the entire welfare-state concept of government. Thus, to the extent that this basic common-heritage right is granted to everyone, many of us will be happy to join Gingrich and company in doing away with welfare. But until that time many of the existing welfare programs must be continued, and some added — all because the ordinary people of the world are mostly being denied their basic right to a fair share of income from our common heritage.

He ends his description of what I am calling his Challenge to Change #1 by stating that "our first task is to return to teaching Americans about America," and that "until we reestablish a legitimate moral-cultural standard, our civilization is at risk."

Reasonable, fair-minded people can agree that there is a crying need in America — indeed, all over the world — for a *legitimate* moral-cultural standard, and that lacking it "our civilization is at risk." Let us, then, put our attention and energies into determining what constitutes such a truly "legitimate moral-cultural standard" rather than taking the easy way of claiming legitimacy for old standards which are not only of questionable moral merit but which never had either the general acceptance, continuity, nor moral integrity which Gingrich claims for them.

In Chapter III we will have another opportunity to evaluate Gingrich's much more detailed description of what he would have us teach our children and ourselves about what it means to be an American, and presumably what one must believe in order to legitimately claim participation in American life. For the remainder of this chapter we turn to consider Gingrich's descriptions of the other five Challenges to Change which he would set before us.

## I-2: *Change #2: Gingrich Embraces "The Third Wave"*

Gingrich's first sentence describing this "Challenge" evidences as much as anything else in his book his basic interest in helping corporate America build *power* per se in almost complete disregard for the tendency for power to corrupt: "We must accelerate America's entry into the Third Wave Information Age."

The Third Wave terminology, of course, is Alvin Toffler's. In Toffler's view, the first two "waves" were the agricultural revolution and the industrial revolution. But the electronic revolution is predicted by him to have a far more revolutionary impact on life on this earth than the other two.

I agree with Toffler, and with Gingrich, in this regard. The question is, what is our social and ecological responsibility in view of this momentous "Wave" descending upon us? There have been many books and articles expressing concern that unless prompt precautions are taken the rich will continue to get richer and the poor poorer all over the world. In that case, we can expect even more of the poverty and violence which Gingrich claims to be concerned about — even to the point of violent revolutions as its victims increasingly find themselves with their backs to the wall and with nothing to lose!

But Gingrich doesn't seem concerned about this. He evidently retains faith that "trickle-down" will sufficiently satisfy those who are largely marginalized in the process. Problems of the kind raised in Paul Kennedy's *Preparing for the Twenty-First Century*, in Robert Reich's *The Work of Nations*, or in William Greider's *Who Will Tell the People?* don't seem to concern Gingrich. All he seems to see is economic opportunities for corporate America to beat out those economies in the rest of the industrialized world also entering "The Information Age."

His response is not only socially and ecologically irresponsible, it is downright foolhardy. *Accelerate* America's entry into the Third Wave Information Age, he says. And the result he predicts is typical of his power-seeking mind-set: " . . . we can lead the world into the Information Age and leave our children with a country unmatched in wealth, power, and opportunity." If we fail, he says:

> . . . we will at best have a lower standard of living and at worst find that another country has moved into the new era so decisively that it can dominate us.

I rest my case. This is the frame of mind of someone looking at life in the simplistic terms of economic warfare, doomed one day to come to military warfare. And in this nuclear age that is not only folly; it is socially and ecologically irresponsible. It is literally to flirt with global disaster, as we will see more clearly when, in Chapter IV, we evaluate more fully Gingrich's suggested response to The Third Wave.

## I-3: *Change #3: Gingrich's America in the Global Marketplace*

Again Gingrich's first sentence is revealing: "We must rethink our competition in the world market." Again, the main emphasis is on becoming powerful as well as competitive in what comes across as a dog-eat-dog global competition.

But if corporate America is permitted by a permissive and Gingrich-manipulated U.S. Government to trade with foreign corporate entities which are exploiting and enslaving marginalized workers even more than does corporate America, there will be several serious consequences.

First, corporate America and its stockholders will be in complicity with such exploitation. Second, the only high-paying jobs will be those which contribute (1) to the advancement of high-tech, or (2) to the personal needs, enjoyments, and outright addictions of people, especially of the wealthy. Category (2) would include jobs filled by doctors; lawyers; psychological counselors; people who excel in sports, entertainment, and any of a number of esoteric services of great variety, and those offering personal companionship to the wealthy.

On this much there is widespread agreement. In fact, one of the chief economics advisors to the Clinton administration, and its Secretary of Labor, Robert Reich, says as much in his *The Work of Nations*.[1] A major difference between Reich and Gingrich, however, is that Reich is concerned about those who will get left behind in this rat race. Gingrich doesn't seem to be. Reich urges corporations to take it more slowly, keep their workers, and help them to get ever new training, even if it is costly to the corporation in the short run. Gingrich seems to have no such concerns.

In Chapter V, we will evaluate further Gingrich's proposals for participating in the global marketplace. At that juncture I will offer a more complete analysis of what is happening world-wide, both economically and politically, and how we might respond in ways which are *truly* socially and ecologically responsible. At this juncture this much seems clear: Gingrich's attitude of "full speed ahead" is the road to continued world-wide tragedy and turmoil.

## I-4: *Change #4: Gingrich's "Opportunity Society"*

Gingrich begins this section with a statement I can agree with provided the word "opportunity" is expanded to be *fair, just, equitable*, etc. Here are his opening words:

> We must replace the welfare state with an opportunity society. Every American is entitled to a life filled with opportunity. After all, we are endowed by our Creator with certain inalienable rights, among which are life, liberty, and the pursuit of happiness.

As indicated earlier, I agree that the welfare state should gradually be replaced. But the "opportunities" must be spread before us in a fair way. As it stands, the U.S. Constitution doesn't provide for such fairness. It permits

---

1. See Chapter 23, especially Section 6.

the most aggressive and acquisitive among us to have many more opportunities, and much more lucrative ones, than the rest of us.

Thus, the first to seize this continent from the Native Americans were allowed to claim it as their private property. George Washington, among others, found this to be very lucrative. While fighting the Native Americans in the French and Indian wars he was able to identify choice pieces of property. As people flocked to America, land became increasingly valuable. In Washington's case, he invested in so much land in so many states that he didn't live long enough to reap the harvest. But he was part of the first wave of the most aggressive and acquisitive in the history of America, a wave which continues today because there is no constitutional or other provision for restraining the most aggressive from seizing or inheriting what I have called our common heritage.

The result is that today the most aggressive are still using power gained from previous ventures to establish their economic and political power positions ever more solidly. Thus, what we find today is that "elites" of the kind Gingrich would further enrich have acquired private ownership of the bulk of the productive facilities of this country. That means that most people who work at all work for them, either directly or indirectly.

As Robert Reich points out, in the three decades after World War II there was enough residual patriotism among the power elites, and sufficient need for labor of all kinds, so that most people benefitted — even though not equally and not in a truly fair way.

What is causing this to change rapidly today, however, is "The Third Wave." It is a high-tech wave, in which both manufacturing and service industries are becoming rapidly automated at the same time that cheap labor is becoming available in Third World countries. Labor-saving technology and low-wage labor obviously increases the profits of the owners of the production facilities while leaving all but those who can contribute something technologically (either in skill or knowledge) literally out of a job.

Later in this volume I will argue more fully that all this would change if the "opportunity" which Gingrich speaks were shared in a just-fair way, beginning with income from our common heritage. Only as such fair-sharing actually takes place is it socially responsible to do away with the welfare state. But to the extent that this does, in fact, take place — and I consider it inevitable, as the justice of it becomes obvious — we really can gradually reduce the welfare state to zero and leave the role of government limited in the way it should be: to preventing and remedying injustice, period! More on this subject in Chapter VI.

## I-5: *Change #5: Decentralizing Power, Gingrich Style*

In this section Gingrich is calling for a decentralization of *political* power. The emphasis on political power is crucial, because it reminds us that at the same time he is calling for increased *centralization* of *economic* power. Why? So that corporate America can successfully "compete" with other global, corporate entities who trade with global power brokers — and who do so with almost no questions asked about employee working conditions, livable wage, environmental impact, or human rights violations generally.

Realizing this global agenda, it becomes clear why Gingrich wants political power to move out of the central government and into the 50 states. It is the old strategy of "divide and conquer." No single state is powerful enough to place social and ecological restraints on American multinational corporations — only the national government could have either the monitoring perspective or the policing power to exercise such restraints.

Gingrich accused a "cultural elite" of a "calculated" effort to undermine his agenda. In truth, we now are in position to see that the agenda of Gingrich and company is the real calculator and the real underminer of an American Dream we could be proud of — one based on justice-fairness throughout, beginning with the fair sharing of the financial and other benefits derived from our common heritage.

We will have occasion to enlarge on this evaluation several times in the course of the following pages, especially in Chapter VIII. At this juncture we go on to evaluate the last of the six Challenges to Change.

## I-6: *Change #6: Budget Balancing, Pros and Cons*

Gingrich's final suggestion for a challenge is that "we must be honest about the cost of government programs and balance the budget." We can generally agree (with some reservations[2]), but we note how he proposes to do so —

---

2. Whether or not going into debt is justified depends on many factors. For instance, as we shall see in Chapter VII, the modern corporation couldn't compete in the global marketplace without constantly borrowing at a low rate of interest in order to get a higher rate of return from investing the borrowed money in improving efficiency and product line. On the other hand, going into debt in order to buy consumer goods (which do nothing to generate profits or minimize losses) should be avoided. As we shall see, what Gingrich will not consider are the possible advantages in improved quality of life, or even in long-range

not by charging corporate America and its beneficiaries, even though they benefit from the governmental protection they get around the world from the U.S. Government and its military. Rather, the budget is to be balanced by cutting social programs which now serve as the only remedy the marginalized are receiving for being denied their fair share of the financial and other benefits from our common heritage.

What, then, is the justification for favoring corporate America in this way? We are told that not only is it the only way to "compete" in the global power race, but it is also the only way to replace those jobs lost through labor-saving technology and by going south and overseas for cheap labor. On the other hand, if each family received its rightful share of income from our common heritage, jobs would be plentiful. Many persons would choose not to seek a job, or they would return to having one breadwinner rather than two, or to each working half-time, or part-time, and would then have time to spend with their children. They would also have funds with which to join with others in educating their children in how to live wholesome and socially-ecologically responsible lives. The only promising option for most students at this time, with corporate America at the helm, is educational programs with emphasis on science and mathematics, so that they will be able to "compete" in the increasing, high-tech, global competition. As with all instruments of power, science and math have their place; *but only within the moral bounds of justice for all — not to be confused with equality for all. For instance, equal treatment for oppressor and oppressed is not justice.*

A large part of the problem of today's global injustice and poverty is related to entering the global marketplace. Again, it is the route naturally preferred by those who seek power per se rather than wholesome, socially-ecologically responsible living. Truly socially responsible Americans would reject trade with foreign corporate entities which exploit child labor, women labor, and human beings in general. They would favor trade with those who made a commitment to human rights, and who would agree to monitoring and policing systems which could assure that their commitments would be honored.

As noted in the Preface, if all Americans were given their rightful income from our common heritage they would have leverage for bargaining for truly fair wages and salaries over and beyond their common heritage

---

financial gain, from borrowing for the purpose of investing in preventing illness, crime, etc. *and especially in a more just society.*

income. Then corporate America would again have customers at home with money to buy their products. Then Americans would once again have a sense of community, because their economic and political system would be based on policies which are truly fair rather than on a corporate structure which seeks to accumulate the maximum economic and political power in order to be sure to have enough to compete with any corporate entity in the world and to militarily defeat any military force in the world. Much more on this in Chapter VII.

Gingrich ends his first chapter by quoting Franklin Roosevelt's 1936 statement that "Our generation has a rendezvous with destiny." Ours is different, he says, but just as demanding. I agree to a large extent, but as already indicated in the previous pages, my conception of the challenges before us are radically different from his. They are different in the most fundamental way imaginable. He envisions corporate America as the supreme power in the world, aided by a national government strong enough in ways needed to protect its corporate interests both nationally and globally and too weak in ways needed to effectively either monitor or govern its ominous "free enterprises." In contrast, I see our challenge as one of envisioning and then implementing a truly *just* world order, with America taking the lead toward that quite different goal.

I close this chapter with some relevant words from Thomas Paine:

> These are the times that try men's souls.
> When it shall be said
> in any country in the world,
> "My poor are happy;
> neither ignorance nor distress
> is to be found among them;
> my jails are empty of prisoners,
> my streets of beggars;
> the aged are not in want,
> the taxes are not oppressive . . ."
> when these things can be said,
> then may that country boast
> of its constitution and government.

# Chapter II

# *Gingrich's Basic Principles*

In his Chapter 2, Gingrich gives us a bit of insight into his childhood as the son of a career military man. His account helped me to understand why so much of his thinking is in terms of "security," especially military security. Because of the devastation he witnessed in Europe as the result of World War II, he was impressed by "the terrible risks a country and its people run when they underestimate the effort it takes to remain safe and free." He decided to dedicate his life "to understanding what it takes for a free people to survive and to helping my country and the cause of freedom."

He tells how he was permitted to write a paper for his sophomore history class "on the balance of world power." He states that "that high school experience was the beginning of an in-depth grounding in military history and military analysis *that has served me well ever since*" [emphasis added]. He was about 15 at the time.

Two years later he reached another momentous conclusion "that there was no moral choice except to immerse myself in the process of learning how to lead and how to be effective." That led to his joining the Republican party and volunteering in its campaigns.

Thus, at a very young age he committed himself to enter the military and political power games, and to learn how to become an "effective" leader in such games. No wonder he thinks in terms of "renewing America" by way of military and economic power, rather than in terms of moral values like "justice for all," compassion for the marginalized, passing on a healthy environment to the following generations, or building wholesome family and community life based on moral integrity.

To be sure, if he were asked if he believed in these things he would likely say he did. But in laying down his basic principles for "renewing America," these values are not factored in.

In the entire chapter there is no reference to a "just" society. His motivations for becoming a student of history were, rather, in terms of what it takes for a country to remain powerful, and safe in its position of power. Again, I do not argue against power as such, because it can be used to accomplish good things as well as bad. But what I see in Gingrich's motivation is the pursuit of power per se — for his country, supposedly, rather than for himself only, to be sure; but nevertheless pursuit of power per se.

He tells of becoming an Eisenhower Republican. This fits in with his admiration for the military. Yet he doesn't seem to be influenced by the warning about the military-industrial complex which Eisenhower delivered at his retirement.

He tells of being influenced by Toynbee's *A Study of History*. In keeping with the power concepts in terms of which he was thinking, he states that "Toynbee's thesis was called "challenge and response." This is true, in a sense. But Toynbee was primarily concerned about challenge and response in relation to moral issues. He called for less attention to developing what he called "the head" — i.e., math and science — and more attention to values of "the heart." Gingrich seems to have missed that distinction.

He says, "Again and again, I realized, large scale events create the framework within which ordinary people lead their lives." I agree. But such frameworks can emphasize the "head" and its economic and military technology primarily, or it can emphasize the "heart," with concern for such technology primarily as it serves the passions of the heart.

Ideally, it seems to me, the "head" serves the heart. We need intellect to help us reconcile our feelings (of hate, love, fear, courage, lust, dread, aggressiveness, etc.) to each other. But what is crucial is the nature of the moral *scale* upon which these to-be-reconciled feelings are to be weighed. I suggest that the first weighing must be on the scale of justice. Nothing which fails that test is morally acceptable, no matter what its merits might be in other ways.

He does make reference to America's "moral decay from within" but doesn't elaborate except to say that "we are definitely *the first generation in American history* to face such a challenge" [italics his]. Again, he doesn't elaborate at this juncture, but in the next chapter he declares that this is the first generation in which God isn't accepted as the supreme power and as the One to whom we owe our final and complete allegiance. This is an important issue, one which receives extended discussion in the next chapter. At this juncture we merely note that, as with everything else, what Gingrich considers important about divinity is its source of *power*.

Next, attributing the statement to Toynbee, he asserts that "it is not the nature of these challenges, but the *quality of our response* to them that will determine our future." He doesn't give us the source of his claimed support from Toynbee, so we can't check its accuracy. But, we note that placing most importance on effort expended and less on the nature or extent of the challenge conveniently supports his policies of giving ever more "freedom" and license to corporate America.

By placing all the emphasis on effort expended to meet a challenge, he more easily dismisses the complaints of those who are victimized by the escapades of corporate America and its trading partners around the world. He can then call the victims of these escapades "whiners" (See end of III-3), thereby implying that the problem is with "the quality of their response."

Thus, he can say to corporate America, "Full speed ahead into the Information Age. Don't worry about those who can't adjust and adapt. That's their problem, not yours. They just aren't making the necessary "quality of response."

So, again, my basic disagreements with Gingrich are regarding the answers to certain key questions: Who is responsible for the various challenges we face today? Who are the victims of them? What *kind* of qualitative response is called for on the part of whom?

He ends the chapter by urging us on to the next six chapters, in which he deals with each of the six challenges in considerably greater detail than he has in Chapter 1.


I agree that we face a civilization crisis.
I agree that what Americans do
has global consequences.
I agree that we are challenged to be "effective."
The question is:
effective in doing what?
By what means?
Toward what end for whom?
Measured by what moral yardstick?
Who will be the winners in our effectiveness?
Who will be the losers?
What will the winners win?
And the losers lose?

# Chapter III

# *How Gingrich Would "Renew America"*

## III-1: *Introducing the Issues*

Gingrich again makes reference to changes that took place in the "mid-1960s." He gives us a clear picture of what he considers the basic American way of life he would "renew" and what he regrets is being put in its place.

He would evidently like to see a return to school ceremonies like "the Pledge of Allegiance, the opening prayer, "The Star-Spangled Banner." He would like to see a return to certain historic holidays, mostly of a patriotic nature, such as "the study of the Pilgrims at Thanksgiving, Washington and Lincoln on their birthdays." He regrets no longer having "Washington seen as the indispensable man, the individual on whose character and moral strength the nation was founded."

I agree that it would be nice if we could all accept some simple moral standards, in both ceremony and stories — *provided they are truly worthy of being such.* But, could it be that there are good reasons why they are no longer practiced as he knew them as a boy growing up in a military family? Could it be that some of these patriotic myths have been shown to be morally tarnished?

In Chapter XI, I seek out the truth about how the U.S. Constitution came about, and about Washington's role in it. As a result, I am persuaded that anyone who does this cannot but have doubts. In any case, if Gingrich would have us go back to adopting these myths as guides in our lives, he must present evidence in support of their moral validity, not just urge them on the grounds that we need such myths as a way to unite us around his agenda and thereby motivate us to make corporate America #1 in the world.

Next, he reiterates his thesis that what he considers deterioration in America's values and patriotism began in the mid-1960s, and for the first time makes reference to "the counter-culture." Living as I did in Berkeley, California, when it all began in 1964 with the Berkeley Free Speech Movement (the FSM), I can sympathize to a considerable extent with Gingrich's concern. I was not enthusiastic about some of what was being offered in place of dominant American values. But most of the counter-culture was nevertheless a sincere response to what were seen as moral flaws in the dominant one.

I knew personally the leaders of the Berkeley Free Speech Movement; they were honorable human beings. Mario Savio, the sophomore philosophy student who became its charismatic leader, had just come back from risking his life in voter registration work in the segregated South. It was a segregation which has its roots in the U.S. Constitution itself, and in the life style of Gingrich's hero, George Washington, with his hundreds of African American slaves. (See Chapter XI).

I am sympathetic with Gingrich's criticism of the position that "there are no general rules of behavior," and that there are no "universal standards of right and wrong." In fact, in subsequent pages I am going to suggest some. But, again, it is not enough to express dismay. There must be arguments presented, and they must be sound arguments. And alternative standards must be presented, and reasons given, with *senses* of right and wrong appealed to, rather than offering only standards which at one time were merely "handed down" and which since have been challenged. If he would re-establish these old standards, then he must answer the substantive arguments against them.

In defense of Washington he refers to the 1888 biography of Washington by Henry Cabot Lodge. But Lodge bent over backwards in his attempt to paint a rosy, but unconvincing, picture, a picture which I feel has since been largely discredited by historians with access to more detailed information. In Part II of this volume I shall do a bit of discrediting myself.

Gingrich then sets the stage for introducing what he calls "five basic principles that I believe form the heart of our civilization." He begins to set that stage by referring to "Gordon Wood's two great books, *The Creation of the American Republic* and *The Radicalism of the American Revolution.*" He then writes as follows:

> As Wood observes, America in 1830 is as thoroughly recognizable as the America of the first half of the twentieth century, where mass tastes and a common popular culture prevailed. Even today, this democratic culture remains the common, everyday experience of nearly all Americans. This is the America of voluntary associations, practical problem solving, active local leadership, and an ethic of getting the job done as efficiently as possible. *What is different today is that this practical, democratic culture has been overlaid with an elite culture — predominant in the upper echelons of Washington and the media — that says that American history is nothing but a story of racism, oppression, genocide, disenfranchisement, and constant violation of the norms to which we all thought we subscribed* [emphasis added].

The above quotation gives insight into Gingrich's views regarding "the ways in which these elites have been deserting us" (thus responding to Question B of the five questions raised at the beginning of Chapter I).

Apparently, what Gingrich objects to is "elites" pointing out moral flaws in America and Americans down through history. But he attacks his critics in the weakest way possible: by unfairly attributing to them the charge that America is "nothing but" the moral flaws he names. Yet no one with credibility sufficient to cause Americans to "abandon our culture" has been taking that ridiculous position. So, what Gingrich has done is set up a straw man.

Having done so, and having attributed to it a ridiculous position, he evidently feels he can dismiss it without further comment. In this way he evades dealing with the criticisms as they really have been stated. That is, he evades dealing with the *actual* criticisms regarding "*racism, oppression, genocide, disenfranchisement, and constant violation of the norms to which we all thought we subscribed.*"

For instance, he evades dealing with the criticisms voiced by Martin Luther King, Jr., not only regarding racism in America in 1965 but also regarding the Vietnam war. It took a great deal of courage on King's part to oppose that war, especially since he was criticized for doing so by other leaders in the civil rights movement. Some of them saw the Vietnam issue as at least a distraction. But, worse, taking a stand on such a controversial issue could lose them the support of those who took the position of supporting the war.

Gingrich also doesn't address the charge that American policies were contributing to oppression in countries where, in order to "fight communism" U.S. policies were supporting oppressive dictators around the world, especially in South and Central America.

He thereby avoids dealing with the charges of disenfranchisement, both in regard to women and African Americans within our country, and to victims of oppression in countries where U.S. policies were supporting virtually any dictator, no matter how oppressive, so long as s/he would oppose communism. Granted, communism showed itself to be a "cure" in many ways worse than the "disease." But it would not have gotten a foothold as a claimed cure if it were not for the moral flaws in Western civilization generally, to which communists could then conveniently draw attention as a way of recruiting supporters.

Gingrich also avoids addressing departures from the supposed American values of "freedom and justice for all" in relations with those few remaining groupings of Native Americans from among the thousands of tribes which inhabited this continent before the European invasion in 1492. He acknowledges nothing of the rape, torture, and, yes, genocide and ethnic cleansing which began with the arrival of Christopher Columbus, and which continues to some extent to this day.[1]

Nor, as we were reminded again recently at the U.N. Conference in Beijing, has the issue of women's rights been as yet adequately addressed. And it is also well to remind ourselves, in this regard, that the early American values and culture which Gingrich would have us blindly embrace didn't even provide for voting by women — only finally achieved in 1920. Nor did it provide for an end to slavery. Indeed, in determining numbers of representatives to the national congress, states were permitted to count not only the number of white males but three fifths of their slaves. Thus, the hundreds of slaves "owned" by people like Washington and Madison not only were denied representation in Congress, but were used as political tools for carrrying the self-interests of their masters to the national con-

---

1.  See Howard Zinn's *A People's History of the United States,* pub. by Harper & Row, NY. 1980

gress, the political influence of the latter thereby being expanded hundreds of times beyond that of the more socially responsible non-slave-owners!

Gingrich then states that "In my reading, I found five basic principles that I believe form the heart of our civilization:

1. The common understanding we share about who we are and how we came to be [what Gingrich goes on to call "The Spiritual Dimension"]
2. The ethic of individual responsibility
3. The spirit of entrepreneurial free enterprise
4. The spirit of invention and discovery
5. Pragmatism and the concern for craft and excellence, as expressed recently in the teachings of Edwards Deming."

In preparation for enlarging on each of these in detail Gingrich makes a convincing case for America's being "unique." But then he makes one of his typical claims without giving evidence to support it. He simply asserts that "America is a series of romantic folktales which just happen to be true." And therein lies the heart of his credibility problem. It would be great to be able to present American history in an inspiring way. But it must, first of all, be *true!* It must, of course, also be morally sound. What we find is that what Gingrich offers as a moral standard for America's future has credibility problems in regard to both truth and moral soundness. For he has yet to evidence either the extent or quality of moral purity he would have us attribute to those who laid the foundation for American society today.

## III-2: *The Spiritual Dimension*

He begins this section by asserting that "In America, *power* comes from God to the individual and is loaned to the state" [emphasis added]. We note, again, his emphasis on "power." The implication is that if power-seekers like him are politically smart they will acknowledge Who holds the basic power in the universe. In short, Gingrich's devotion to "God," such as it is, seems to derive from the fact that God's got the power. And Gingrich wants *power*.

He would, however, be more effective in inspiring some of us if he were to present evidence that this Supreme Power is, as I believe, primarily concerned about *justice* among this earth's inhabitants.

In fairness to Gingrich, he does then go on to quote a statement by Thomas Jefferson arguing that God does not approve of slavery. Similar quotes follow from statements by Abraham Lincoln and Franklin D. Roosevelt. But he still doesn't seem to recognize the distinct contrast between the *moral* concerns expressed in these statements and his own emphasis on who has the ultimate *power,* and whom we therefore had better acknowledge *if we want our power-building efforts to be "effective."*

In any case, what he quotes are mere words. It is our actions that count most — the kind of action taken by Thomas Paine when he sacrificed his position as hero in the French Revolution by arguing against beheading the French king. He insisted that the problem wasn't this particular king (toward whom Paine may well have felt grateful for helping in America's own revolution at a crucial time), but the *system.* The result was that Paine was incarcerated in Luxembourg prison and scheduled for the guillotine.

Incidentally, of no avail were appeals to Gingrich's hero, President Washington, to help his old friend get released. At that point Thomas Paine was an embarrassment to America's power interests in the world. Indeed, when he was finally released through the efforts of James Monroe, who eventually replaced Gouveneur Morris as Ambassador to France, and returned to the country he had served so faithfully during the revolution, he was denied American citizenship!

I still find the treatment of Thomas Paine truly incredible! The author of the very pamphlet, *Common Sense,* which so inspired Americans to rise up against the British royalty like no other historical event, denied citizenship? Thomas Paine, the author of the *Crisis Papers,* those crucial morale-boosters issued from time to time to remind his fellow Americans of the ideals worth fighting for — and to alert Congress and the American people to Washington's plight in field — denied citizenship in the country to which he so selflessly gave of himself in its struggle to be free from tyranny?

How is this to be explained? As implied above, it is partially explained by the fact that the American government had by that time become one of many sovereignty-claiming power-seekers in the world. It may have been considered an offense to Britain, America's main trading partner, to release from a French prison, or even to give citizenship in the country he had been so central in forming, the man who had been so critical of British royalty in both his *Common Sense* and the *Crisis Papers.*

How quickly the new power brokers in the new American government forgot the heroism of the man who wrote those now famous lines: "These are the times that try men's souls." I hope that women will forgive Tom Paine for using the accepted masculine terminology of the times. He did, also, speak out for women's rights as well as those of African Americans.[2] In this way also, and in his defense of women's rights, he may have seemed too radical to the power brokers of his day.

Near the end of this section Gingrich also has something to say about relations between men and women. But he thereby displays the shallowness of his views on the subject.

> One of the most absurd of modern practices is the 'war between men and women' — as if God didn't make us both male and female, as if both were not necessary for the propagation of the species.

I doubt if there are many women who don't realize that they are "necessary for the propagation of the species." To imply that acknowledging this biological fact is relevant to the much larger social, political, economic, and spiritual issues involved in the women's rights movement is to reveal an incredible naiveté and spiritual insensitivity. One wonders, therefore, about the sincerity and spiritual depth of his beautiful words about "a divine spark that makes us all equal in the eyes of God." He ends this section as follows:

> Only by immersing ourselves in our own history do we begin to pick up the rhythms of America and the simple themes that underlie the extraordinary complex tapestry of its diverse peoples.

There is truth in that. But when we do thus immerse ourselves we must do so with the kind of moral integrity which "says it like it is." We must not claim virtue beyond what actually exists. When Gingrich says that "we have also been a nation of sinners and sins" he speaks in the needed spirit. But it is a spirit which is rare in his seemingly blind praise for previous leaders and for the Constitution which they established. Both they and it must be carefully scrutinized in terms "of sinners and sins," as well as of moral

---

2. Paine's first published essay upon arriving in America was called *African Slavery in America*. It was written with such passion and lucidity that it aroused the interest of Dr. Benjamin Rush, one of the most respected signers of the Declaration of Independence, who then introduced Paine to the anti-slavery movement, such as it was at the time. Paine's later essay on women's rights was called *An Occasional Letter on the Female Sex*. Imagining how women might plead for justice he wrote: "How great is your injustice. If we have an equal right with you to virtue, why should we not have an equal right to praise? The public esteem ought to wait upon merit. Our duties are different from yours, but they are not therefore less difficult to fulfill, or of less consequence to society. . . ; From Volume I of *Writings of Thomas Paine*, edited by his major biographer, Moncure Daniel Conway, AMS Press Inc., New York, 1967.

standards and actions worthy of being emulated. And before the last page of this volume is turned, I hope not only to show that this is what he doesn't do but also to present a picture of parts of our American heritage which is morally worthy — not in order to present it as an ideal to be emulated, but as a tradition worthy to be improved on.

There is yet one more important issue to be raised under the heading of "The Spiritual Dimension." I have indicated why it seems to me that the God to whom Gingrich basically appeals is a God of power. This fits with his central concern about power, instilled, as he recounts in his Chapter 2, at an early age. But those of us concerned with "justice for all" are not inspired by power terminology or symbols of power, whether "supreme" or otherwise. We look for moral leadership in the sense of leadership in actually securing justice for all on this earth.

I join Gingrich in believing that there is some form of divine, Supreme Power in the universe. I join him in believing (assuming he does really believe, and isn't merely playing politics in deference to the religious right) that this Supreme Power is in the form of conscious entities, sentient beings, as distinct from some abstract principle. Whether there is one supreme conscious being among them, or there is some form of democratic community in overall charge, I do not know. Basically, I stand in awe of it all. In the last analysis, I think of ultimate reality as "The Wonder of Wonders."

But the more important point in all this is that I do not think of a Supreme Being as requiring of us blind obedience to some divine destiny laid out for each of us in great detail. I do not think of "God" as " a jealous God." I think of the Divine as like a loving parent, one who doesn't lay down the law on everything; rather, one who encourages us to, as Gingrich advocates in economic activities, take creative initiatives. *However, what is crucially important is that we are at the same time urged by this parental-like Divinity to keep these initiatives at all times within the moral bounds of justice to our fellow sentient beings here on earth.*

Such urging comes, for me, and I suspect for you, my reader, in the form of two crucial moral guides. The first is what all healthy persons experience as *a sense of justice.* It is an intuitive sense which emerges at a very young age. One of the first passionate utterances of children is, "That's not fair!" This moral guide, I suggest, is divinely given as a constant companion.

Whereas my sense of justice indicates (at its best) what would be a *just* outcome in a situation, entirely apart from how it might be accomplished, the second moral guide is very personal, and refers to actions to be taken in the light of the justice or injustice of a situation. It is commonly known as the individual *conscience*. It urges me personally to *act* according to my best sense of justice, and thereby to maintain my creative initiatives at all times *well within the moral bounds of justice for all.*

I believe it is a view of Divinity which is presented either explicitly or implicitly by many religions. And it is the *moral* guidance we receive from Divinity, in this and other ways, and not the evidence of divine *power*, which makes that Divinity worthy of our worship.

Both of these moral guides function in both individual and corporate affairs, if we will but remain open to "that still small voice." One of the most beautiful manifestations of it appears in Micah. In answer to the question, "What does the Lord require of thee?" Micah replies simply, "To do justice, love mercy, and walk humbly with your God."[3]

## III-3: *Individual Responsibility*

Gingrich begins this section with a very strange statement:

> Precisely because our rights are endowed by our Creator, the individual burden of responsibility borne by each citizen is greater than in any other country. This is why our new-found sense of entitlement and of victimization is exactly wrong — and so corrosive to the American spirit. In America, the fact that God, not the state, has empowered us puts an enormous burden on our shoulders. Our rights are pale shadows of our responsibilities.

Looking at the first sentence, he is clearly implying that it is the rights of Americans *only* which are "endowed by our Creator." Otherwise, why would our responsibilities be "greater than in any other country"? As if to affirm this conclusion, the third sentence implies that it is only in America that "God, not the state, has empowered us." Thus, Gingrich's position has all the earmarks of a "chosen people" mentality. It also implies a God who plays favorites, and who lays agendas on people. As noted in the above section, this is not the God I know. It is a conception of Divinity in sharp contrast to one in which everyone (not only Americans) is encouraged to set

---

3. Issues regarding spiritual realities as they relate to modern science will be addressed at length in my forthcoming book, tentatively entitled, "Transcending Both the Mechanistic and Biological Paradigms.""

one's own agenda — *provided only that all such personal agendas are maintained within the moral bounds of justice toward other sentient beings*.

Turning again to the first sentence, he outrightly says that "precisely because" of this special relationship between Americans and the Divine, "the individual responsibility borne by each citizen is greater than in any other country." Granting his "chosen people" thesis for the sake of argument (only!), how does special responsibility logically follow? We *take on* responsibilities. We take them on by the commitments we make. Gingrich would almost surely argue that parents "take on" the responsibility for caring for children by knowingly engaging in the act of conception. But by this meaning of "responsibility," it is God, not God's creations (just as it is parents, not their children), who takes on responsibilities with the act of creation.

It might be reasonably argued that any normal child would *feel* a certain sense of *loyalty* (as distinct from responsibility) toward parents who "brought her into the world." Similarly, Gingrich might argue that a normal American would, again, *feel* a similar loyalty toward a God who did the same in a much more fundamental way. If he were to make that argument I would be inclined to agree with him. However, any one of a number of persons born with a disease from which s/he is doomed to die in a few months or years after long suffering might not be expected to feel the same way. In any case, we are considering here what a normal person would *feel*, not what s/he *would be responsible for*.

The difference is important. Again, responsibilities are things which are *taken on*, which one "assumes" by free choice, by a creative action, such as by parenting a child or, in the role of a god, choosing to "take on" a chosen people.

Turning now to the second sentence, he says that the whole concept of entitlements is inconsistent with his stated role of Divinity in the lives of us Americans. Again we note that Americans are being singled out in this matter, thereby again implying that Americans are somehow Divine favorites. Knowing Gingrich, we assume that he is referring to things like welfare payments. Is he implying that chosen people shouldn't be asking for anything more, that to do so would be to display a lack of gratitude? I, for one, am not clear about this.

But this much does seem clear. Entitlements are not claims which are laid on the Giver of life, of Nature, of Nature's land and resources, and of Nature's laws by which the universe operates. In short, gratitude is not the issue here. The God-given gifts Gingrich refers to are already *given*. Nor does there seem to be any threat of removal. There is a problem, however; and it is a major one. Entitlements have to do with how these above-mentioned God-given treasures are to be *distributed* among us earthly sentient beings *by human beings. Again, the problem is that the most aggressive and acquisitive have an unfair share of them.*

*Because it is not only life itself that is God-given, to use Gingrich's terminology, but much, much more, we face the challenge of distributing that much, much more in a truly fair manner. That is, the question then becomes, "Who is entitled to what portion of God-given Nature and Nature's resources"?*

In the Preface (P-4), I have argued, and reaffirm here, that every sentient being, human and non-human, born into this earthly life is "entitled" to a fair share of these God-given resources. And as long as those in the upper 5% of income in America are unfairly getting nearly all the financial and other benefits from our common heritage, it is only fair that they be forced to give remedy to those who have been unjustly denied their fair share for so many years, and to "do justice" henceforth.

At the present time, the only form of such remedy in place and operating is the governmental social services which Gingrich and company would eliminate. Therefore, they should not be eliminated at this time. In fact, until our common heritage is fairly shared, if anything equivalent to the $36,000 per year for the average family of four mentioned in the Preface (and calculated in Appendix A) is to be achieved many existing programs would have to be increased and others added.

And if this common heritage income sounds to the reader like a figure which would bankrupt the American economy, consider this. I have calculated (see Appendix A) that if such distribution were to take place, then America's income distribution would change in roughly the following way:

Whereas at present America's upper fifth in income are receiving about half of total American income, and its lowest fifth are receiving about 3%, after a fair distribution of income from our common heritage the upper fifth would still be receiving about 34% and the lowest fifth about 10%. That is, the upper fifth would still be receiving more than three times the lowest fifth.

So, even after such a distribution there would still be a wide spread of income and of wealth in America. There would still be incentive to increase personal wealth. Individuals would still be able to become extremely wealthy. Some of the rich would still get ever richer. *But the big difference would be that none of this would be at the expense of someone else.* And in such a truly just society the amount of happiness which would abound from the good feeling everyone had toward one another would accrue to everyone. That, in any case, is my belief.

Gingrich makes much of the courage displayed by those who by signing the Declaration of Independence "pledged their lives, their fortunes, and their sacred honor." He says they meant it literally. I don't know how he could know this, but they certainly didn't carry its words about "all men [sic] being created equal" into their personal lives, nor into the wording of the subsequent Constitution. Nor were they putting their lives in danger nearly as much as was Thomas Paine in writing *Common Sense,* because Paine's was the first forthright and widely publicized call for rejecting the British monarchy.

On a related subject, Gingrich repeats his attack on "the counterculture." He says they blame "everything" on society. Here, again, he goes to extremes. As with his previous "nothing but" straw man, he is at it again. It is true that there were those, are those, who blame a large part of the injustice in this world on the economic and political *structures* which dominate. But anyone who praises the U.S. Constitution and its founders to the extent that Gingrich does implies that it is important the way a society is structured. He implies as much in his observations while growing up in a Europe in disarray during the period of salvaging and rebuilding in the years immediately after World War II.

But the counterculture criticism which began in the sixties and which extends to the present was not *primarily* directed at society in general, nor at its structural level. It was directed at specific U.S. policies and at the individuals in Congress and in the U.S. administration who were promoting them.

In contrast, Gingrich targets those who have been marginalized. He approves of saying to them, "If you don't work, you don't eat." He calls them "whiners." This is so ironic, because the basic reason the poorest 20%

are thus marginalized is because the bulk of the upper 5% in income don't get that income from "working." They get it by investing wealth which has largely been made possible by the head start they received in the form of the bulk of the income from our common heritage. Yet they not only "eat" lavishly, but live lavishly in every other way, *thanks to the work of others!*

So, I would suggest that his calling those who have been denied their entitlement rights "whiners" is disgustingly misplaced. In fact, I feel that his display of arrogance in this section is so extreme that I do not wish to honor it with further comment!

## III-4: *The Spirit of Free Enterprise*

Gingrich begins this section with this statement:

> Americans get up every day hoping to put in a good day's work, create a little more wealth, provide a little better service to their customers, or invent a slightly better mousetrap for the world.

I hope I have made it clear that I applaud private initiative *provided it remains within the moral bounds of justice.* But Gingrich doesn't add that proviso. Instead, he ignores the fact that those who have become most wealthy in America have strayed far beyond such moral bounds, and continue to flourish in such "elitist" territory. Instead, he criticizes the "taxes, regulation, and litigation" that "have all thrown a blanket over the entrepreneurial spirit." In short, he is critical of all efforts to maintain such free enterprise within the moral bounds of justice.

Even Adam Smith placed moral restrictions on the free enterprise system he fathered. He was basically a moral philosopher, as he clearly demonstrated in his *Theory of Moral Sentiments.* In fact, his was a moral crusade against the near monopolists of his day.

Again, Gingrich evidently cannot resist a slap at "the welfare system." Either he is not aware of the fact that the wealthy in this country are the ones who receive the greatest "welfare" in their near-monopoly of the financial and other benefits from our common heritage, or he approves of it. Either way, what he advocates is a continuation of a fundamentally unjust distribution of that part of the "wealth," which is given by God and previous generations as our *common* heritage.

He again shows his bias in favor of those who live "to create wealth." In fact, he ends the section by saying that "the lesson of American civilization is that inventing new forms of wealth is the key to a better future." Nothing about the need for justice, compassion, neighborliness, caring community, and the fair sharing of what is God-given to all of us, but nearly monopolized by the most aggressive and acquisitive among us.

## III-5: *The Spirit of Invention and Discovery*

Again, his opening sentence: "More than any other country in history America has been committed to the spirit of invention and discovery." I have little argument with his main thrust in this section, except for his sweeping claim of "more than any other country in history." Again, he overlooks the long history of invention which laid the groundwork for both the industrial revolution and the Third-Wave electronics revolution. Again, his bravado for America is a display of arrogance. Again, he seems to need to think of America as a chosen people, in some sense — indeed, in almost every sense — superior to every other. It's as if, because Americans are a chosen people, they will somehow let down their Creator unless they dominate the world in every way.

And it is "American individualism" which, in his mind, is the main expression of this superiority — not compassion for the suffering and the marginalized, not remorse for past injustices, not commitment to "do justice, love mercy, and walk humbly" in the future, not all those wholesome virtues which our senses of justice and consciences would rise to applaud and urge us to continue to develop and enhance. His closing statement in this section displays his distorted myth about what is admirable about America, and what we should continue to emulate:

> Whether displaying determination in the battlefield, persistence in pursuing new inventions, or dedication in spending long, hard work making an invention or dream come true, American individualism has been an enormously powerful force for good.

Perhaps it has, but for me he hasn't made the case, given his failure to acknowledge that "power tends to corrupt" and that he objects to every effort to contain America's and Americans' economic and political power *within the moral bounds of justice.*

## III-6: *Pragmatism and the Spirit of Quality Thought*

In this section Gingrich justifiably praises the work of Edwards Deming in promoting worker participation in all production of goods and services. But the following quotation requires some minor comments:

Deming argued that in order to improve the quality [of work and its products] *everybody* has to get involved in designing and improving a manufacturing process, and they have to improve the system. No longer can workers be passive participants.

I would modify this statement only enough to say that every worker should be given the *opportunity* to thus participate. At age 17, and fresh out of high school, I worked a year at Underwood Elliott Fisher Typewriter Company in Bridgeport, Connecticut before going on to college. The routine, non-participatory nature of the job suited me just fine at the time, because it left my mind free to think of philosophical matters which then were of prime importance to me. My only point is that this quotation again reveals Gingrich as one inclined toward simple, absolute formulas with which "everyone," especially all Americans, somehow *must* comply.

Nevertheless, as Gingrich goes on to describe Deming's philosophy and his conception of human persons, I confess that, with some residual reservations, I am favorably impressed. Gingrich says that "although Deming's work defies any easy summary," his teachings generally focus around four basic points:

1. The customer should be the focus of any business.
2. Systems rather than individuals should be the focus of improved production.
3. There has to be a theory or hypothesis before each change or action.
4. Every employer can be a key player [I like the inclusion of the word "can" rather than "must"] in improving a process or product.

I do have the following comments. In regard to #1, it is not clear what is meant by "the focus." If he and Gingrich are arguing in favor of "giving the customer what s/he wants," this is, of course, only "good business." But it may not always be ethically responsible business. If what the customer wants is harmful to her-him and loved ones (such as harmful drugs or addictive consumerism) then such wants need to be moved out of "focus." Also, the working conditions of workers, degree of pollution emitted, and impact on the environment generally, are all due their respective considerations.

As for #2, I agree that *systems* are much more fundamental determiners of both good and bad consequences in our lives than individual actions. This is why most of my comments in this volume relate to systems, economic and political systems. However, individual and group actions can be important, and usually essential, in changing systems. They may also be crucial in contributing what is needed at a particular existential moment in ways the operative system is too rigid to take into account.

As for #3, I agree that hypotheses are important, in general. They are especially important in helping to identify what *systems* are operating, whether these be natural or human systems. Systems do not generally reveal themselves in the way physical objects do. Systems reveal themselves in processes and operations. Testing hypotheses regarding what systems are operating, and how, is crucial to gaining knowledge about them.

As for #4, I have already agreed that each employee is due personal consideration. This consideration derives from our roles as sentient beings, as conscious entities capable of experiencing pleasure, pain, joy, despair, remorse, and compassion. Indeed, it seems to me that there can be no value apart from sentient beings and their conscious experiences. And humans deserve special — though not exclusive — consideration because they have such experiences more intensely than other sentient beings.

Those who would improve American civilization
had better first establish
morally worthy standards of measurement,
standards which
give due consideration
to sentient beings and their possible experiences,
including all humans
and non-humans
worldwide
under various hypothetical scenarios.
Only then
can either past or hypothetical models
be appropriately evaluated
for their worthiness
to be adopted.

# Chapter IV

# *Gingrich Embraces The Third Wave*

## IV-1: *Gingrich Fantasizes*

In Chapter I, Section I-2, we were introduced to Gingrich's views on the coming "Information Age." In his Chapter #4 he continues his optimistic predictions about how there will be "enormous improvement in the lifestyle choices of most Americans," and how there will be a "revolution in goods and services that will empower and enhance most people." In each case, the benefits are predicted to accrue to "most" people. Whether this is true or not evades the more important moral question: "Will the distribution of benefits be just? Or will the rich get even richer at the expense of the poor getting ever poorer?" In Chapter I, I suggest that unless the financial and other benefits of our common heritage are more equitably shared, the latter will be the result. In this chapter, we consider the realistic practicality of some of the benefits which Gingrich is claiming for at least some people, if not "most," — such as in the following fantasy:

> Imagine a morning in just a decade or so. You wake up to a wall-size, high-definition television showing surf off Maui. (This is my favorite island — you pick your own scene.) You walk or jog or do Stairmaster while catching up on the morning news and beginning to review your day's schedule. Your home office is filled with communication devices, so you can ignore rush hour traffic. In fact, since most [that word again] Americans now telecommute, rush hour is dramatically smaller than it used to be. Telecommuting has proved to be the best means of dealing with pollution.

We can begin by questioning his prediction that pollution will have been greatly reduced. This may depend on how many of the resulting affluent people generate even more pollution in their global jet travelling, and the extent to which American industries generate more than they do now because of the relaxed environmental standards and the reduced budget for monitoring legislated by the Republican-controlled Congress. Even if the one balances the other, there remains a major pollution problem. And Gingrich gives no indication that he realizes the seriousness of it.

Let us also take a look at the fantasy life-style which Gingrich envisions "for most Americans." With the marginalized getting still poorer, and feeling even more frustrated than they are now, I wonder how much peace, either physical or "of mind," Gingrich and his fellow non-commuters will have. Can they be sure that there won't be demonstrations outside their homes? And what about when they venture out occasionally? Will their travel be uninterrupted, or will there be homeless people lining the roads, and fears of bombings at various junctures? Or will this problem be solved by America's continuing to lead the industrialized world in imprisonment of those who "aren't going to take it anymore"?

And what kind of family and community life will he be having? Will his children be doing all their learning at home also? If so, what about their lack of fellowship and companionship with fellow students? Also, what about the ambiance of the workplace? Work isn't only a way to get income for paying the bills. It also, at its best, serves as a place for comradeship with fellow workers, in which the meaning in the work is not limited to what one contributes, but includes what is contributed as a team. In fact, Gingrich himself seems to imply this, as noted in Section III-6 of this volume.

To be sure, there can be teams of a sort while individuals work at computer terminals. But is that any substitute for a pat on the back, a poke in the ribs for fun, and for all that intangible fellowship which accompanies a working group at its best? Americans are already doing many more things alone than they were in the past. What does this do for our sensitivity (or lack of it) to the subtleties of human touch and feeling?

And what of community life for the family? Will family members feel safe in venturing out alone, or together? Will it be safe to hold community gatherings? And even if it will, how much joy will there be in such community groups while realizing that "the poor are always with us" and that an increasing number are behind bars in an ever-increasing number of prisons?

These are some of the questions which Gingrich simply doesn't address. He is so locked into his thinking in terms of "competing" in power games, whether for individuals or for corporate America as a whole, that he almost completely ignores the most important considerations in what constitutes a wholesome quality of life.

## IV-2: *Gingrich's Do It Yourself Health Care*

When you are sick, you sit in your diagnostic chair and communicate with the local health clinic. Sensors take your blood pressure, analyze a blood sample, or do throat cultures. The results are quickly relayed to health aides, who make recommendations and prescribe medicine. The only time you visit a doctor or hospital is when something is seriously wrong. Because information is now readily available, the guild-like hold of the medical profession has been broken. Health care has become more flexible and convenient — and less expensive.

First we might ask if he has considered in his pollution calculations those that will be created in manufacturing all those private diagnostic chairs. And what of the natural resources that their manufacture will consume?

But what may turn out to be the biggest problem of all will be the extent to which the "information" given by such a chair is truly reliable. In order to be certain, it presumably will have to be checked frequently. And more ominous still might be concern about the reliability of the diagnosis, and of the prescription which is to be filled at the pharmacy. With Gingrich advocating, and legislating, so much "freedom" combined with such widespread relaxation of restrictions on corporate America, who will be able to be sure in his Third-Wave world of another's competence or conscientiousness on the job?

Thus we are reminded that it is not merely "information" per se that will be needed, but *reliable* information. And even reliable information isn't enough. It must be reliable information based on reliable *knowledge*. It would seem best to be denied information that relates to <u>un</u>reliable knowledge. One can imagine that there will be considerable competition among the suppliers of all these high-tech services. How is the ordinary person to evaluate each one, especially with the comparable increase in selling and manipulation skills and with the reduced governmental monitoring which he advocates?

We have only to recall how these manipulative skills are even now making it difficult to know what products are as they are claimed to be, and to know whether politicians will really carry out what they have promised in their reach for political power. Even now we can see how little concern politicians have with maintaining integrity in this regard. Their expectation is that all will be forgiven if they perform well enough to get the votes of "most" of those who vote in the next election. And, given the present majority-vote political structure, they are right, aren't they?

Add to the above considerations the fact that all this high-tech in the medical field will permit people to live longer, with illnesses lingering longer. Thus, though certain medical expenses *may* be reduced as Gingrich predicts, others will be greatly increased — and prolonged. There will certainly be more need for individual home care.

## IV-3: *Wishing Away Attorneys*

But Gingrich is most subject to skepticism when he argues as follows:

> Your legal problems will work the same way. You can write your own will, file your own adoption papers, form your own partnership or corporation — all with software programs available in your home. Then you will e-mail them to the proper authorities. Any disciplined and educated person can now "read the law." Once again, the "legal guild" — so similar to the medieval craft guilds that were scattered by the Industrial Revolution — has been broken. People now bring their law suits, file their own briefs, even represent themselves electronically in court. This democratization of the law — plus the astonishing decline in government regulation — has drastically reduced the demand for professionals. Fortunately, since most lawyers were reasonably smart and well educated people, they have been able to find other lines of work.

I begin to fear that Gingrich has "lost it." He seems to completely overlook the fact that the more complex and free-wheeling life becomes the more complex the resulting legal problems. Earlier he suggested that precisely because of ever new complexities, and the fact that no one could know everything about a field, there would be specialists for many more things than now. Each such new specialty presents new problems for monitoring agencies, such as governments — in the meantime reduced in size and power under Gingrich's "leadership." Eventually the need for truly justice-serving government will have been realized, laws will have become more complex than ever, and these will spawn more specially trained lawyers than ever. Witness the O.J. Simpson trial and the number of man-hours of lawyers for both prosecution and defense that were employed, even without considering the many legal consultants of various kinds which both sides had to engage in order to keep one step ahead of the other side.

Gingrich tends to assume that advances in high-tech will simplify *human* problems in the same manner as purely physical ones. Thus, if a computer will make a factory more efficient in turning out mechanical gadgets, he tends to assume the same will be true for legal, medical, educational, and governmental problems. The truth is, however, that the more high-tech increases efficiency in the physical world, and thereby increases power in certain hands and the pace of life generally, the more complex and baffling become those areas of human relations and development serviced by lawyers, health professionals, educators, and the most essential government officials — those we call upon to make those difficult judgments about justice and injustice and how to minimize the one and maximize the other. The fact is that the faster the pace at which high-tech gives us answers and performance in the physical areas of our lives, the more difficult, more prolonged, and less clear are the answers we get in the most important personal-relations areas of our lives.

It is a truth deriving from the fact that mathematics can only be applied in those areas of our lives that are appropriately analyzed into discrete units, where any unit can be substituted for any other — *that is, where uniquenesses can safely be ignored.* On the other hand, in human relations and in our most personal lives we ignore uniqueness at our peril; thus, we apply mathematics at our peril.

In short, by assuming that high-tech can necessarily increase efficiency in human relations as it does in the physical world, Newt Gingrich shows his ignorance of the essential nature of high-tech and his insensitivity to the unique nuances of human relations.

## IV-4: *Fantasy in Education*

The problem of reliability takes on a general and sweeping form in the area Gingrich deals with next: the area of education. Here is the way he pictures an end to educators, along with medical technicians and lawyers, in a world in which everyone simply self-educates:

> Now imagine that you want to learn something new, solve a personal problem, or enter a new profession. Do you have to go to night school or trek twenty-five miles to the nearest college? No, you simply enter the on-line learning system and describe what you need. . . . In less than twenty-four hours you can launch yourself on a new profession. In a society of continuous, lifelong learning, these options will be available to everyone.

Here is where the matter of reliability in the "knowledge" thus gained comes to a head. Where a person supposedly could become a professional in such an easy way, consider what little confidence we could have in anyone posing as a medical, legal, or technical expert. Yet, in the following quotation Gingrich shows what little appreciation he has for this simple truth even when he himself states the evidence for it.

> Living in a world that is bathed in information — *too much information for any one person or company to absorb* — your livelihood and security are likely to come from becoming an expert — maybe the world's greatest expert — on one small corner of this vast infosphere. You may become the authority on some obscure medical procedure or accounting principle. You may know more than anyone else about the incorporation laws. . . . Corporate giants are finding it just doesn't make sense anymore to try to bring all their expertise under one roof. It's much easier to "outsource," relying on small, mobile, independent contractors for information. *The world of information these companies must master is exploding* [emphasis added].

Again, the significance of the statement about "too much information" seems to escape him. And the problem of *reliability* among such "too much information" evidently escapes him still more. It seems he is pre-programmed to see only the positive outcomes. And that is a formula for disaster in today's exploding civilization. But such is Gingrich's ominous blindness in his passionate, obsessive devotion to corporate America. But why? Why is he on this "trip"? He gave us his answer in his Chapter 2 (See our Chapter II): He sees corporate America as the only hope for again making America "#1 in the world" in the same old materialistic, militaristic, power-dominating way he thought of America in his own power-seeking youth.

Therefore, I conclude that in the scenario he portrays, the exaggerated legal claims would be so great, the sloppy workmanship in all professions so extensive, the disappointment in performance so deep (and often tragic), and the resulting law suits so overwhelming that law and order would break down almost completely, and civil war of some kind would be the likely outcome.

Nor would the resulting tragedy be confined to the industrialized countries that follow his lead. Because of their influence in the world and the widespread dependence on them world-wide, the conflicts would be global. That is my prediction if the blind faith Gingrich displays in his Third Wave fantasies is not realized for what it is. Indeed, a major reason for my writing this particular book is in order not only to challenge these fantasies but also to alert everyone he might influence to their ominous nature. And in the following paragraph we again see the basic motivation behind all of them:

> There will also be enormous advantages for America and Americans if we lead the world in the transition to the Third Wave Information Age. Just as Britain profited enormously by leading the world into the industrial era, so the United States can profit enormously by being the leader in the development of the new goods, services, systems, and standards associated with a technological revolution of this scale.

Here we see again the major motivation behind all his fantasies. This is the way to make his childhood dreams come true: Newt Gingrich, the great leader and teacher, leading America into becoming the greatest *power* in the world. We remember his youthful conclusion that he had to learn "how to lead." We remember his preoccupation with power per se, and the significance for him of that English paper he wrote on "the balance of world power" (Chapter II).

Roughly speaking, his economic message seems to be this: Don't worry about jobs being lost through downsizing and their being sent overseas. A constant flow of new jobs and local markets will be developed by having America become the major producer of high-tech in the global marketplace. In that way, there can also be enough trickle-down to make the safety net of welfare only minimally necessary. Everyone will be educated as to "what it means to be an American," a pursuer of wealth in high-tech in every home! It's as if Gingrich himself had been unthinkingly swept up in some auxiliary "wave" of the very Third Wave which so intrigues him.

## IV-5: *Gingrich on Why Governments Don't Work*

In the next chapter we shall see more completely how this fantasy for America relates to his fantasy for the distribution of power in the world, with America again #1. But, before leaving this one, we note Gingrich's theory about why governments tend to become bogged down in inefficient bureaucracies:

> The basic reason is that governments are not customer driven. Governments almost always grant monopoly status to their own operations so they won't have to compete . . . Because government operations don't have to please consumers, they end up catering to employees. That's why most government operations are overstaffed. Unionization has only made things worse . . . Change inconveniences employees, and that's why governments end up lagging in technology. Installing computers means employees have to learn new tasks. It's also likely to put a few people out of work.

There may be some truth to his charges of government lethargy. If so, then both the rational and socially responsible approach is to inquire what can be done about it. But that wouldn't serve Gingrich's purpose of freeing corporate America from governmental restrictions. Also, again, Gingrich doesn't note what is a significant difference between the role of government in dealing with the delicate nuances of human relations and the role of industry in applying mathematically structured high-tech. To be sure, there are jobs in government which are purely technical and clerical. But, again, the key jobs in governments ought to be held by people who are unusually committed to justice and sensitive to injustice in its increasingly multitudinous forms. Put simply, no computer can substitute for a mature and committed *sense* of justice. Over and over again, Gingrich fails to enter that crucial consideration into his thinking and proposals for America, and the world.

## IV-6: *A Summary Evaluation*

Finally, Gingrich summarizes the economics part of his fantasy in the closing statement of his Chapter 4:

If we liberate entrepreneurs and make it relatively easy for them to discover and invent our new world, we will be rearing a generation that increases our wealth and improves our lives to a degree that we can now barely imagine.

I also believe that there can be a great future for life on this earth, and that technology, including high-tech, must play a part if the growing number of human beings on this earth are to have anything like America's middle class lifestyle. But such a scenario will only be realized in a good way to the extent that we can bring about economic and political *systems* which are truly *just*, and which therefore give a high degree of assurance that there truly will be *justice for all* on this earth.

Gingrich quotes Toynbee. I have also been impressed by Toynbee's study of civilizations. But I draw a different lesson from it. Toynbee notes that civilizations collapse when challenges come too fast. And what constitutes "too fast"? I am persuaded that it relates to power, and the significant fact that power tends to corrupt. From this simple fact it follows that unless systems designed to assure the *just* use of power "keep pace" with the development and employment of economic and other forms of power, then it will corrupt!

But economic and political systems have not kept pace. They have not kept pace in their commitment to justice and their ability to prevent and remedy injustice. Power has grown faster, and continues to grow faster, than the institutions designed to assure that it will be developed and employed within the moral bounds of justice for all. Indeed, it is now clear that most governments are manipulated by the very power brokers governments most need to control. The "foxes" are indeed in charge of the chickencoop, and Gingrich would have it be even more so. If he has his way, corporate America will not only dominate all economic activity in the world but all political activity also.

Corporate America not only has its way in America's political life today, but also in what Clark Kerr, former President of the University of California, has called "The Knowledge Industry."[1] This is the industry which — centered in our major research universities — constantly turns out knowledge-power in almost complete disregard for how it is used, or whether there are adequate safeguards in place to restrain its tendency, as with all power, to be misused. The heart of our modern tragedy, therefore,

---

1. *The Uses of the University*, by Clark Kerr, pub. by Harper & Row, New York, 1963

consists in the fact that the knowledge industry — with the major universities of the world producing most of the basic knowledge — has largely become a servant of the military-industrial complex that Dwight D. Eisenhower warned us against.

What is most needed, therefore, is for the major universities of the world to STOP feeding that complex with indiscriminate knowledge-power until there is assurance that it will be justly used. And this will happen only when economic and political systems are in place which provide such assurance.

*This is why I challenge the major universities of the world to use their intellectual and experimental facilities to envision, and then to show us how to establish, the economic and political structures which will thus assure that the ever-increasing power coming into the world will be maintained within the moral bounds of justice for all. To the extent that this is done, they can then gradually return to producing knowledge-power for the marketplaces of the world. But not until then.*

Indeed, we do face a civilization crisis.
In this I agree with Gingrich.
But it is not
as he portrays it to be.
He would have us generate power
without adequate assurance of its just use.
But that is the road to even more
misuse of power
than we see today.
So, what we are really challenged to do
is to at all times
have in place and working effectively
safeguards against such misuse of power,
and to keep developing ever new safeguards
at a *pace* at all times greater
than that at which power,
especially knowledge-power,
is developed, distributed,
and employed.

# Chapter V

# Gingrich's America in the Global Marketplace

## V-1: *Gingrich Embraces the Multinationals*

On page 65 of his Chapter 5, Gingrich begins to state his views on the global marketplace as follows:

> If we intend to give our children the best job security, the best quality of life, and the best take-home pay in the world, then we are going to have to rethink our entire approach to being competitive in the world market.
>
> If we are serious about American success, we must begin by learning *from our multinational corporations* under what circumstances they would create the next thousand high-value-added jobs in the United States . . . We also need to approach our major exporters and ask what help they need to compete in the world market [emphasis added].

Again we see Gingrich's preoccupation with making America #1 in the world in economic wealth and wealth production. We also see again the deference Gingrich proposes to show to America's multinational corporations and their eagerness to export their goods and services and reap their profits, to and in all corners of the earth. The supposed reason is that they are the only remaining source of "high value-added jobs." This is largely true, and will continue to be true so long as corporate America has a near-monopoly of the country's productive capital. But Gingrich's reasons go far deeper — to America as #1 in the world, with Newt Gingrich as its "leader."

Job creation with the interest of the workers at heart really does seem to be central to the Clinton administration's program. But, so long as ordinary people are denied a fair share of the financial and other benefits of our common heritage, there is no other way for most of them to get even survival income — apart from the humiliation of welfare payments — without their having decent-paying jobs. And with low-skilled jobs being rapidly lost to automation and the availability of cheap labor in other countries, the only hope for such income, especially for the level of incomes that Americans have come to expect, is in jobs in the high-tech industries.

In his *The Work of Nations*, Robert Reich paints the American and global picture in a much clearer and more realistic way than does Gingrich. The big difference between the job-creation programs of Gingrich and Reich is that the latter shows considerable compassion for the marginalized, whereas Gingrich speaks of them as "whiners," and treats them as if they were mere nuisances in his drive for achieving what he sees as America's God-given destiny as God's chosen people, to be #1 in the pursuit of ever more power and wealth in a power-brokering world.

Of course, for Gingrich, America virtually **is** corporate America. That we are reminded of in the above quotation. The American multinationals are to be catered to so that they will "create the next thousand value-added jobs in the United States" rather than somewhere else. Thus, America's multinational corporations are envisioned to be in the driver's seat of America's effort to again be the major wealth and power producer in the world. This means that their lobbyists in Washington and elsewhere will have to be catered to, and their financial contributions to political campaigns accepted as the order of the day. In effect, they are to be considered as speaking for the true interests of the American people. In the twenties a common expression was, "What's good for General Motors is good for the country." That motto has now been revived in its multinational form. Today, under a Gingrich agenda, the American military-industrial complex has a new lease on life.

Let us be clear in all this that the basic problem is not what some pacifists would have us believe. The basic problem is not the U.S. military. To be sure, they have their vested interests, and they want to keep their jobs. But, in America, they have not yet gained the upper hand. That remains with the corporate world of Big Business. The American military is paid by the stockholding *owners* of America's multinationals. Stockholders generally have a very impersonal relationship with the corporation in which they hold stock; they have bought it for its money-making potential, and they will sell it when it seems to lose that potential. The managers of the corporations draw salaries only so long as they deliver profits to their stockholders. So, they pay politicians like Gingrich to see to it that the U.S. military serves their interests in the global marketplace.

## V-2: *The Big Money Makers in America*

And who are these major stockholding owners and power brokers in the American corporate world? The owners are sometimes also power brokers, but not necessarily so. The owners of corporate stock get their dividends even when they are vacationing in the Bahamas or in the Mediterranean. The power brokers, along with the military, do the bidding of these ultimate owners; at least they must appear to do so. The "symbolic analysts" (Robert Reich's term) are the managers and technicians of the American corporate world. They are the ones who have become skilled at knowing how the existing economic and political systems of the world work — at knowing who holds what kind of power, and how to use these power sources and the laws of Nature in such a way that, for instance, a factory turns out its products as "automatically" and reliably as possible, by way of impersonal high-tech and impersonal managers.

Many of the owners of America's productive capital have their owner-ship by way of inheritance. George Washington invested in so many thousands of acres in so many states[1] that he didn't live long enough to reap the profits from selling it to the expanding population — but his descendants must have reaped a tremendous harvest. And if they continued to invest wisely what they inherited and didn't squander too much, they continued to get richer and richer by the profits from the first investment added to the amount to be next invested. And so the original nest egg mounts. One can see, then, the big disadvantage suffered by those denied their share of income from our common heritage, their rightful source for that initial nest egg with which the investment process can then begin.

The nice thing about income from investments is that the amount from which the investment income derives keeps mounting, provided only that one is reasonably frugal and one invests wisely. Nor need it take one's constant attention. The income from investing one's current surplus wealth gives one freedom to investigate other investment opportunities. At some point one can just sit back and wait for the ever-increasing dividends to come in. That's when one can as well be in the Bahamas as anywhere else.

But the marginalized, being denied their rightful share of the original common-heritage nest egg, never get a chance to get started on that road. Not only don't they get their rightful common heritage dividend as a means to get started, but they don't even have the time or energy to think about it, and certainly not to figure out how this extremely complex economic system works to their disadvantage. They may suspect they are being cheated somehow. But they never quite figure out why or how. So, they live in frustration, from which they occasionally, and understandably, strike out wildly, or turn to drink, or drugs. That's the route by which increasing numbers of Americans end up in America's increasing number of jails. The overt slavery of the corporate America of the Hamilton-Madison-Washington days has been replaced by today's more insidious kind of slavery. The

---

1. Paul M. Wolf (*Land in America, Its Value, Use, and Control,* Pantheon Books, NY 1981) has this to say about Washington's land holdings: "George Washington, who kept a regular agent in the upper Ohio country staking out claims on choice territory for himself, wrote in the 1760s: ' ...Any person who neglects the present opportunity of hunting out good land will never again regain it.' "

slave-plantation owners of the 18th century have been replaced by the more manipulative corporate owners of our day. Indeed, some of the 18th century slave owners may have taken better care of their slaves than corporate America does of its wage-slaves of today.

In contrast to living in the Bahamas from income from investment capital, income from "a job" usually requires one's constant attention. Because of limitations on time and human energy, it is difficult to hold more than one job at the same time and thereby build an original nest egg.. There are those who have done it, such as original immigrants, but it takes unusual physical and mental stamina, and determination. It is an effort which no one should have to make — and wouldn't have to make if everyone received a fair share of financial and other benefits from our common heritage.

We must look to the economic and political systems for answers. Each corporate head pleads innocence, saying that they are forced to do what they do in order to "compete" in the present system. And yet, they continue to support the system which rewards aggressiveness and acquisitiveness. They have come to like the power game. People like Gingrich have become "good" at it. That's all they have been trained to do. So, they don't want to give it up; they don't want to change to a system which would force them to give it up.

Those beneficiaries of large inheritances who prefer to oversee their investments more closely, and even to supplement them with some power brokering — i.e., as "symbolic analysts" — participate in the corporate world in some administrative way. They supplement their investment income by serving on Boards of Directors. Some may even take on technical or administrative roles, such as assistant vice president in charge of this or that. Those who become "chief executive officers" supplement their investments handsomely while at the same time being in position to greatly enhance the income from such investments — thus making the difference between getting a dollar return of 8-10% and one of 20-50%. It doesn't take knowledge of higher math to see that one's total wealth can mount exceedingly fast at either rate of return, but especially at the latter rate.

## V-3: *A Crucial Distinction Between Owners and Non-owners*

In all this, it is important to maintain the clear distinction between owners and power brokers. The former get their income essentially as landlords. They rent out their production facilities, or their money, to those who actually make the production and service wheels go around. And to the extent that they can achieve a near-monopoly of such ownership, they can demand of their lessees ever higher "rents" — in the form a of percentage of profits in the case of a production facility, or interest payments in the case of cash investments in the open financial market.

Reich does an exceptionally skillful job of making this kind of analysis except (as noted in the *Preface*) for failing to make the distinction between owners and symbolic analysts. Thus, he almost completely ignores the category of owners as such. Amazingly, he attributes almost all income to "jobs." To be sure, the jobs held by his symbolic analysts are not the usual jobs. Their special skills in manipulating and managing increasingly complex (and human infested) economic and political *systems* are so much in demand that they can set their own hours, weeks, months, and years for "working on the job."

But so long as they don't additionally have legal ownership of production or service facilities — whether as stockholders or by holding title to physical property — they still must get all their income from some form of service they render with their minds and their bodies. Some may even spend all their time in the Bahamas, but  they cannot spend all their thoughts on recreation in the Bahamas and still have money coming in. The owners of sufficient investments, however, as noted above, can do precisely that.

So, it is among the *owners* of the production and service facilities of the corporate world, in partnership with the symbolic analysts, that we must look for the largest American incomes. The owners (of land, factories, machinery, computers, franchises, patents, etc.) get income apart from a job. The symbolic analysts offer their services to these owners, and get paid according to how much return on investment they can deliver for the owners. The rest of the jobs in the economic and political systems are held by people of more ordinary skills: secretaries, mechanics, maintenance personnel, sales clerks, etc.

## V-4: *How Our Common Heritage is Now Distributed*

As noted above, it is the owners and symbolic analysts who derive the bulk of the income from our common heritage. In the case of owners of land, they do so in the course of charging rent for land which production facilities occupy (especially when this land is in conjunction with complex urban infrastructure). Thus, those who hold title to urban land get income from both Nature's land surface and from technology incorporated in it.

The symbolic analysts, on the other hand, use the technical *knowledge* part of our common heritage. It is a bit more difficult to identify, but, as noted, the technical and intellectual skills which they offer for sale are founded on technical knowledge and know-how developed over centuries by many unidentified persons in many cultures. Some was developed in recent years, with patents issued to their "inventors." When, after 17 years, their patents run out, that "intellectual capital" should also be acknowledged as our common heritage. But it isn't considered such by our legal systems. Rather, it becomes available to those symbolic analysts and owners who have been educated to make use of it.

Again, what I am suggesting is that (1) the common heritage part of land and its resources, and (2) the common heritage part of technical knowledge and urban infrastructure inherited from previous generations should both be held in trust, leased out to both ordinary people and Gingrich-type entrepreneurs (though for socially and ecologically responsible uses *only*), and the income distributed to the residents of the earth *as a common heritage right*.

## V-5: *Summary and Closing Comments*

Now we are in position to see the relevance of this proposal to the problem of securing income for those who lose their jobs to high-tech through downsizing and to foreign workers who work cheap because they're deprived even more than Americans of a fair share of our common heritage.

If everyone received a common heritage dividend as a basic right there would be no job crisis. Not only would everyone, in addition, have leverage for bargaining for truly fair wages and salaries, but as high-tech made for ever-more-efficient, more "labor-saving" production of goods and services, the market value of our common heritage of land, resources, and technology would increase with it, and thereby our common-heritage dividends. In this scenario everyone, instead of just an elite few, would share in the benefits of increased technological efficiency — *provided, of course, all this takes place within the moral bounds of justice, in turn assured by truly just economic and political systems.*

To the extent that such common heritage dividends are assured, there won't exist the desperate need to constantly generate new jobs, especially high-paying ones in high-tech. Thus, it won't be necessary to find foreign markets in places with questionable human rights records. We can develop a largely self-sufficient American economy, with foreign trade limited to those foreign markets which we can be assured are being maintained within the moral bounds of justice. In this way, we will be setting a moral example for other economic and political systems around the world. Additionally, because we Americans will apply moral standards in choosing trading partners, we will be giving incentive to those wanting access to our markets to meet our moral standards, not only in dealing with us but also with their own people.

In contrast, we note again an example of Gingrich's thinking in relation to America's role in the world:

> No nation can lead the world if it can't economically sustain itself. Unless we accept our role as world leader, our planet will eventually be a dark and bloody place. No other nation is in a position to assume our mantle [as God's chosen people?]. We therefore have an absolute obligation to our children and grandchildren to commit ourselves to a strategy of winning the economic competition within the new world market.

Again, I suggest that adopting the Gingrich agenda would lead this country, and the world, down the path of increased power brokering with increasingly inadequate safeguards against the corrupt misuse of the economic, political, and military power it generates. I leave readers with some closing quotes from Gingrich's Chapter 5, quotes which simply serve as further evidence of the ominous agenda which Gingrich would impose on the American people, and, if he could, on the people of the world.

I say "impose," because that is what he proposes as far as the young are concerned; they are to be given little choice but to be indoctrinated with Gingrich's view of America as God's chosen people, and of America as defined by the power-seeking principles and questionable moral values of those he calls Our Founding Fathers of over two centuries ago when both America and the world were, as he also notes, radically different from what they are today. Thus, we read the following three paragraphs on page 68:

Economic growth is the most important social policy objective a country can have other than keeping its people physically safe. Without economic growth there will be no jobs for current welfare recipients to go to when we reform the system. Without jobs there will be no resources to sustain the Medicare system. Without economic growth the baby boomers will not be able to rely on their Social Security benefits. Without economic growth our children will not be able to earn enough to pay interest on the national debt, help pay for their parents' and grandparents' Social Security and Medicare, help pay for their own generation's government, help save for their own retirement, and still have some income to live on.

Economic growth is that central to a sound social policy for the whole country. When the pie is getting bigger everyone stays busy trying to cut a bigger piece for themselves and their families and neighbors. When the pie starts shrinking people begin to get selfish and jealous. The whole social fabric of the country is strained.

America's future depends on economic growth. Economic growth depends on our ability to compete in the world market. Competing in the world market is going to require a lot of reforms, a lot of work, and a willingness to face reality and then be more creative, more energetic, and more optimistic than any of our competitors. We can do it. In fact, we have to do it. We owe it to our children and our country.

What Gingrich says here is pretty close to the truth unless moves are made to assure everyone her-his fair share of the financial and other benefits of our common heritage. Unless this is done, virtually all that Gingrich says will come true, and with ever-increasing poverty, desperation, and social turmoil. And what the Clinton administration and Robert Reich propose constitutes only temporary bandaids so long as the most aggressive and acquisitive among us are permitted to continue to accumulate a larger and larger chunk of the ownership and benefits of our common heritage of land, resources, and technology.

In the next chapter we deal with further dimensions of these same issues.

Only when it becomes generally recognized
that income from capital
is all but monopolized
by the most aggressive and acquisitive
in the world
will we come to acknowledge
the natural, moral right
of each resident of this planet earth
to a fair share
of the financial and other benefits
derived from
*our common heritage*
of productive capital
as distinct from
that productive capital
which someone generates over and beyond this.

# Chapter VI

# *Gingrich's Opportunity Society*

## VI-0: *Gingrich's Eight Steps*

Gingrich's proposal to replace the welfare state with "the opportunity society" has already received my initial comments in Chapter I, Section I-4. Readers may want to review what was said there before entering upon this chapter. The following comments are directed specifically at some key statements in his Chapter 6. After criticizing some of the ways the existing welfare system is subject to misuse, he asks us to "consider the facts:"

> Welfare spending is now $305 billion a year. Since 1965 we have spent $5 trillion on welfare — more than the cost of winning World War II. Yet despite this massive effort, conditions in most poor communities have grown measurably worse . . . We owe it to all young Americans in every neighborhood to save them from a *system* that is depriving them of their God-given rights to life, liberty, and the pursuit of happiness [emphasis added].

The question remains: What "system" is it that is making it necessary to spend increasing amounts just to keep the marginalized at a bare subsistence level? Clearly, the culprit is *the dominant economic and political system,* not the welfare system. The latter is only there to pick up the pieces strewn across the landscape by the more fundamental system.

More precisely, as argued several times in previous pages, the welfare system is needed *in lieu of* everyone's getting her-his fair share of the financial and other benefits from our common heritage.  So, Gingrich's criticism of welfare is misplaced.  Furthermore, his supposed sympathy for the children of welfare parents seems ingenuous:

> We have an obligation to improve the lives of the poor from day one. . . .
> When people tell me I am intense on this issue, I ask them to imagine that their children were the ones dying on the evening news and then tell me how intense they would be to save their own children's lives. That is how intense we should all be. [page 73]

Such statements strike me as disgustingly ingenuous. If he really cared about these children he wouldn't be so indiscriminate in cutting welfare payments. Again, what he fails to factor into his proposals is "welfare" to the most aggressive and acquisitive by way of a near-monopoly ownership and income from what ought to be recognized as our *common* heritage. Most people of compassion feel there must be something wrong with the rich getting ever richer as the poor get ever poorer, even though they haven't yet realized that the cause of it lies in the unfair distribution of income and other benefits from our common heritage. But Gingrich seems perfectly willing to blame the victims rather than even *consider* the possibility that the riches which the most aggressive among us are hauling in, and of which the poor are increasingly being deprived, may be not so much the result of the efforts of either the rich or the poor as of an unjust *system.*

But let us hear from Gingrich what are  the "eight major changes" that he says will be required in order to replace "the welfare society with an opportunity society." Presumably trying to sound compassionate, he calls them "the eight steps we need for improving opportunities for the poor:"

1. Shifting from caretaking to caring
2. Volunteerism and spiritual renewal
3. Reasserting the values of American civilization
4. Emphasizing family and work
5. Creating tax incentives for work, investment, and entrepreneurship
6. Reestablishing savings and property ownership
7. Learning as focus of education
8. Protection against violence and drugs

Then he suggests considering each of these in turn. So, that is what we shall do, following his format.

## VI-1: *Shifting from Caretaking to Caring*

Quoting from *Working Without a Net*, by Morris Schechtman, he makes a distinction between:

> (1) caretaking — a more casual attitude, in which the important concern is to make the provider feel good, no matter the outcome and (2) caring — a more selfless but positive approach, in which the outcome for the person being helped is the first concern.

This does seem to be an important distinction. But we withhold comment until we see what use he makes of it. In the meantime we go on to consider a distinction which he attributes to *The Tragedy of American Compassion*, by Marvin Olasky, that between "the deserving and the undeserving."

> Olasky emphasizes that indiscriminate aid actually destroys people. In addition, the sight of undeserving people getting resources while refusing to be responsible for themselves sends a devastating message to those working poor who are trying to make the effort to improve their lot. Besides undermining individual morality, indiscriminate aid undermines society as a whole.

We begin by granting some truth to this statement. Oxfam and other groups seeking to reverse world poverty employ this principle. Instead of constant handouts of milk, they give a family a cow. Better still, instead of providing food lines, let us help people to get their own rightful share of land, on which they can then grow their own food. Better still, see that they get a fair share of the financial and other benefits of our entire common heritage — then they will never be at our doorstep again.

Again, what Gingrich fails most to consider is the possibility that the basic reason so many are poor in the first place is that the most aggressive and acquisitive in both America and the rest of the world are the *most* "undeserving" of all, because they are undeserving of the near-monopoly financial and other benefits they are constantly receiving from our common heritage. In thus "ripping off" the cream of our common heritage they are the greatest contributors of all to the poverty of hundreds of millions of people over the entire world.

Gingrich closes this section by concluding that "true caring requires a level of detailed knowledge that is not possible for government bureaucracies." But this is a too sweeping and hasty conclusion. Careful structuring can assure that those persons *administering* governmental programs at the grass roots level are sufficiently sensitive, compassionate, and committed to make the necessary distinctions with the "effectiveness" Gingrich so highly values (See XIII-2).

## VI-2: *Volunteerism and Spiritual Renewal*

In this section Gingrich carries a step farther his argument for helping the needy in ways which will put them on the road to caring for themselves. He suggests that the best kind of caring includes doing so from a religious motivation — better still, one which leads to a religious conversion. For this reason, he argues, religious groups do a better job of caring than secular governments.

Readers will not be surprised that my first comment on this is that the thing which the poor need most is their basic economic *right* to a fair share of the financial and other economic benefits of our common heritage. Whether or not a person needs something beyond that is a separate issue, and one having little to do with poverty. Again, in the present state of affairs a religious conversion among the most aggressive and acquisitive would be far more "effective" than among the poor. If they would agree to be limited to only their fair share of our common heritage there would be no poverty (See Appendix A).

In fact, in my *Liberating the Early American Dream* I have argued that the discrediting blow which has been given to the mechanistic-materialistic conception of the universe by quantum physics may serve us in this regard. We now know that the picture presented by the older Newtonian physics of the universe as an impersonal machine, and with human consciousness a mere temporary "epiphenomenon," has completely lost its scientific and philosophic credibility. That long-standing mechanistic view of life contributes nothing to the sentiment of compassion. Rather, it gives support to the dog-eat-dog philosophy which the American free enterprise system (with its inadequate moral bounds) and Western culture generally have largely accepted.

Might it be, therefore, that a religious rebirth based on a more spiritual conception of the human person might well be the more "effective" means of bringing about a new level of fair dealing among the most aggressive and acquisitive among us? I consider this possibility also in Section XIII-8.

Returning to Gingrich's manner of thinking, whether or not a particular religious person would do more harm than good would depend on many things, including the beliefs and commitments of that person and her-his religion. Religions which advocate cutting off hands of thieves or blinding peeping Toms would be suspect from the start.

Gingrich ends this section by putting in a plug for volunteerism. He says, for instance, that he makes a point of volunteering to help build houses under the sponsorship of Habitat for Humanity.

Again, however, the volunteerism that's most needed on the part of the most aggressive and acquisitive among us is of a different kind. If they were to begin basing their lives on simple fairness, beginning with economic fairness, those who finally benefitted from such fairness would be inspired to follow.

## VI-3: *Reasserting the Values of American Civilization*

Gingrich begins this section by deploring the fact that "everyday on television and radio poor people see and hear things that reinforce the message that income transfer is what matters and spiritual transformation is unimportant." This is another indication that he believes the basic problem with poverty is the poor people themselves. All they need, he implies, is "spiritual transformation." Again I am struck by his presumptuous and callused arrogance. He then continues as follows:

> I believe we are at the end of the era of tolerating alcoholism, addiction, spouse and child abuse, parental indifference, and adult irresponsibility. We have all seen society change for the better in recent years in its view on smoking. drunk driving, and racism. There is no reason that views on unacceptable behavior for the poor cannot change as well.

And so, he keeps hammering at the victims of our unjust systems rather than at the systems themselves, and the privileged elite who benefit from them. Then, in a further slap at some of the more tragic figures among the poor, he declares that "it is shameful to be a drunk at three in the afternoon, and we ought to say so." But we are not told why it is more shameful for a desperately discouraged, poverty-stricken, unemployed person to get drunk in the middle of the afternoon than, for instance, for a Wall Street broker to be so when he comes home to his family late in the evening. He then goes on to make a point which has considerably more credibility:

> It is shameful for radio stations to play songs that advocate mutilating and raping women. Governments can't and shouldn't censor it, but decent advertisers could announce they will boycott any station that plays that kind of music. Within weeks these brutal, barbaric songs would be off the air.

Why governments "can't and shouldn't" censor such verbal violence is not clear. I would suggest that they both can and should. They can fine stations which present it, both individual stations and networks. They can also shut down any station which persists. That would get the obscene programs off the air sooner than leaving it to the consciences of corporate bodies who have their eyes primarily on profits for their stockholders. For most of the producers it would take a considerable amount of shame to bring them to the same effect. What we are considering here is grossly unjust behavior, with countless victims in the making. And I will argue that it is precisely the role of governments to prevent, and remedy, this and other forms of injustice.

As for concern about violating the right to freedom of speech referred to in the Bill of Rights, it is important to remember that these amendments were added specifically to protect against the use of governmental power. They are presented as absolutes because any deviation from absoluteness might otherwise give U.S. Government officials a foothold with which to gain powers they should not have. Thus, the right to freedom of speech should not extend to the right to vilify or preach hate. *It should only apply to the right to be critical of the government, of its government officials, its structure, its policies, or its actions.*

What Gingrich seems to be doing here is gesturing toward people concerned with public morality — of whom I am one — while also being true to his friends in the corporate world who want to see an end to all regulating of their activities. Again, to me, Gingrich's moralizing comes across as ingenuous.

That's about all he says here about "reasserting the values of American Civilization." Nothing about the need for strengthening and deregulating the corporate world — except, as noted, by implication in what went unsaid.

## VI-4: *Emphasizing Family and Work*

This section is primarily his argument against features of the welfare system which discourage marriage and normal family life while supposedly encouraging young girls to become pregnant and remain single.

This may well be a valid argument against certain features of the existing welfare program, but, again, I would counter that the welfare system is not the primary cause of broken families. The wealthy "elite" are notorious for a great variety of "relationships," as are the affluent generally. He closes with the following statement, the first sentence of which I largely agree with:

> We need to revise welfare so that going to work never lowers your standard of living. When you add up housing, health care, food stamps, aid to family and dependent children, and other programs, there is actually a substantial disadvantage in joining the labor force. We need to redesign the system so that people have a sense of reward at each step up the ladder of opportunity.

We can agree with Gingrich that people should not be discouraged from working. But he would have us *force* them to work (even if there are no decent jobs) by denying them that mere token of welfare payments which serves as a poor substitute for the $36,000 per year for the average family of four (See Appendix A) which they would get if they were getting their fair share of income from our common heritage, the bulk of which is presently going to people who are getting so much money from invested capital (including our common heritage capital) that they not only don't have to work but they can vacation all year long.

## VI-5: *Tax Incentives for Work, Investment, Entrepreneurship*

He opens this section with the following:

> People can work only when jobs are available; job creation requires investment. Today America's poor neighborhoods offer such poor returns on investment that people simply won't go there to create jobs . . . As a result, the poor are cheated out of jobs.

Whereas it is true that the best jobs are those in production facilities in which there has been substantial investment — provided such investment makes that part of Nature more efficient in producing something worthwhile — such increased efficiency in productivity doesn't depend on investment by any particular person, such as by one of those who now have a near-monopoly of capital. If the income from our common heritage were truly equitably distributed, then *many* people would have money to invest. In fact, investment would take many more innovative and productive forms than it does today when those who have a near-monopoly of money to invest tend to leave investment decisions to someone else. When one is directing the investment of one's own money one is most likely to invest wisely.

He then goes on to praise Jack Kemp for his leadership in getting "enterprise zones" created in the inner cities. He encourages people to create their own jobs through investments in small enterprises — though he gives as examples working for large enterprises, such as Amway and Tupperware. Then he makes a closing pitch for opportunities in the American free enterprise system:

> Anyone with a little money, some free time, and a willingness to learn marketing can make money [a bit of an exaggeration]. It is just as important to convince the poor that they can create their own jobs as it is to help them find jobs.

I agree that in an increasingly capital-intensive economy it is important to help people turn from getting all their income from a job to getting it from increasing amounts from capital investment. But, again, those who are denied any substantial inheritance, exceptional intelligence, or good looks, or, most importantly, a fair share of the financial and other benefits from our common heritage, have great barriers to overcome in getting started on that capital-investment ladder.

## VI-6: *Reestablishing Savings and Property Ownership*

It is difficult to disagree with the principles advocated in this section: the need to encourage people to own property, especially property which generates income, and most especially that which will generate still more income by putting one's personal labor into it. A carpenter who owns his own truck and tools is a good example. Another example would be producer cooperatives, such as ESOPs.

But, again, with the most aggressive and acquisitive taking over both ownership and income from our common heritage, it becomes more and more difficult for the rest of the population. Because the rest are forced to get all their income from lower-and-lower-paying jobs, they find it almost impossible to get any significant initial foothold on either savings or property ownership.

## VI-7: *Learning as the Focus of Education*

Most of this section is devoted to blasting the public education bureaucracy, especially as it operates in many inner cities. I find little to criticize about the concerns he expresses in this section. Having myself taught from 7th grade up to and including the university level, roughly following in each case the level at which my children were studying, I sympathize with many of the criticisms he voices here.

I have concluded that governments should have a very limited role in education, only that necessary to inform people of what the government will consider unjust behavior, thereby subject to coercive censure.

How, then, will children get educated? One way would be by parents (who get a regular income from our common heritage and truly fair wages and salaries) who join together to form their own schools, preferably guided by socially responsible and truly spiritually rooted religious organizations to which they belong.

I can say, for instance, that the Friends (Quaker) secondary schools in which I taught (one was a "day" school and the other a boarding school) were both superior to any public school I either taught or studied in. Even the best public schools, and there are some very good ones (two daughters of mine teach in them), are handicapped in having to remain completely secular. Not only that. It is almost impossible to avoid having the school serve as a means of instilling a narrow patriotism, even to the point of brainwashing. This is why I have expressed concern about what Gingrich would have our children taught in public schools — namely, that Americans are in some sense God's chosen people, that America is destined to be #1 in the world, and that our entire economic future depends on corporate America's competing in the global marketplace.

My views on the appropriate role of government in our lives is presented in Chapter XIII. Readers may want to turn to it to receive further clarification of the views expressed here, but my recommendation is that they first read the ground-breaking chapters which precede it.

## VI-8: *Protection Against Violence and Drugs*

The opening paragraph in this section states Gingrich's view of the role of government. It bears some resemblance to mine, but there are significant differences:

> Safety is simply the most fundamental concern of government. After all, none
> of our God-given rights matter much if we can be raped, mugged, robbed, or
> killed. And the poorest neighborhood is entitled to be as safe as the richest.
> No economic incentives a government can devise will entice businesses to

open factories in a neighborhood where employees are likely to be in constant physical danger. Nor will any amount of education make up for your child being preyed upon by drug dealers and pimps. Addiction and prostitution will quickly wipe out the fruits of any educational reform.

The big difference is that Gingrich fails to mention the one role for government which justifies its near-monopoly coercive powers: namely, that of preventing and remedying injustice. Assuring personal safety is only a small part of this larger responsibility.

Again, what is left unsaid is the desperate plight in which ordinary people are placed when an aggressive elite gets a near monopoly of the financial and other benefits from our common heritage, and then uses that springboard to build a near monopoly of all forms of capital. Again, also, his emphasis is on moral standards for individual persons only, thereby failing to consider moral standards for systems, especially for economic and political systems.

## VI-9: *Gingrich's Summary*

In his summary, Gingrich returns to his blaming all that he sees as wrong — and much of it is wrong — on "the welfare bureaucracy." The welfare state serves as the ultimate whipping boy, whereas, again, welfare programs were established to help remedy the harm done to victims of an unjust economic and political system by its beneficiaries, the most aggressive and acquisitive among us.

"Let's keep our eyes on the prize,"
*A truly just world order.*
The welfare state is not the problem
any more than
it is the solution.
The crisis in our world civilization
arises from
the pursuit of economic power
at a pace faster than the development of truly *just* political controls
which are designed to maintain that power
*within the moral bounds of justice for all.*

# Chapter VII

# *Budget Balancing Pros and Cons*

## VII-1: *Evaluating Gingrich's Reasoning*

It is especially important, before going ahead with this chapter, to reread I-6, the Section in Chapter I dealing with the budget.

Going into debt to each other from time to time is part of the many ways we share with each other, and trade with each other. *Loaning, borrowing, and paying and charging interest is a way of trading different forms of economic power.* In return for one party's voluntarily giving up to a second party a certain amount of fully negotiable economic power in hand, usually in the form of the most liquid of assets (money), the first party receives the promise of a larger amount over a period of time extending into the future.

Moral problems arise when such trading is forced upon one of the parties by an unjust system — especially when an aggressive few are legally permitted to secure a near-monopoly of the economic benefits from that most basic of all economic goods: namely, access to Nature's land and resources, and to the knowledge and skills needed to convert such basic resources into high-tech production facilities. This is one reason why, as stated in Section I-6, whether going into debt is justified or not depends on many factors. In what follows I will evaluate Gingrich's position in relation to what I consider the most important of such factors. We begin by noting his very first paragraph and the first two sentences of the second:

> There are three essential reasons to balance the federal budget. First, it is morally the right thing to do. Second, it is financially the right thing to do. Third, each of us has a personal stake in it. In fact, your personal stake is probably a lot bigger than you realize.
>
> Let me start with the morality of balancing the budget. Historically, it has always been self-evident in America that each generation has the obligation to live within its means . . .

Gingrich never does address each of these three points in any distinguishable manner. He evidently feels that they have all been covered in the course of his general treatment. In any case, having just told us that there are three main reasons for staying out of debt he assures us that there are circumstances in which going into debt is justified. In doing so, he shows his military bias by citing the necessity to pay for major wars, such as "the Revolutionary War, the Civil War, and World Wars I and II." The question then becomes: What is the moral principle by which one should decide whether or not to go into debt, either at all or still deeper? Until we answer that question it would seem to be very difficult to evaluate Gingrich's views on balancing the budget.

In the case of family debt, Gingrich suggests such a principle in the very next paragraph:

> The principle was that we would pay off the mortgage and leave the farm to our children . . . Now we are borrowing against the farm to pay today's living expenses and leaving our children to pay off that debt.

Again Gingrich shows his inclination to think only in monetary terms rather than quality of life terms. But even in monetary terms he engages in careless thinking when he measures inheritance in terms of debt rather than equity.

Gingrich's corporate America goes into debt deliberately, and as a matter of course. It does so in order to make profit at a rate greater than the rate of interest on the debt. A family may be wise to do the same in order to get title to a home or a farm. And even if parents are not able to completely pay it off during their lifetime, they almost certainly would pass on to their children capital *equity* over and beyond the debt. After all, it's not the amount of debt that will matter to those who inherit it, but the remaining equity. One may wonder how Gingrich could be so careless in his reasoning about a matter he considers of such great moral import.

## VII-2: *The Quality-of-Life Issue*

As noted above, there is an even more important moral issue here: the quality of life issue. What I am suggesting is that even if there wasn't a monetary advantage to purchasing a family homestead in this way, there might be a much more important quality-of-family-life advantage, especially to the children growing up in that home. Thus, they might be grateful to their parents all their lives for going into debt in order to make such a quality of life possible.

I suspect that this kind of rational and moral reasoning escaped Gingrich because he was so determined to persuade readers of policies which would serve the monetary values of *corporate* America. In any case, neither the monetary nor quality-of-life values of ordinary Americans, nor that of their children, received his attention in the way he so passionately claimed.

Thus, in the following statement on page 90 he states facts and reasons much more carefully when considering the importance of low interest rates in serving the monetary values of "industry." After anticipating the debt level which will be reached by 2010, Gingrich asserts the following:

> This level of indebtedness has two immediate and profound impacts. First, the amount you have to pay in taxes just to pay off the *interest* on the debt keeps going higher and higher. Second, the government's need to borrow forces interest rates higher for all borrowers — including industry, small businesses, families, home buyers, and state and local governments.

We note in passing that "industry" is first on his list. And we keep in mind that we are still looking for a moral principle to guide us. So, we ask if there is any such principle implied in the above quotation. It seems that there are three at least partial principles suggested here. One is that taxes should be kept as low as possible. A second is that interest rates should also be kept as low as possible. A third is that all borrowing tends to drive up interest rates.

We are not given any reason to accept any one of these principles as a *moral* one. Clearly, the third is not. It simply states a relationship which results from the law of supply and demand. As for the first two, if either could be related to maintaining "justice for all" in the world it might qualify, at least in some limited way. But no such causal relationship is even attempted. Instead, the rest of the chapter is devoted to trying to convince his readers that failure to balance the national budget at this time will lead to higher taxes and interest rates in the future. The implication is, of course, that these are both undesirable outcomes.

In the case of Medicare and Medicaid, he gives projected figures which supposedly show that they both will be bankrupt in a few years unless something is done soon. He implies that balancing the budget and reducing administrative inefficiency might save them, but doesn't say how. In any case, these are side issues to the main topic of this chapter.

## VII-3: *Evaluating the Least-Taxes Principle*

We consider, first, the possible moral value of the principle that taxes should be as low as possible. Whether it is a moral principle or not, it is one which might give one considerable "political mileage." All other things being equal, most voters would rather pay less taxes than more. And political power is granted to those who can get the support of such "most voters."

But, in order to test this principle on moral grounds we must first ask what justification there is for taxes in the first place. Presumably, the answer is that the government cannot function without the income from them. What, then, is the justified role for government?

To govern is to coerce, either overtly or by threat. Thus, the further question becomes, "What is the moral justification for coercion?" My answer is that there are only two such moral justifications, and both are designed to minimize injustice. They are (1) to prevent injustice from being perpetrated in the first place, and (2) to provide remedy in the form of compensation to the victims of whatever injustice was not prevented.

Therefore, *while differing with them regarding what constitutes injustice,* I join Libertarians and some Republicans in maintaining that taxes for any other purpose is a form of robbery or conscription. However, I hasten to insist, as my readers by now can predict, that the economic and political structures presently dominating life on this earth have for centuries permitted, and are still permitting, a basic and widespread economic injustice to take place, and to increase with each day. I refer, of course, to the fact that an "elite," aggressive, and small percentage of the population of the world have secured to themselves the lion's share of the financial and other benefits from our common heritage.

Since this gross injustice has now been taking place for centuries, continues today, and is mounting, governments have the dual responsibility of (1) taking steps to prevent it from continuing to take place in the future; (2) taking steps to provide compensation to those who have been and continue to be victimized.

We first note that the changes called for in this present volume are so radical that they should be brought about gradually — otherwise those who are counting on existing programs and policies will themselves be done an injustice.

But attention to a better, long-term correction and remedy should be promptly pursued. In general, the policy should be to temporarily utilize existing social programs to provide financial aid and services somewhat equivalent to, and in lieu of, the fair share of income from our common heritage presently being denied most people in the world. Such social programs could be dropped gradually as, over a transition period, we move toward assuring that everyone in the world receives her or his fair share of the financial and other benefits of our common heritage. Thus, what I am suggesting is that the needed changes take place by way of radical evolution rather than violent and disruptive revolution.

Clearly, to make such a radical shift in present governmental policies will cost in both administrative expense and financial outlay. In order to cover such costs there will have to be taxes levied in addition to those presently in place, and perhaps others eliminated or reduced.

*What economic justice requires, therefore, is that we lower the present level of U.S. taxes for those who have been denied their fair share of income from our common heritage, and raise taxes on persons to the extent that they have benefitted from more than their fair share.*

Thus, even a preliminary evaluation of the principle which advocates reducing taxes on corporate America reveals its moral inadequacy. The additional funds, which the governments of the world, like the U.S. Government, will need in order to govern the corporate world adequately and to force them to give compensation for past injustices, will have to be raised by some combination of additional taxes and likely by additional borrowing. Additional borrowing would be necessary in order to spread the impact of higher taxes over an extended period. How much additional borrowing, over how long a period, will best serve "justice for all"? That would presumably become clear in due time. The interest on the borrowing plus the repayment of the principle would eventually have to be paid for by taxes.

In any case, we can now clearly see that the principle of keeping interest rates "as low as possible" cannot, *by itself*, be our moral guide. *In a truly just economy* it is only fair, as well as practical, that the market determine interest rates as well as prices of all kinds. Again, the most socially responsible, and most practical, way to control interest rates is to assure that the economic realities which determine the market rate for them and other prices *are maintained within the moral bounds of justice for all.*

## VII-4: *Who Should Pay for Governing?*

But, who, then, is justifiably taxed to the extent needed? We remember that there are two parts to the job (See P-5): (1) the cost of providing a truly just economic system, and (2) the cost of providing remedy for past injustices.

*The principle I suggest for accomplishing (2) is a simple one: Where, as in the situation we are dealing with, the injustice is attributable to an unjust system, the cost of remedying should be borne as much as practical by those who have benefitted from that system.* In the case of the U.S., those who have benefitted from the system which legalizes monopolizing the benefits from our common heritage are largely to be found within corporate America. It's almost as simple as that.

*The principle I suggest for (1) has already been stated in P-5, and is also a simple one: The cost of preventing and remedying injustice should be borne by individuals and corporate bodies <u>to the extent that they behave in ways that require governing</u>.*

This principle is already applied to a large extent in the case of paying for policing traffic. When someone drives on the highway s/he requires governing, because s/he is thereby in position to do a grave injustice by way of accident on the road. So, most states require drivers to subscribe to liability insurance. In addition, they are required to quality for a driver's license. Further, they are required to *pay* for a driver's license as a way of helping to pay for the price of "behaving in ways that require governing."

As also noted in the *Preface*, since power tends to corrupt, it requires governing. For this and related reasons, it will become clear that those entities that most require governing are the large corporations, especially the multinational corporations. Yet, these are the very entities which have been largely left free of governing. When governing has been applied even to a small extent to corporate America, both it and Gingrich have complained. They have complained of paper work, inefficiency, and bureaucracy. Much of what they say may be true. But, if so, most of the bungling is the result of trying to catch up on governing too long neglected in the past. Today there is so much injustice that has gone unattended for so long that a tremendous job lies ahead in both preventing further injustice and remedying that which hasn't been prevented in the past.

Therefore, again, our verdict is that Gingrich's proposed principle of minimum taxation as applied to corporate America is that it also fails to pass the test of a deeper moral scrutiny, though tax-relief may appropriately apply at times to those who are due remedy for past injustices.

# VII-5: *Evaluating the Low-Interest-Rate Principle*

What, then, of the principle that lowest possible interest rates should be our guide? Clearly, from the borrower's standpoint, the lower the interest rates the better, for the reasons Gingrich refers to in the above quotation. But, from the lender's point of view, the reverse is true. What, then, determines a fair rate of interest?

It helps, in such matters, to take an extreme case. If one party, or one group, owned all the wealth in the land, then they could demand extremely high interest rates; rates so high that we would intuitively feel them to be unfair. But we would also quickly realize that this unfairness would derive from the unfairness in the distribution of wealth.

Therefore, it would seem that the rate of interest determined by the market is fair to the extent that the distribution of wealth is fair. In our day we know that it is unfair to the extent that there exists a near-monopoly of private ownership of, and income from, our common heritage capital. How much this basic unfairness influences interest rates is difficult to say. But it does seem clear that, *considering the "near-monopoly" factor only*, governments should try to bring about a lower, rather than a higher, interest rate. But, in an economic and political atmosphere as complex as ours is today, there are many other factors which would influence fairness. For instance, to what extent should the interests of senior citizens (who get most of their retirement income from investments) be considered? In short, there seems to be no easy answer to this question. For lack of one, there seems to be little justification for disagreeing with Gingrich in his plea for lower interest rates. But we might still disagree with his motivation.

If, on the other hand, everyone were to receive a fair share of income from our common heritage, the economic picture would change radically. With more money in the hands of ordinary people, new economic and educational ventures would spring up from the grass roots. Local marketplaces rather than the global marketplace would become dominant. These would require much less governing than the multinational ones. Therefore, the cost of governing would be reduced as multinational corporations died out or were greatly reduced and local ones took over. The transition process itself would, of course, require some innovative governing, but much of this could be assumed by local governmental bodies.

The result likely would be that interest rates would vary greatly from one kind of economic enterprise to another. Again, local ones, being generally safer, carrying lower governing costs, and being easier to evaluate, would be able to borrow at much lower rates than the highly governed and precarious global enterprises. This fact would also contribute to their reduction in territorial sweep, power, and influence.

## VII-6: *Global Crisis As Opportunity for Global Community*

What bearing does all this analysis have on whether to reduce the national debt, or on its rate of increase or decrease? Gingrich has allowed that going into debt is justified in case of national emergency. I would call the present situation a national emergency far greater than the one which prompted the Gulf War or the Vietnam War, or even the Cold War with the Soviet Union. We definitely have not only a national emergency on our hands, but a global one. We survey the list of crises around the world and we see that about the only thing needed to generate a total global emergency is to add a U.S. crisis to the list. This, I feel, we must now do.

But "we can overcome." We have only to "keep our eyes on the prize," which is not only a sustainable environment and economy, but also sustainable justice for all. In the sixties we heard the simplistic motto, "All we need is Love." Our revised motto might be "All we need *from governments* is justice for all." Many more blessings will follow, to the extent that we actually achieve that. To paraphrase a biblical verse: "Seek ye first justice for all, and many other blessings will be added unto you."

*The U.S. economy is at present vigorous enough to withstand radical changes, provided they are made gradually, intelligently, and, most importantly, "with justice for all." This is the advantage of proceeding by radical evolution rather than violent and disruptive revolution.*

We see, then, that when we apply truly moral principles to the question of taxes and interest rates, our conclusions are almost the reverse of those of Newt Gingrich. This has not been intentional. It has been the result of applying morally responsible and rational reasoning to the realities we face today.

Personally, I am not discouraged about the outlook for the future. I believe that we finally have the opportunity to return to sanity and true social responsibility in our political and economic lives. By emphasizing quality of life, with emphasis on justice for all, we have the opportunity to recover and carry forward what I have called "The Early American Dream." We shall find that by building economic and political structures "from local to global" around the commitment to justice for all that we will experience a quality of life, and a quality of *community* life, from which we will never want to regress to what so many of us have today. And in the next chapter we shall build on this theme and its implementation.

In any cost-benefit analysis suggested to us

we must ask in advance:

What is to be considered costs?

And to whom?

What is to be considered benefits?

And to whom?

And throughout any analysis

it behooves us to beware,

on behalf of both present and future generations,

of what former President Eisenhower warned us

in his farewell address:

*The American military-industrial complex!*

# Chapter VIII

# "Decentralizing Power"

# Gingrich Style

### VIII-1: *Gingrich Identifies His Nostalgic Era*

In Section I-5, Chapter I, it was pointed out that Gingrich's main reason for wanting a weakened central government is in order to free corporate America from effective monitoring and governing. Evidence for the correctness of this perception has mounted in each subsequent chapter. In this chapter his basic motive becomes more obvious than ever. His very first paragraph reveals his view of the ideal.

> We may well be nearing the end of the century of big government. It is hard for those of us who grew up with today's bureaucratic, centralized systems to realize that only a century ago our current scale of government would have been rejected as unimaginable by both Britain and America. During the Victorian and Edwardian eras people expected dramatically more self reliance and local initiative and control than anything we have today.

Let's take a look at the period he idealizes: the last part of the last century and the first part of the present, covered, as he says, by "the Victorian and Edwardian eras." Let us recall what these times were noted for.

As for the last part of the nineteenth century, in America it was the age of the robber barons. It was the time when huge fortunes were made, especially in oil and steel. Both were built by exploiting our common heritage of its basic resources, mined and drilled from the earth itself, resources which cannot be replaced. It was only after such exploitation became so obvious that it couldn't be ignored that the national government finally stepped in to partially restrain corporate America, at that time in the form of the Sherman Anti-Trust Act of 1890. But it does sound like the kind of time that Gingrich would have liked: lots of "opportunity" (See Chapter VI) for the most aggressive and acquisitive to make lots of money.

It was, of course, also the time of the depression of 1892. But that didn't bother the robber barons very much, because they had our common heritage to draw on for the basic source of their profits. Here is the way the Encyclopaedia Britannica describes it.

> Despite the depression of 1892, marked by the bloody Homestead strike, the Carnegie companies, aided by favorable tariff legislation, prospered.[1]

Homestead was the name of the community in which one of Carnegie's steel mills was located, and the strike was "bloody" because the strikers were confronted with militia hired by the Carnegie steel works. The "favorable tariff legislation" was, of course, evidence that the national government was then, as now, basically supportive of corporate America. Nor is this surprising considering the way the U.S. Government has been structured since its founding. (See VIII-6 and Chapters XI and XII.)

Andrew Carnegie wrote an essay called *The Gospel of Wealth*, in which he stated that a rich man should, after acquiring his wealth, distribute the surplus for the general welfare. And it can be said that he made a considerable effort to practice what he preached. As Gingrich points out, Carnegie devoted his retirement years to giving back to society a substantial amount of the wealth he had acquired.

But such philanthropy is no substitute for making sure that everyone benefits in a fair way from our common heritage in the first place rather than permitting it to be the near-exclusive springboard for corporate America and a few "robber barons" on their road to super wealth. If this basic right were assured there could be a great many more people getting that

---

1. Volume 2, page 880 of the 15th edition of Encyclopaedia Britannica

crucial initial boost into the world where income is increasingly from capital and less and less from labor.

So much for the robber baron times. What of the Edwardian era, the second of the times of which Gingrich also speaks so highly? That took place at the beginning of this century. Webster's Third New International Dictionary defines "edwardian" as "characterized by opulence and a complacent sense of material security."

And so it was. And we all know what emerged out of that opulence and complacency: World War I, a few years later, then more opulence until its bubble burst in the crash of 1929, followed by a deep depression culminating in World War II.

## VIII-2: *Injustices in the Wake of Opulence?*

Is it possible that the robber baron era and the age of opulence and complacency which Gingrich looks back on with such nostalgia was a time when there were a few structural injustices brewing in the world? Was it possible that the robber barons and the rise of corporate America had something to do with these injustices and the tragic events that followed? We know that it was a time which provoked the beginning of the Labor movement in America, beginning with the founding of the American Federation of Labor in 1886. It was during the period that followed that organized labor was attempting to do something about the plight of the American worker in the face of this corporate surge in power. But with the basic structure of the U.S. Government designed to give a budding corporate America an almost unlimited amount of the kind of economic "freedom" that Gingrich would have us so thoroughly embrace, the labor movement had a constant up-hill struggle.

We also know that in this period which Gingrich idealizes, racial segregation was rampant in America, and not only in the South. He acknowledges as much when, later in the chapter, he expresses his support for the civil rights movement that emerged a half century later, in the sixties. In fact, it was during this period, between the Civil War and World War, I that African Americans were hounded, beaten, and hung with virtual impunity. The armies of the North, having defeated the armies of the South, abandoned the former slaves to receive from the white segregationists the wrath and revenge which they could not inflict on their fellow whites in the North.

But, again, understandably, Gingrich doesn't mention all this because matters of justice and injustice aren't given any consideration at all in his evaluation of the quality of life during that period. Indeed, as in most of his book, it is not quality of life but "initiative," "efficiency" and America as #1 in the world economically and militarily that occupy his entire attention.

We also know that this was a period in which American women still didn't have the right to vote, despite the outstanding efforts to secure it by women like Elizabeth Cady Stanton and Susan B. Anthony. So resistant to women's rights was budding corporate America during that period that despite the many efforts of courageous women to continue to build on the work of Stanton and Anthony it was not until after the shake-up of World War I that women's suffrage was finally given legal status via the legislation of 1920.[2]

Gingrich doesn't consider the possibility that the aggressive "initiative" which powered the rise of corporate America, and disregarded the injustices that accompanied it, might have had something to do with the social turmoil that followed. Indeed, I don't remember his expressing any concern about justice or injustice in his entire book. Nor are there any references to either in the Index.

He has a great deal to say about "freedom," though not the kind of freedom Martin Luther King, Jr. spoke of in his *I Have A Dream* speech. Again, the freedom Gingrich argues for is freedom for corporate America, free from any monitoring or governing by a government strong enough to be effective in doing so.

He has much to say about voluntary initiative. And this is fine. But he has nothing to say about making sure that the power generated by such initiative doesn't "corrupt" in the way power tends to do.

---

2. For a grass roots and pictorial history of the Movements for Racial Equality, Women's Rights, Worker's Rights, and Civil Rights generally during this period and thereafter, see *The Power of the People*, edited by Robert Cooney and Helen Michalowski, pub. by New Society Publishers, Philadelphia, PA, 1987

He is concerned about government corruption and, of course, inefficiency, though primarily at the national level. He doesn't mention corruption at the state level, with its history of notorious political bosses, except as he observed it in the Democratic party during his teen years (his Chapter 2) when he was first entering politics.

Again, the reason Gingrich doesn't say anything about the tendency of economic power to corrupt seems to be because that would argue for a strong national government designed to assure that it doesn't happen.

In view of the above analysis, I suggest that during this entire period that Gingrich would have us accept as some kind of ideal the groundwork was being laid for what has now become a corporate America of international scope. World War I gave it such momentum, and it got so drunk with power during the twenties, that the crash of 1929 and the great depression which followed now seem to have been almost inevitable. Yet, despite the tremendous, international power of the corporate America that has emerged from its beginnings a century ago, Gingrich would have us give it even freer reign at this time.

## VIII-3: *Gingrich's Careless Thinking Continues*

As in the last chapter, Gingrich's enthusiasm for a more limited national government leads him to careless thinking. It leads him to open his Chapter 8 with a pitch for reducing the power of the national government, as we have seen. But then he realizes he may have gone too far, because later in the chapter he returns to his original position, only to again recant somewhat. In short, in this chapter, although he wants to make a rational case for reducing the power of the national government, every time he tries to build a case in support of his agenda he comes to realize that he can't really pull it off.

For instance, though he begins Chapter 8 with arguments for a weaker national government, the justification he acknowledged in the previous chapter for a *strong* one during "national crises" (such as during America's wars) is supported by implication in this one. But then he claims that the need is now past, except, as we shall see (VIII-5), for the continuing need for a strong military to fight for corporate America around the world. Here is what he does say on Page 102.

> With the end of the Cold War, the case for a strong central government has been dramatically weakened. The time has come for a revision to first principles. In America, one of those first principles is that power resides first and foremost in the individual citizen.

Evidently we can now safely reduce the power of the national government because we are not to be concerned about any "national crises" in the future (except that we must always be prepared for military ones). Then, for the next couple of pages he pours out praise for the "voluntary associations" which characterized the last part of the last century and the beginning of the present, especially those established and encouraged by Andrew Carnegie.

We get the impression that as long as we remain militarily strong, strong enough to protect corporate America as it moves out into the global marketplace as the leader in high-tech in the new Information Age, we can just let private initiative run free, free, free — free and unmolested by a national government no longer needed for anything but financing the military and "keeping America strong" in the global marketplace. Thus, by page 104 he has again built up the courage to really come down hard on any notion of a strong national government:

> We are not simply trying to move a few offices out of Washington while retaining the heart of the twentieth century behemoth. We are trying to reestablish the American rule of individual liberty and the citizen's first claim to their own money. What we have done so far is only one step in that direction..
> . . . Power in fifty different cities is better than power centralized in one city.
>
> Yet our ultimate goal is to move power even beyond the state capitals. . .
> However much I sympathize with both state and local governments, what we really want to do is to devolve power all the way back to working American families.

At this point he sounds as if we hardly need a national government at·all. It is as if he wanted a populist ring to his message: give government back to the people. Away with Washington and its bureaucracies. Who needs them? He continues in the same vein on Page 105:

The liberal model is that an enlightened national capital will establish the correct laws and hire the bureaucrats to enforce them. . . *Instead, Republicans envision a decentralized America in which responsibility is returned to the individual.*

We will come back to this sentence when we recognize its similarity to the theory behind the structure of the U.S. Constitution as set forth by Hamilton in his Federalist Paper #15 (See XI-8). The strategy set forth there, and largely adopted by Gingrich here, is that of so dispersing the power that it can be manipulated in a way in which it cannot when it is subject to reasoned argument and clearness of motive. But at this juncture we simply note that in his current mood Gingrich is ready to dismiss almost entirely a national government of any kind, whether strong or weak. It's a bit bewildering, considering his strong pitch for a strong America at the beginning of the book, an America which would lead the rest of the world into the Information Age. But such is the confused logic of his position.

Then we come to the first recanting section, an implicit admission that not all national crises take the form of wars. It comes on the very next page, #106:

There was certainly some justification for a centralized bureaucratic effort when one third of the nation was legally segregated. The federal government had to be prepared to intervene to protect minorities from the legal oppression of state and local governments. In 1965 there was perhaps a good case for centralized supervision during an era of change.

What? An admission of oppression by *state* and *local* governments? Is he really referring to that level of government to which on the previous page he would have us turn over virtually all national responsibilities? Not only is he here offering a justification for a non-wartime, strong national government, but "a centralized bureaucratic effort"!

There are those who would be interested to know that our racial problems are essentially solved. Clearly, they are not. What seems much more likely at this time of corporate America's downsizing and moving so rapidly into the foreign regions of the global marketplace is that racial tensions will increase. But the context will be different. In the Information Age they will increase as a derivative part of a more generalized sense of outrage and sense of injustice — that deriving from the rich getting so very much richer while the poor are getting so very much poorer. And this more pervasive "crisis" may require a stronger national commitment than any we Americans have ever before been called upon to make. I refer to the commitment to "justice for all," regardless of race, ethnicity, gender, or sexual preference, and extending worldwide "from local to global."

## VIII-4: *Calling for An Expanded Civil Rights Movement*

What I am suggesting is that not only hasn't the need for a civil rights movement completely disappeared, the need has expanded far beyond race. And this author predicts that it will not be satisfied until each resident of this earth is assured *a fair share of the financial and other benefits of our common heritage.*

As this expanded civil rights movement gains momentum it will also become clear that only a national government would be strong enough to restrain the corporate America which is at the causative core of this expanded civil rights crisis.

Yet, at the bottom of the very same page on which Gingrich offers the above-stated admission of the occasional need for a strong central government, he returns to his Washington bashing — this time with the aid of his bountiful faith in the healing power of the Information Age:

> Our desire to devolve power out of Washington and disperse it to local governments is reinforced by everything we are learning about the Information Age. Virtually every effort to create more competitive companies has involved returning authority to the person closest to the problem. . . . The Information Age will actually make it easier for these positive changes to be transferred to other systems. A model that is working in one place can rapidly be adopted by others.

As he has done before, Gingrich is failing to realize that the process for *generating* power is basically different from that of restraining it and containing it within the moral bounds of justice. The former can achieve important breakthroughs by way of individual effort. The latter takes a careful, consensus-building process. Why? Because *justice* can only be achieved by weighing the concerns of everyone who might be impacted by a decision. And these not only vary greatly, but they are constantly changing and becoming ever more complex (See XIII-2 and XIII-3).

Again, however, Gingrich can avoid this crucial distinction because he is not really interested in either establishing justice or preventing injustice. His sights are almost exclusively on *power-building*, and not power-containing. *And a major reason his political leadership is so ominous at this time is that the potential for the unjust use of power is greater in the Information Age than it has ever been.*

A weakened central government would permit corporate America to become stronger and more centralized while the only government which could possibly monitor and govern it becomes less so. In this way, corporate America would be able to go on to dominate not only all economic life in America, but also, Gingrich hopes, the corporate world at the global level. And with no single state, or foreseeable combination of states, capable of even monitoring, let alone governing, it, corporate America would rampage through America and the world with its growing power largely ungoverned. It would be like the proverbial "bull in a china shop." And that is an ominous prospect, indeed!

## VIII-5: *More Backtracking, Some Specifics, & Confusion*

Arguments against Gingrich's position as socially irresponsible and as a way to seek unharnessed power for its own sake have been given in virtually every previous chapter of this volume. They have been further strengthened in this chapter. But there is more, because there is still another instance of Gingrich's backtracking to be noted on the very last page of his Chapter 8:

> This drive to decentralize should not be  mistaken as a plea for weak government. I strongly favor the Constitution over the Articles of Confederation [the form of national government established following the Declaration of Independence in 1776, and in existence up to its replacement with the present Constitution in 1787]. The Constitution is a device for strong central government, and so it should remain. Keeping our money honest, regulating our

trade in the world market, maintaining our national defense, breaking the back of illegal drugs, sustaining a nationwide database on convicted felons and the mentally ill so that we sell guns only to honest and law-abiding citizens, sustaining a nationwide system of retirement, investing in research and development at the level of basic knowledge so we can continue to advance (as we did as early as the Lewis and Clark Expedition) — all of these are but a few of the legitimate duties of the federal government.

. . . Government would be leaner but more focused, more effective at its designated responsibilities. Beyond that, as the Tenth Amendment states: "The powers not delegated to the United States by the Constitution, nor prohibited by it to the States, are reserved to the States respectively, or to the people.

Gingrich thereby abandons his several efforts in the body of the chapter to make a case for transferring power to the states in some sweeping way. After switching back and forth several times, his current mood favors "a device for strong central government." Also, no longer is he talking about a temporary situation, such as during a national "crisis." No, now he says "it should remain" strong. And he implies that one reason he favors "the Constitution over the Articles of Confederation" is precisely because the former assures such a "strong central government."

Favoring the Constitution over the Articles in this way places decentralist Newt Gingrich in a truly self-contradictory position. It is the opposite of what an objective observer would have expected upon reading the title of Gingrich's Chapter 8: "Decentralizing Power." The 18th century supporters and critics of the Constitution alike would have been especially surprised, because the very purpose of the main promoters of the Constitution — notably Alexander Hamilton and James Madison — was to substitute a political instrument with highly centralized political power for one which very much *de*centralized it (See Chapters XI and XII).

So, if Gingrich really is concerned about decentralization of power he should go back to the Articles of Confederation, and consider how they might be amended to correct their defects. I have done this. In doing so, I have shown (Chapter XIII) that the issue is not in terms of strong versus weak government; we definitely need strong government of the kind which can assure that power brokers will be kept well within the moral bounds of "justice for all." The issue is in terms of *moral quality* of government, moral quality in terms of effectiveness in maintaining justice for all. And this, in turn, becomes an issue on the level of governmental *structure*.

A strong central government which is imposed from the top for the purpose of serving the most aggressive and acquisitive, such as the one structured by the U.S. Constitution (See Chapters XI and XII), will lead to the kind of government we have today. On the other hand, one which is a true federation of genuine communities, from local to global, where each one is organized around a solid commitment to justice for all, will, as we also shall see (Chapter XIII), yield precisely that to which they are committed. The logic is quite simple. We harvest that to which we truly commit ourselves, whether as individuals or as a society. So, each of us must choose. Do I commit myself to acquisitiveness and aggressiveness, or will it be to justice for all? Do I commit myself to work for societal commitment to the former, or to the latter? On the answers to these questions hang our futures as individuals, as families, and as societies, "from local to global."

How, then, do we make sense of the title of the chapter: "Decentralizing Power"? Clearly, the amount of decentralization he is now advocating doesn't extend to changing the Constitution. It, he says, "should remain" as it is, "a device for a strong central government." Nor does he give us any guiding principle, moral or otherwise, by which the extent of the "decentralizing" he presumably still advocates is to be determined. He doesn't even say, for instance, that such and so roles now filled by the central government should be transferred to the states. What he does do in closing his Chapter 8 is list certain roles which he now claims the central government in some sense *should* fill without indicating in what "sense." So, let's take a look at the list. Let's see if we can detect any principle implicit in it. If so, we can evaluate such a principle on social and environmentally responsible grounds. If not, all we can do is evaluate each part of the list on those same grounds.

## VIII-6: *One More Fruitless Search for A Moral Principle*

Here, then, is the list of the roles he suggests the U.S. national government should fill. The rest, as directed by the Constitution, "are reserved to the States respectively or to the people."

1. keeping our money honest;

2. regulating our trade in the world market;

3. maintaining our national defense;

4. breaking the back of illegal drugs;

5. sustaining a nationwide database on convicted criminals and the mentally ill so that we sell guns only to law-abiding citizens;

6. sustaining a nationwide system of retirement;

7. investing in research and development at the level of basic knowledge so we can continue to advance (as we did as early as the Lewis and Clark Expedition)

8. plus additional "legitimate duties of the federal government."

He doesn't say what these "additional duties" are, nor, again, indicate by what principle they might be added. But, apparently, whatever they are, they are not relevant to his present purpose. How, then should we proceed with our evaluation"?

As a start, since Gingrich seems to feel that what he advocates is perfectly in keeping with the U.S. Constitution, it might be interesting to review what roles for the U.S. central government are specified in that historic document. In short, what is the Constitution's "list"? We get our first indication in the preamble:

> We, the people of the United States, in order to form a more perfect union, establish justice, insure domestic tranquillity, provide for the common defense, promote the general Welfare, and secure the Blessings of Liberty to ourselves and our Posterity, do ordain and establish this Constitution for the United States of America.

We note one item common to the two lists: providing for the common defense. But that's all. None of the other items in Gingrich's list are mentioned in what might be called the Constitution's mission statement.

In fairness to Gingrich, elsewhere he has argued for "forming a more perfect union," though primarily around materialistic, economic values rather than what I have called "quality of life values." As noted several times, nowhere does Gingrich express concern for "establishing justice." Can it be that he believes that rounding up criminals, drug users, dealers, and putting even more people in jail, will contribute to "domestic tranquillity," will "promote the general welfare," and will secure "the blessings of liberty to ourselves and our posterity"? In terms of his interests and values, perhaps so!

Again, the most serious omission from Gingrich's list is the role of "establishing justice." As I have argued several times, this role should not only should be at the top of the list for every governing body, but should be the *only* thing on the list. All else should be spelling out the details of what this entails and how it is to be accomplished. As we shall see in Part II of this volume, the Constitution fails in this regard almost as much as does Gingrich.

Again, the reason "establishing justice," or some equivalent wording, is crucial is because that goal, role, etc. is the only moral justification for *coercing* anyone — and "to govern is to coerce."

Libertarians and some Republicans are right in saying that in order for a government to give goods, services, or money to some, it must take it from someone else. Thus, such taking must be morally justified if it is to be morally acceptable. My position is that forcing people to share in a fair and largely equal way the financial and other benefits from our common heritage is morally justified, provided it is done in a humane way. And my further position is that if governments were to force such sharing, then "domestic tranquillity" would reign. Whatever additional safety net was needed by some could be supplied by voluntary associations. Again, this will be fully explained in Chapter XIII.

But neither the U.S. Constitution nor Gingrich take that position. Thus, my summary evaluation of Gingrich's Chapter 8 is roughly as follows:

It has been confusing from the start. As in the previous chapter, it has revealed confusion in Gingrich's own mind. It confirms Gingrich's seeming lack of interest in "preventing and remedying injustice." It confirms that his main interest is in governing those who are victims of corporate America rather than corporate America itself, even though we can largely attribute the desperate straits of increasing numbers of people today to the failure of governments all over the world to govern the corporate power structures in their midst.

I also must conclude that Gingrich is still not being completely honest with us, because he doesn't mention among the purposes of his "strong central government" that of militarily defending corporate America's economic interests all over the world, a purpose made so crystal clear in his very first chapter. All in all, I must conclude that the challenge Gingrich poses for us is almost completely devoid of genuine social and environmental responsibility. Therefore, I repeat the concern I have expressed or implied several times in the preceding evaluation of his proposals: that Newt Gingrich and his proposals for America presents one of the most serious threats to all that is dear to me and my friends in America. And my main reason for challenging him as I am doing is in order to persuade the American people, and the people of the world generally, of this ominous threat.

In all our meanderings,
considering and evaluating,
let's keep our eyes on the prize:
Sustainable Justice,
as assured by
truly just economic structures,
established and enforced
by truly fair
political structures,
thereby assuring "Justice for All"
These are, indeed, times that try our souls!

# Chapter IX

# *Gingrich's Contract With America*

This Chapter IX will be an evaluation of all of Gingrich's chapters dealing with the Contract with America. Each of Gingrich's chapters to be evaluated will be assigned a Section in this chapter. Thus, Section IX-9 will be an evaluation of Gingrich's Chapter 9. Section IX-10 will be an evaluation of Gingrich's Chapter 10, and the last Section, IX-28, will be an evaluation of Gingrich's Chapter 28.

The reason for dealing with all of his chapters from 9 through 28 in this single Chapter IX is that the heart of Gingrich's proposal and philosophy has already been dealt with in the previous eight chapters. There just isn't *enough* new in Gingrich's chapters 9-28 to warrant a separate evaluation chapter for each one. On the other hand, each of his chapters on the Contract with America does give a bit more insight into what Gingrich is up to. Each Section in what follows will bear roughly the same name as that given by Gingrich to the chapter being critiqued.

## IX-9: *The Contract with America and the Campaign of 1994*

In Gingrich's Chapter 9 he tells us how he feels about the Contract with America. As we now know, it is a document and a political strategy which he personally largely initiated and made into the 1994 political campaign for generating a Republican Congress. He tells how the idea was originally suggested by Charlie McWorter, a vice president at AT&T, who had "a reputation as a great innovator in Republican politics." He tells how the idea was first tried in the 1980 campaign.

He tells how they were encouraged by the "new faces" which were being attracted to the Republican party.

> They were mostly young, educated people with professional backgrounds — many were religious — who had grown up questioning the legacy of the 1960s and were critical of liberalism both on economic and social grounds.

He tells how several of these "new faces" were getting good public support in their various districts, with the help of the religious Right and those critical of "liberalism." Then he gives us the first hint of their basic political strategy.

> Revolutions have to be built one step at a time. The first step was to commit the party to the idea that we should run on idealistic bold reforms and be prepared to keep our word. By June we had agreed to hold a Capitol steps event in September involving ten major program statements. The ten points basically selected themselves as deeply felt desires of the American people. We knew from long experience that people were desperate for a law requiring Congress to obey the same laws as everyone else. We knew that there was overwhelming support for the balanced budget amendment, the line-item veto, and term limits. As the party of small businesses and family farms we knew that litigation reform and regulatory reform were strongly supported. As conservatives and advocates of a prowork and profamily America we knew that welfare reform, a child tax credit, increased savings opportunities, and capital gains tax cuts to increase economic growth would strengthen America. Finally, as conservatives we felt the liberals had weakened our national defense and our laws against criminals and child pornographers. We believed that these should be strengthened. It can literally be said that the Contract with America grew out of our conversations with the American people and out of our basic conservative values.

Gingrich then goes on to tell how he felt the White House helped draw attention to their gathering on the Capitol steps, how on the day they actually gathered it was windy but beautiful, and how "the event got substantial press coverage and we were on our way."

What, then, is to be said of all this? First, we notice that the very idea of the Contract was indeed a very innovative strategy. There has indeed been a problem, since the beginning of America's political parties, with being able to count on the fulfillment of promises made during the campaigns. Making such a specific point of so many specific promises was indeed an impressive display of putting their integrity on the line.

Next, we note that the strategy included selecting for the contract — *among those policies they and their conservative friends were most eager to have legislated* — those which they felt could get the support of a healthy majority of the electorate, especially of the young conservatives who were well established with the money and youthful energy needed to persuade and manipulate those who were undecided, and who were thus able to generate majority support where it didn't yet exist, or increase it where it did. So, in the world of political strategy they clearly emerged from the election as big winners.

Who among the American people could also be counted as winners is quite another matter. Certainly corporate America came out a winner — at least temporarily. Also at least temporary winners are the symbolic analysts who do the high-tech leg work for corporate America in the global market-place. But, again, the already marginalized were, by this dramatic "victory," destined to have their basic "unalienable right" to a fair share of the financial and other benefits of our common heritage (and all the springboard advantages which follow from them) even more surely denied them.

At the end of his Chapter 9, Gingrich tells of sitting with about forty of their strongest supporters at two-thirty in the morning discussing "the scale of our victory."

We got into an interesting discussion about the word "growth." In several interviews I had already said that being speaker would be a much bigger responsibility than being minority whip. I hoped to learn and grow in the job. I would have thought these words were positive, but several of my conservative supporters joined my friend John Uhlman to reject the phrasing. In their view "growth" is what the Washington press corps likes to say about someone who comes to Washington and betrays grass roots people. "We don't want you to grow in the eyes of the Washington news media," they said. "We want you to remain the guy who fights for our values, protects our pocketbooks, and explains us to Washington rather than explaining Washington to us." Here we were, only two and a half hours into the majority, and already I was beginning to get a taste of how challenging it might be.

In closing this Section, we note the kind of values his supporters want him to fight for — not "justice for all," but for "our pocketbooks," and to "explain us to Washington rather than explaining Washington to us." The implication of the last point was that the people in corporate America who feel that they put him where he is aren't interested in having Washington interpreted to them. It's his job to understand Washington. And included in that job is "explaining" in the sense of "working for" corporate interests in Washington. And, presumably, his corporate elite friends want him to keep complaining about that "intellectual elite" who just won't get out of corporate America's way in their world-wide rush for domination of the global marketplace.

## IX-10: *Implementing the Contract: Part I*

Gingrich's Chapter 10 deals primarily with political strategy. Apart from such strategy, what, then, can we learn about The Contract's basic commitments from what we find in his tenth chapter?

On the first page he says that "Our opening agenda was to audit the House, cut committee staffs, and shrink the general size of the legislative branch." He then goes on to tell of eliminating congressional committees they thought were no longer necessary (presumably not necessary for implementing their "contract") and reducing the importance of seniority in selecting committee chairs. He tells of placing women in more responsible roles than previously. Very much on their minds was sticking to their promise of radical changes. And it must be said that they largely did so. He then goes on to say what they did in support of the traditional monogamous family.

> We also established a bipartisan Committee on the Family chaired by Congressman Frank Wolf. We found both members and their spouses eager to participate, and a number of Democratic members were also enthusiastic about trying to make Congress a more humane environment. It may seem like a small thing, but having a chaotic schedule can make congressional life very difficult. Failing to plan recesses so they coincide with children's school vacations had made family life hard to preserve . . .

Three practical steps made Congress a little more family friendly. First, we guaranteed that we would always end our sessions by three o'clock on Fridays so members could catch planes home for the weekend.

Second, we cut the one hundred days [during which time period they promised to bring all ten issues to the floor] to ninety three when someone realized that most children had their school vacation the week of April 10. Technically, one hundred days didn't end until April 13. This earlier recess made our job harder, but it meant that families would have some time together around Easter and Passover [One may wonder if, in view of the principle of the state's not favoring some religions over others, the family gatherings among other religions had been considered].

Third, we announced that floor votes would end after seventeen minutes. Under house rules, the votes must last at least fifteen minutes but can actually stay open as long as the chair desires. . . . Wolf's Committee on the Family calculated that nearly a week could be saved simply by insisting on a seventeen-minute limit. . . . Members quickly adjusted to the new rules and everyone has been happy with the result.

We developed other ways to make Congress more friendly to family life. We turned the Tip O'Neill Room just off the House chamber into a family room, which is now widely used by spouses and family friends.

What, then is to be said for or against these initial actions? It is difficult to find fault with the changes designed to support family life. But, placing a definite limit on time for floor votes did not, I suspect, receive the unanimous support indicated; suppose some special circumstance arises whereby extending the time might be extremely important. Presumably, the 17-minute limit itself would have to be set aside by a vote of the house, which might be a better way to extend the time than by leaving such power with the Speaker.

Gingrich spends the rest of the chapter on the mechanics of getting started implementing their contract. But there is very little of substance regarding how to meet the civilization crisis which supposedly has motivated the publishing of his book. And, again, no reference is made to how to achieve "justice for all," nor the kind of structural change which might help bring it about. One gets the impression that he was primarily overwhelmed with the sense of power which had so suddenly been thrown in his lap:

I will never forget mounting the rostrum and looking over the House for the first time. It was an amazing experience. Until that moment, I had never actually imagined myself standing there as Speaker. I had seen myself as a leader [thus fulfilling his teen-age dream], but this was a moment for which I was not prepared. The House is a large room and on this day it was filled with over five hundred people on the floor. . . . The Democrats were more than polite in their applause. Most of them were gracious and have remained pleasant and conciliatory to this day. The whole scene gave me a wonderful sense of the romance of America and the magic by which Americans share power and accept changes in government. . . .

The courtesy he was shown was from fellow politicians, the overwhelming majority of whom had their offices with the aid of large financial contributions from the very corporate lobbyists that the Gingrich program was designed to please and substantively support. This was not the time to plant seeds of concern among such financial supporters that Democrats might not be cooperative in implementing a contract so largely designed to serve corporate interests.

Again, we see no indication of concern for the injustice and oppression sweeping the world. Perhaps we are to draw some implication of concern for the breakdown of the family from the moves to favor families among the members of Congress. But  the extent of the civilization crisis which supposedly is upon us — and definitely is, though not in the way Gingrich claims — his Chapter 10 cannot be considered a call to anything approaching a revolution designed to address such a crisis.

Rather, what is recounted is the way strategies were developed and carried out for "getting the votes." And despite his expressions of appreciation to Democrats for their courtesies, before he ends his Chapter 10 he makes the following comment about Democratic cooperation in accomplishing this absolutely essential vote-getting when the American political process moves "from push to shove":

Again and again the Democrats would try to undermine or delay a bill through procedural moves but then vote for it on final passage. They knew there was too much popular support for them to be on the record in opposition. But they did their best to gut these bills anyway in little-noted proceedings. That's one reason the Democrats have gotten away with so many things for so long — and why open-door technologies such as C-SPAN have done so much to improve Congress.

## IX-11: *Implementing the Contract: Part II*

The first part of Gingrich's Chapter 11 is about power plays, and their successes and failures in relation to getting the Contract-with-America agenda instituted into legislation.

After ending the previous chapter by saying that "one poll showed 96 percent of the country favored replacing the current welfare system — a unanimity virtually unknown on any other issue" he begins the chapter by saying that "welfare reform nonetheless came the closest of any Contract issue to collapsing (except of course term limits, which failed to get the two-thirds vote needed to pass the House)." And so it went throughout the entire chapter.

All of the substantive issues touched on in this chapter have been, or are about to be, dealt with in other chapters. So, on to the next!

## IX-12: *Learning Versus Education*

In Section VI-7 of Chapter VI, I have already commented quite a bit on Gingrich's views on education, so I will try not to repeat here.  But Gingrich's Chapter 12 is an important one. He spends the first part of the chapter again criticizing the entire American educational system, presumably both public and private. Basically, he complains that "students are not learning the math and science they need to be competitive in the world market."

Anyone familiar with Gingrich's value system will not be surprised at that. Math and science (with emphasis on the physical sciences) is the foundation for high-tech, and that's what corporate America needs in order to "be competitive in the world market." So, no criticism from Gingrich for students not learning how to participate in a truly just society. Again, no concern expressed about the need to educate for intellectual and moral integrity. All education is to be measured in relation to the "Third Wave Information Age."

We need the courage to start anew. We need the determination to abandon the assumptions of the past and begin creating a Third Wave Information Age learning system that is as different from the current bureaucratic model as the space shuttle is from the 1845 coach. There are five major distinctions between Second and Third Wave education. They are:

1. Lifetime learning versus a segmented system
2. Learning focused versus teacher focused education
3. Achievement versus process as a measure of success
4. Society-oriented approach versus isolated systems
5. Technology-embracing versus technology-averse learning

When I first thought of evaluating Gingrich's views on education I considered setting forth my credentials in that field. But, as I read with amazement his outrageous statements it became clear that all that was necessary was to appeal to the common sense of my readers.

The first impression that comes across is another example of Gingrich's arrogance. We must "start anew," he says. "Abandon the assumptions of the past and begin creating a Third Wave Information Age learning system," he says. As usual, he simply offers know-it-all statements without giving rational argument to support them. Even more amazing, his guru-type declarations are so unbelievably extreme. It would be different if these assertions were conclusions reached at the end of careful analysis and after giving credit where credit is due. But no; no need to consider possible merits of what has been done in the past. No, just "abandon" it, and "start anew."

Similarly with what is to be put in its place. No solid and intellectually responsible reasons founded on well established and researched "information." We are reminded of the enthusiasm he displayed in his Chapter 4, on The Information Age, where he all but swallowed it, so to speak, "hook, line, and sinker."

Let's look at his five "major distinctions between Second and Third Wave education." First, he says that Third Wave education is "lifetime learning." To know his total agenda is to understand this emphasis. Because the blind pursuit of high-tech constantly replaces a set of previously established jobs with "labor-saving" devices at each step-up in automation, the only way for working people to be ready for the next level of high-tech when their jobs at the current level are replaced is to have learned while holding a job at one level how to be useful in the next highest level. And with each such high-tech jump the beneficiaries of corporate America become richer and the increasing number of marginalized who can't keep up with the pace become poorer. As for his second point, "learning-focused versus teacher-focused education," I deal with that in a major discussion below.

Turning to his third "difference," he evidently is alluding to those in progressive education who emphasize consideration for human relationships, child readiness, consensus building, etc. as central in education rather than the substantive material being learned. Gingrich wants students to learn math and science by whatever process. That's what corporate America wants. So, that's what he wants.

In his fourth point he is arguing for utilizing all the resources in the society for learning — and, of course, for learning about high-tech by way of high-tech. His views here are not to be confused with those who advocate relating to society in order to help build more wholesome and fair-minded communities. No, Gingrich would virtually *use* society as a stepping stone up the ladder of success in the world of corporate America.

Gingrich's fifth and final "difference" is in the use of technology in learning and in working at a job. There is truth in what he says about the tendency to avoid using technology which is labor-saving. No wonder, when the greatest advantage is always to corporate America and to those most aggressive among us. Because those who constitute corporate America have a near-monopoly of production facilities, they naturally want to make them increasingly technology-intensive and less and less labor-intensive.

In short, the five "differences" Gingrich lists are differences between (1) the present situation in our economy where the rich are getting richer at the expense of the poor getting poorer, and (2) the situation under the Third Wave when the rich will be *even richer* and the poor even poorer. This is because high-tech will make for more profits for corporate America, the owners of America's production facilities, while forcing those who must get all their income from a "job" to be willing to work for less and less in order to compete with fellow workers in a decreasing job market with increasing numbers of takers.

An important distinction Gingrich fails to make is that between an activity and the practitioners of it. Take the activity of teaching. First he makes sweeping statements about the practitioners of it, and the "bureaucracy" into which, admittedly, *some of them* are organized. Then, assuming he has made the case that they have "grown inefficient and expensive," (page 142) he jumps to the conclusion that he has made a case against teaching as such and the teaching profession itself. He simply dismisses all teaching outright in favor of what he calls "learning," as if there were no way to combine teaching with learning in a fruitful combination. As one who has taught on many levels (from seventh grade to the university level), as a father of two daughters who are teachers, and as one who has been helped to learn by excellent teachers, I know him to be simplistic, unappreciative, and, considering his position of power in America today, literally a threat to some of the most promising educational activities going on in our society.

In my studies in Philosophy of Education at the University of Pennsylvania about 40 years ago, I was "taught" some very important things about the relationship between teaching and learning. The professor liked to say, with a grin: "You can't teach a student until you learn him. And that's good grammar." I'm not sure it was good grammar, but it was put in that cute way so that we would remember that in order to be a good teacher one must first *learn* about the particular child to be taught. One must learn what her interests are, and what his conceptual vocabulary includes, and doesn't include. The more one learns about the particular child the more effectively a good teacher can help that child to learn. And what was the teacher urged to help her learn? Not some political ideology about American myths or how to make America #1 in some narrow, materialistic, and militaristic way by emphasizing math, science, and whatever else would feed the "job" requirements of corporate America. Not at all. Not even a small hint of such a thing. Basically, the teacher was to help the child pursue interests which would make for a wholesome, interesting, and socially responsible life.

It may seem to readers of Gingrich's book that he embraces the child-centered approach to education when he writes (page 144) "Children should be encouraged to read whatever interests them." Again, Gingrich's simplistic answer misses the intricate weave of what sensitive teaching is about. A person, whether teacher or parent, who truly has love and compassion for another person doesn't just say, "Do whatever interests you, whether in reading or anything else." That would be to ignore the many pitfalls in life. And it would be to ignore the tendency for power to corrupt when the "interests" a child pursues mature into a position of economic or political power over others. Indeed, I would say that anyone who naively assumes that all "interests," whether of a child or an adult, will turn out to be socially and ecologically responsible is not fit to be a guide to, or "leader" of, others.

Rather, what we were encouraged to do, after "learning" the children and their individual interests and abilities, was to make them aware of *options* available to them which were "within the moral bounds of justice." It wasn't put just that way, but it amounted to that. There was to be moral judgment in suggesting options. The *feelings* of others were to be considered. In utilizing a common facility or resource, one "takes turns." And this reminds me of Lani Guinier's very timely suggestion that politics should not always result in "winner takes all."[1] There must be a place for "taking turns" as well as for the application of a few other civilizing, moral principles (See Chapter XIII).

Alerting the student to options is crucial to both teaching and learning. Young students cannot possibly know of even a small number of the options which might help them pursue their interests. And they couldn't possibly know about the countless intellectual, artistic, emotional, cultural, social, economic, and political tools available to them. These, Mr. Gingrich, cannot be simply "learned" out of thin air. If the child is to have access to them they must be made available by someone more mature. Ideally this will be a teacher, parent, or friend with no corporate-America, or Third-Wave, or Information -Age axe to grind, but who genuinely cares about the individual child. The caring teacher offers only socially and ecologically responsible options, but within those moral bounds s/he is alert to those for which the child may be ready to consider at a particular time of development.

Gingrich has quite another approach, set forth in the section on "Earning by Learning." What he is advocating is motivating students to read by paying them for doing so. Nor is quality of reading a consideration. No, just *numbers* of books.

Finally, it is so ironic that this man, who dismisses with the sweep of a phrase that so beautifully honorable human activity called "teaching," should himself be setting himself up as a kind of super-teacher for our time. Nor is he doing it by a legitimate teaching process. No, it is by a *telling* process. Gingrich simply *tells*. He simply tells us that we must "start anew," that "we need the determination to abandon the assumptions of the past."

---

1. *The Tyranny of the Majority*, by Lani Guinier, The Free Press, NY, NY, 1994

Well, Mr. Gingrich, here is one teacher-student whom you haven't convinced.

*In fact, with every chapter of revelations regarding the way he would apply the "leadership" position and power he now has (which he has told us he has been striving for since a teenager) and regarding the direction in which he would lead America, Americans, and America's children, I am ever more committed to putting out this challenge to him and to his whole philosophy and agenda.*

## IX-13: *Individual Versus Group Rights*

Gingrich's Chapter 13 reflects again his tendency to prefer to see everything in black and white terms. In his Chapter 12, it was either "learning" *or* "education." No combination was even considered. In his Chapter 13, it is either "individual" *or* "group" rights.

> One of the great debates of the near future will be individual versus group rights. It is a debate that must end decisively in favor of the individual. . . . The very concept of group rights contradicts the nature of America. America is about the future, about "the pursuit of happiness," while group rights are about the past. America asks who you want to be. Group rights ask who your grandparents were.

How can one respond to such thoughtless simplicity? Anyone who faces ethical and justice issues seriously knows that in every concrete situation there are many moral considerations which enter into what is just. First, they know that there are no absolute rights, by either individual or group. My right to free speech must be weighed on the scales of justice along with your right to not be slandered.

Thus, whenever *complete* freedom of speech will inflict no injustice on anyone (such as when one is alone in a soundproof room) there exists an *absolute* "right" to engage in it. In a crowded theater, however, as generally acknowledged, that right is very limited. One doesn't have a right to cry "FIRE" in a crowded theater when there is no fire. Why? Because great injustice might result to those who get trampled. And even when there really is a fire, the manner of alerting people contains limitations on "rights."

How, then, does this principle apply to group rights? The same. Any group has a right to do anything which doesn't do injustice to anyone — but not beyond that.

The reason, therefore, there are no absolute rights is because there seems to be no behavior which cannot possibly, under any circumstances, do injustice to anyone. As already noted (VI-2), even freedom of religion cannot *rightly* extend to cutting off a person's hand for stealing, or cutting out her tongue for lying — at least not without weighing the harm thus done against the harm such action is supposedly designed to prevent.

The Bill of Rights was a crucial addition to the US Constitution. Without it the document would be much more supportive of corporate America than it presently is. But, careful analysis will reveal that what it lists are not absolute rights. Rather, it lists kinds of behavior which commonly are due moral *consideration*. Thus, the "right to free speech" is a right to have the behavior of speaking freely, given appropriate moral consideration in weighing it along with other "rights." (See XIII-2).

A recent Supreme Court case brought this out clearly. The issue was whether the practice of using peyote in a Native American religious ceremony was to be permitted in the light of laws against its general use as a harmful drug. Justice Sandra O'Connor argued against those who took an absolutist position regarding upholding the law. Even though she decided that justice was better served by upholding the law in the case at issue, she argued that the religious practice should be given some moral "consideration." In her mind, presumably on the scales of justice as she saw them, the religious consideration was outweighed by the law consideration in this case, but only after giving due weight to all relevant "consideration."

Whether one agrees with the weight she gave to each, her argument against absolutes and in support of weighing various "rights" on a scale of justice seems to me morally sound.

Gingrich evidently likes absolutes because this allows him to reach fast and sweeping decisions in support of simple, clear-cut agendas. But that is largely because he is basically interested in promoting corporate America and its simplistic, materialistic, power-seeking, world dominating, military-supported agenda rather than serving justice and preventing and remedying injustice as we travel along the pathways of life.

## IX-14: *Illegal Immigration in a Nation of Legal Immigrants*

Gingrich suggests ten related principles for determining immigration policies. "First," he says, "anything illegal is, by definition, wrong." Thus, he is logically wrong at the start. A triangle, in geometry, is by definition a plane figure, and also a polygon. Therefore, if something is a triangle, it is logically correct to say that it is a polygon. However, neither the word nor the concept of "wrong" appears in the definition of illegality. That is illegal which has been declared so by some political process. Nothing more. If Gingrich wanted to say that he *believed* that whatever is illegal is wrong he might be able to persuade us. But to claim it "by definition" is to make a claim he cannot substantiate.

Also, the word "wrong" is ambiguous. If he were to say that all illegality is unjust, he would at least have an unambiguous thesis. But then he would come up against explaining the admission of "defense of necessity" in the most just of U.S. courts. He would also have difficulty with "jury nullification," an important part of trial by jury, which was sacred in colonial America but which is being whittled away by those who like simplistic, absolutist rules.

The fact is that what is declared "legal" is at the very best an honest attempt at approximating general rules which, if applied with discretion, can greatly contribute to justice, but never absolutely assure it.

"Second," says Gingrich, "any nation has an absolute obligation to protect its sovereign borders." There is that "absolute" word again. Extensive obligation, yes; but not absolute!

"Third," he says, "everyone knows where our border is." That's a statement that clearly is extreme.

"Fourth," he says, "when people have succeeded in illegally entering the United States there should be a quick and efficient method of deporting them." Gingrich really likes things to be "quick and efficient." No wonder he doesn't like to deal with genuine justice issues. They usually don't have "quick and efficient" answers.

Fifth, he calls for the federal government to cover costs to the state for deportations. Fair enough, but *only* to the extent that a deportation is justified.

Sixth, he calls for requiring "everyone to carry employee identification cards" that are hard to counterfeit. Again, *to the extent that identification cards are justified*, they should be counterfeit-proof.

"Seventh, we should develop a guest-worker program to allow foreigners to work temporarily in the United States." He favors this because it gives agribusiness a source of cheap labor.

Eighth, he says clamping down on illegal immigration will make it easier for legal immigrants to enter. Likely true.

Ninth, "preference should be to immigrants who possess knowledge, skills, and investment capital." No compassion here, either. Only the self-interests of corporate America.

Tenth, emergency care *only*, to illegal immigrants. This seems fair *provided* immigration policies are fair in the first place.

Finally, he calls for "developing a workable plan, and implementing it relentlessly." This also seems in keeping with Gingrich's inclination to be relentless in matters which affect the hard-nosed profit and power interests of corporate America.

## IX-15: *English as the American Language*

I essentially agree, but probably not for his reasons; rather, because I believe that justice is much more effectively served by good rather than difficult communication. And having a common language greatly facilitates good communication. It's interesting that in acknowledging that the rights of African Americans *as a group* had been violated until recently, he is arguing against the position of "group rights" which he himself took in his Chapter 13. I also agree that it *may be* a service to immigrants to put *some* pressure on them to learn the language mostly spoken in the country they are in.

## IX-16: *Health Care as an Opportunity in the World Market*

Here he is essentially arguing that modern technology can not only help provide much better health care, but it can also help bring down the cost. In saying this we are reminded of some of the fantasy thinking he exhibited in his Chapter 4. Technology can, indeed, contribute to better health care. But, to claim that it can reduce costs in any degree comparable to the additional cost of the technology itself is unwarranted. The fact is that there is no limit to what can be spent on health care. The only way to deal with it fairly is to assure every earthly resident a fair share of financial and other benefits from our common heritage. Then, religious, cultural, and other groupings can voluntarily join together to bargain for group health care. (See P-5, plus footnote.)

## IX-17: *Health Care as an Opportunity Rather Than a Problem*

Again Gingrich returns to the fantasy thinking in which he engaged in his Chapter 4. He has so much faith in the advantages in high-tech for increasing "efficiency" and for helping with "innovation" that he seemingly completely overlooks the problem of (1) assuring that the "information" it yields is reliable, and (2) assuring that the power it puts in the hands of its main benefactors of it is maintained within the moral bounds of justice. These are essentially the same problems we noted in Chapter IV.

## IX-18: *Ending the Drug Trade and Saving the Children*

Gingrich opens his Chapter 18 with the following paragraph:

> Future historians who look back on our generation will have a difficult time explaining how we tolerated the invasion of drug dealers and their assault on our children's lives. These historians will have to go back to the counter-culture of the late 1960s and its contemptuous dismissal of middle-class values to understand why we have been so ineffective in saving our children from criminals and foreign agents.

He places the blame on the counterculture, but it was the CIA which had Noriega, the king-pin drug dealer of Panama, on their payroll. And there are those, such as the Christic Institute, who believe that the CIA was involved in considerable drug dealing during the Vietnam War.

In any case, placing all the blame on the counterculture is essentially a cop-out from taking responsibility for the moral breakdown in high places; for the disenchantment with government policies during the Vietnam War; the conscription of young men to kill and be killed in that war; the killings at Kent State University; the continued racism, especially in the South; and then the murder within a few years of the very national leaders who showed some concern about racial and other injustices in America: first President John F. Kennedy, then Martin Luther King, Jr., and then, what seemed like the final evidence of moral decay at the very roots of the American estab-lishment, the murder of Robert Kennedy.

Did corporate America have anything to do with these increasingly dark-ening days? It is difficult to know. But there were suspicions that there might be a connection. The Vietnam War was, after all, the front line in the fight against communism, the main concern of corporate America at the time. And it was the Vietnam War which was soaking up young American bodies and sending them home in body bags.

Living in Berkeley, California, during the period when the counter-culture was growing, I experienced first-hand its flavor and its idealism. That idealism was real. It evoked personal sacrifice from its participants in some ways comparable to that being made by their buddies and lovers in Vietnam.[2] The charge laid on them by Gingrich of "contemptuous dismissal of middle-class values" is misplaced and grossly unfair. What those in the counterculture were basically contemptuous of was those values which continued to support racism in America, continued to be critical of the efforts of Martin Luther King, Jr. to end it nonviolently, and which continued to promote a war in Vietnam which, with its body-count way of measuring progress in pursuing American interests, was becoming increasingly disgusting day by day, week by week, and year by dragging-on year.

In any case, in the face of the above recounted series of blemishes on American idealism, all that corporate America seemed to have to offer was a continued and growing consumerism promoted via the rapidly growing television industry. So, it is basically corporate America that the counter-culture was contemptuous of (and continues to be in a more diffused way), and not, as Gingrich charges, "middle-class values" as such. Whatever contempt some may have come to feel for the American middle class developed gradually with the realization that the middle class seemed to be very slow to join the counterculture in registering the moral outrage which the events of the day called for from anyone with a compassionate heart and a conscience. Then, too, there were those in the middle class who brought on whatever contempt there was by their outright rejection of the moral witness which the most courageous of the counterculture participants and proponents were making.

No, Mr. Gingrich. You have almost completely misrepresented both the flavor and the motivations of the sixties counterculture. And if you want to pinpoint the culprits who are promoting today's drug trade — and I agree that it is disgusting — you must look elsewhere. I suggest that you look to

---

2. The definitive work is by Theodore Roszak, *The Making of A Counterculture,* Anchor Books, Garden City, NY, 1969

those high places which place highest value on profit-making with little concern for who is being hurt in the aftermath. I suggest that it is the values of corporate America which have most influenced the profiteers in the drug trade, and not those idealistic young people who have tried, and still try in the face of mounting frustration, to rehabilitate the spiritual soul of their American sisters and brothers.

## IX-19: *Defense for the Twenty-first Century*

After praising the U.S. military for its performance in "Desert Shield" and "Desert Storm," and applauding the advances that have been made in its military hardware, he warns against resting on its laurels.

> We have to plan on the assumption that somewhere there may be an opponent with the courage and determination to test us in circumstances that we have not considered, using systems that we have not invented ourselves. Complacency is the father of defeat. Vigilance is the mother of continued safety.

And so, again, we see Gingrich's mental set. He pictures America as essentially a competitor with other power brokers in the world for world domination. That one short sentence says volumes: "Complacency is the father of defeat."

Having evidently assumed that his readers are with him in this continuing cold-war posture, he goes on to assure us that "I don't think we ought to salute waste just because it is in uniform." So, he is for maintaining a military force without waste, and prepared to defeat any challenger. No thoughts about what quality of life Americans might pursue which would inspire others in the world to take a friendly stance toward us. No thoughts whatever in that direction.

Yet, Gingrich's attitude is understandable, considering his support of corporate America's goal of dominating the global economic marketplace. During the entire recent history of Western civilization it has been a small step from economic competition to military confrontation. In short, if the goal of corporate America is to dominate economic life in every corner of every culture in the world, it is perfectly rational to expect that not just one or two, but many, power brokers will feel that challenge, and will work hard to try to bring it down. So, as long as Americans accept the values of corporate America as their own, life in the global market place will certainly be a constant economic battle, a steady military posturing, an occasional major military challenge, and possibly an eventual and inevitable ultimate one.

So, I suggest that we examine very closely any concern for "safety" which justifies in Gingrich's eyes the continued bleeding of American economic, cultural, and spiritual life. Does the aggressive and precarious "safety" promised by Gingrich's corporate America and backed by the U.S. military, represent the quality of life we want to have for ourselves, our children, and their children? Is it the quality of life that we want to set before the world as a kind of ideal, as something we encourage others to emulate? Or does it constitute an abandonment of what I have called "the Early American Dream"? (See Chapters XI and XII.)

I know not how others may answer this question, but I choose, rather, to encourage my American sisters and brothers to rise to a challenge radically different from that posed by Mr. Gingrich. The vision for America, and for the world, is closer to that posed by Martin Luther King Jr., and, yes, in many respects to that posed by the best of the counterculture of the 60s. It is a challenge to establish in America truly just, fair, humane. compassionate political and economic structures. And it is my faith that to the extent to which we do so we can then lay down our high-tech armaments, pull back our challenge to all comers in the world to compete with us if they can, and again become a spiritual inspiration to the poor, the refugees, the marginalized, "the huddled masses" in this spiritually sick world civilization.

## IX-20: *New Frontiers in Science, Space, and the Oceans*

Once again, this time in his Chapter 20, Gingrich has thrown to the winds all restraints and inhibitions which might prevent him from realizing all of his childhood fantasies. Again he urges us to embrace high-tech in all its imagined manifestations and not to worry about what it does to the environment. That's for kill-joys. That's for people afraid to take risks.

Again, nothing about the real environmental problems that face us. Nothing about those who are victimized by the reckless abandon of the power brokers of the world. Nothing about the mounting injustices in the world, resulting in more refugees than even in history, more homeless people than ever on American streets, more moral and cultural decay in our largest cities. All that is something he might allude to in passing in other chapters in the course of beating on the counterculture. But this chapter is for forgetting all that. This chapter is for advocating a thorough and absorbing embrace of high-tech as it is and high-tech as it could become if, in his view, we don't lose our courage.

> I believe that space tourism will be a common fact of life during the adulthood of children born this year, that honeymooners in space will be the vogue in 2020. Imagine weightlessness and its effects and you will understand some of the attractions. Imagine looking out at the earth from your honeymoon suite and you will understand even more why it will be a big item. For those who have everything, a long trip in space will be the equivalent of today's sailboat or yacht or private airplane.

This is the fantasy thinking of someone who hobnobs with people "who have everything." This is the mental state of someone who doesn't want to be told about the injustice rampant in the world and at the very heart of America's economic and political life. This is the mentality of someone who just doesn't want to hear about any of that. It's not that he has faced these things and has given a rational and socially responsible response. He just doesn't want to hear about them. He wants to be left to imagine his childhood fantasies coming into reality.

> Now, at fifty-one years of age, I am still convinced that this positive vision of my childhood was the right one. . . . I believe more than ever that much remains to be discovered and that many great adventures remain to be launched.

Gingrich is almost exactly the same age as my own son. I imagine them growing up with the same world events going on around them, but how different they were. Gingrich was deep into the culture of military life, the first part of which was experienced overseas. My son was at the same time growing up in a cooperative community of thirty families about thirty-five miles west of Philadelphia, a community in which all children were welcome in any family, and felt safe in any family. It was a social experiment begun by people challenged to live in such a way as to, as George Fox said, "take away the occasion for war." And it was quite successful in that regard. Then, in Gingrich's later teen years, when he was joining the Republican party in Georgia, my son was experiencing some of the counterculture of Berkeley. And Gingrich is right in saying that it was a culture which was challenging the one he had experienced in the military, and which he was experiencing in Republican politics.

So, as I make this comparison I can begin to get a feeling for Gingrich's frame of mind. And I also get a feeling, especially from his Chapter 20, for his present mood. It's as if the main problem with American life today is boredom. And such may well be the case with people he fraternizes with in Washington and related circles.

Especially in this chapter, Gingrich is trying to give them some excitement in their bored lives. Here they've got "everything" and it's still not enough. There's still something missing. So, this chapter is directed at his bored friends.

> The next time people tell you they are bored, ask if they have thought about any of these [space flight?] opportunities. See if you can get them to join us on the great adventures of the twenty-first century.

## IX-21: *Scientifically Based Environmentalism*

Suddenly, in his Chapter 21, Gingrich is an environmentalist! Well, at least in his eyes.

> My interest in the environment goes back to my childhood. I was fascinated by animals and nature long before I went to school. . . Whenever I could I would talk my relatives into visiting zoos and museums.

He goes on to be quite persuasive in convincing us that he is genuinely concerned about the environment; indeed, about the entire ecosystem. He tells of his finding himself "coordinator of environmental studies at West Georgia College." He tells of taking students on field trips, of participating in the first Earth Day. As I said, he is quite convincing! And he remains convincing throughout most of his 21st chapter.

What he does not deal with, however, is the whole justice issue in relation to the environment. One aspect of the justice issue is in regard to whose environment is to be given top priority, and who is going to pay the most? Will distant wilderness areas which only the wealthy can afford to drive to be funded before or after addressing pollution in drinking water and air in urban centers? And who will end up paying for such distant wilderness areas? In short, in environmental matters, as in all others, the justice issues come down to the same old question of who benefits and who pays. In an unjust *system*, it is the already wealthy who benefit and the already poor who pay.

Also, he doesn't discuss the impact on human rights or on the environment resulting from corporate America's global agenda for world-wide economic competition, and its related military competition. What about environmental regulation in countries in which corporate America sets up factories? How will their pollution be monitored? How will children's rights and women's rights be respected in distant countries? He doesn't discuss these issues. It isn't in the interest of corporate America to do so.

Rather, his emphasis, again, is to put faith in high-tech and scientific research, designed to make all environmental efforts more effective, and to help with cost-benefit analysis, where both costs and benefits are in terms of dollars, even when dollars can't measure them.

His closing paragraph reflects his insufficient concern about who pays and who benefits, and about justice issues generally, both in this country and in those whose markets are sought by corporate America. His limited analysis makes it all sound like just another challenging political issue. And it is as if "we" are all in this together, whereas that's not the way the economic and political systems dominating life in today's world are structured. In today's global marketplace there is the "we" who benefits and the "we" who pays.

> From serious scientific surveys to new technologies, from recycling to commonsense management of ecosystems, we have the opportunity to launch a new era of environmentalism. We can craft an approach which is scientifically sound, economically rational, and politically popular. That is a worthy goal for the twenty first century.

## IX-22: *Violent Crime, Freedom from Fear, Right to Bear Arms*

Gingrich makes it clear in his Chapter 22 why he is in favor of "the right to bear arms." He says it is not in order to go duck hunting. It "has nothing to do with target practice or owning collector's weapons":

> The Second Amendment is a political right written into our Constitution for the purpose of protecting individual citizens from their own government. . . .
> If the American colonists had not been trained in how to shoot and fight, they could not have become American citizens.

This may seem like a childish argument. "How," one might ask, "could a few armed militia resist the policing and military might of the U.S. Government?" It's a good question, and Gingrich doesn't answer it. But he might, I suppose, have argued that they would at least give any government agency a considerable amount of hassle; perhaps enough to generate national publicity, as the Ruby Ridge incident certainly has. In short, he would not be arguing for effective resistance against the full might of the U.S. military. Even the relatively minor firearms possessed by the Weavers were sufficient to give pause to government agents and to generate a national incident.

Gingrich does acknowledge that there is a problem in keeping guns from criminals. He suggests solving it in the following ways:

1. Accelerate the instant identity-check system that would compare a thumbprint against a national record of felons and people who have been in mental institutions. No law-abiding citizen's thumbprint would be kept, but the lawbreaker and the insane would be picked up immediately if they tried to buy a gun.

2. The second step would be to make it illegal for convicted felons to carry guns under any circumstances unless they had received pardons.

3. Establish that prisoners should work forty-eight hours a week and study twelve hours a week. Numerous people in poor neighborhoods say that young men in their areas refer to prison as "vacation time." . . . Prison in its present form is more an inconvenience than a deterrent.

4. Eliminate all weight and muscle-building rooms and break down the cult of macho behavior in prison. Prisoners should be learning job skills and doing penance. We must reclaim the prisons just as we must reclaim the streets. [His argument here is that their increased strength and resulting macho image of themselves constitutes aggressiveness armed with added muscle.]

Finally, we ought to teach in school once again why there is a Second Amendment and why the Founding Fathers thought the right to bear arms ought to be part of the Bill of Rights.

What, then, are we to say about Gingrich's arguments? First we give him credit for presenting relevant arguments rather than mere declarations, such as we have noted in other chapters. But, I am not going to argue these points with Gingrich. With some qualifications I would accept his arguments, and there are more important issues to be raised.

What I would again contend is that basic injustices in America's economic and political systems are such that they provoke much of the criminal behavior to which Gingrich's only answer seems to be imprisonment and deterrence. Again, I suggest that if each person on this earth received her and his rightful fair share of financial and other income from our common heritage we would witness a major step toward a general climate of *fairness*. This, plus other steps toward more justice in our economic and political systems would bring about a dramatic reduction of crime of all kinds and a comparable reduction in the need for prisons. It would also greatly reduce the present felt need among American militia groups to remain armed against a government in which they see the rich getting richer, the poor getting poorer, and increasing grounds for distrusting it in many ways and on many levels.

## IX-23: *Why Rush Limbaugh and His Friends Matter*

Gingrich feels that radio talk-show hosts like Rush Limbaugh are important because they challenge what he calls "the elite media." That in itself endears at least some of his listeners to him, at least those who support Gingrich's own "elite" ideas and culture.

The impression I get in reading his Chapter 23 is that Gingrich sees in talk show hosts like Limbaugh a channel to people who are vulnerable to being persuaded that (1) "liberal" policies give handouts to people and that somehow the ordinary "law-abiding," patriotic person gets the bill, and that (2) an "elite media" favors that "liberal" message. What these radio audiences are not asked to consider is whether the people who are really giving both them and the welfare recipients a difficult time might not be corporate America and the economic-political structure designed to serve its corporate interests. In short, are they perhaps being *used* by those who want to "conserve" corporate America. Are they perhaps manipulated into directing their ire at fellow victims rather than at those who are victimizing all who are not included within their "elite" corporate circle? My readers may judge for themselves with the help of the way Gingrich evaluates the talk shows in the next to last paragraph of his Chapter 23:

> Talk shows have done three big things for the country. First, they give people a place to ventilate and have a public dialogue rather than simply being lectured to by the elite commentators.

Second, they have created a unifying sense of confidence among millions of listeners that it is okay to be conservative and challenge the liberal wisdom.

Third, when the elite media have tried to distort the news, the talk shows have a pretty good record of setting things straight over the following four or five days.

We note some key phrases here which might make us question the complete objectivity of Gingrich's evaluation. In his "First" point, we note the pejorative phrase, "elite commentators." In his Second point we note his admitted pleasure that so many listeners are on the "conservative" side. In the Third point we note again the reference to "the elite media" and "setting things straight," the implication being that there are always things to be "set straight." These pejorative and self-serving words and phrases are not the kind which a truly objective observer would use.

## IX-24: *The Flat Tax and the IRS*

Gingrich begins his Chapter 24 with the following statement:

A taxpayer's rebellion is brewing in America. It is going to force us either to adopt a flat tax or to replace the entire income tax system with a consumption tax.

He spends most of this chapter giving evidence of dissatisfaction with the existing income tax system. He doesn't present arguments in support of the flat tax, or the consumption tax, but these may roughly be described as follows:

The main argument for the flat tax is its simplicity. Briefly stated, all income from whatever source would be taxed at the same fixed amount, for rich and poor alike — except that there presumably would be a level specified below which no tax is paid. It is argued that all existing loopholes would thereby be eliminated. Thus, it is argued that it would be more fair. Supposedly it would also be more fair because everyone would pay at the same rate. But this is a simplistic way to measure fairness. It ignores the fairness of requiring those who have benefitted from an unfair structure to compensate its victims in some way.

Except, for major necessities like food and medicines, the consumption tax would simply tax all purchases. The main argument here is that this would encourage savings, and thus investment, such as in corporate

America, which is always looking for money at an interest rate low enough so that it can get a return at a greater rate, and thus make a profit. The more money people have to loan, the lower the law of supply and demand will send the interest rate on the money corporate America borrows.

With either of these two forms of taxation those who comprise corporate America — the rich and super-rich among us — would benefit in relation to the rest of us.

But in order to evaluate each of these proposals against principles which truly would be fair we will have to consider much more carefully (1) the moral justification for governing itself, and (2) what moral principle should guide us in determining who pays for such governing. These questions are addressed in the Preface and Chapters XI-XIII.

We shall see that in truly just economic and political structures neither the present tax system nor the flat tax is fair. The consumption tax could be fair if applied in the following way:

First, producers of goods and services are forced to pay for governing to the extent that they behave in ways that require governing. The large polluters and the producers of hazardous goods and services would be taxed heavily (because they would require much monitoring and governing), and their taxes would be passed on to their customers by way of higher *prices*. Trivial polluters, and producers of benign or socially beneficial goods and services, would be taxed only lightly if at all (because they would require little monitoring and governing), and so they would pass on little or no such tax to their customers. A fuller explanation appears in Chapter XIII.

## IX-25: *The Coming Crisis in Higher Education*

Gingrich's message in his Chapter 25 is quite simple. He doesn't like the fact that his myths about the American economic and political structure, and the values of those who founded them, are questioned. As we saw in his very first chapter, he has a view of American history which he wants to promote; and he doesn't like to see it questioned. Thus, he again shows his bias in the following:

> Most tenured positions in higher education are now held by passionate advocates of the Anti-Vietnam War movement. These former radicals have now become the comfortable, all-purpose "deconstructionists" of American culture. When I talk to older faculty members who still study such traditional

figures as Jefferson, Franklin, and Washington, there is a sadness in their voices as they describe the atmosphere of intolerance and petty barbarism that has invaded American campuses.

Gingrich not only doesn't want his conservative politics questioned. He wants unqualified acceptance of his agenda for promoting high-tech in American colleges and universities. To question these positions is to hold up the agenda of making corporate America the means for making America #1 in the world in every way he considers important.

Let us also realize that Gingrich is most familiar with colleges. Apparently he has never taught at a university. In some ways he would find more reason for concern there, especially at a university like the Berkeley campus of the University of California. But at both colleges and universities what he is complaining about is to be found almost exclusively among the humanities faculty.

Many of the physical science and mathematics faculties at both colleges and universities are "on his side." Many are generally cooperating with the military-industrial complex. The faculties of the social sciences have their feet in both camps. Some faculties and faculty members are supportive of corporate America, and get funded by it, while others are even more critical than the humanities faculties because they, especially the political science and economics faculties, are closer to the power brokers, and thus have more reason to be apprehensive about their agendas for corporate America and their political and military friends.

The faculties of the physical sciences and mathematics are generally feeding into our culture the high-tech which corporate America and Gingrich increasingly are calling for. This is especially true of the major research universities. Basic research is the key to technological advance. It is the key to the superiority of corporate America in the global marketplace. And the science and mathematics faculties, especially at the university level, and most especially at the graduate level where basic research is done, are the ones who are getting the bulk of both federal and corporate funding. It is their constant flow of knowledge-power into the *applied* research laboratories of U.S. corporations that energizes the entire global agenda of the American military-industrial complex.

A major reason, therefore, that the humanities faculties are generally unhappy is not only because they are constantly given the short end of funding, but because they see at close range how their colleagues in math and the physical sciences are, in a sense, selling out their intellectual souls. I'm not sure what academic battles Gingrich is referring to, but I suspect that it largely goes on between the humanities faculties and those of mathematics and the physical sciences.

Before closing this section, let us grant that he has a point. The faculties at this country's colleges and universities do tend to be resistant to change, especially to their roles being taken over by electronic classrooms. There is, no doubt, a degree of self-interest motivating their resistance. It is also true that there is competition for advancements to a *limited* number of positions which not only offer more pay but also more freedom for writing and research. This does tend to set up a competitive atmosphere.

But, the situation is much more complicated than Gingrich's remarks or my comments on them. The colleges and universities of America are at the very center of the power struggles going on at this time. We are, after all, as Gingrich rightly states, at the threshold of what he calls the Information Age and what I would call the Knowledge-Power Age.

# IX-26: *Corrections Day*

Gingrich begins his Chapter 26 with the following paragraph:

> Corrections Day is a brand new concept that is going to have a dramatic effect on the way government does business in Washington. Correction Day will be held one day a month. On that day, the House will see that particularly destructive or absurdly expensive bureaucratic rules and regulations are overturned by narrowly drafted actions.

Then Gingrich indicates whom he is targeting:

> . . . the arrogance of institutions such as today's Environmental Protection Agency, Occupational Safety and Health Administration, and Fish and Wildlife Service. . . . No matter how clean or dirty our water may be, no matter how many industrial accidents we may or may not have, if we have to live in a society in which citizens constantly feel harassed, then the whole point of a free society is lost.

We know from evaluating Gingrich's other chapters that what he wants to be "free" is the enterprising of corporate America. Over and over again we have seen that he is strong on initiative, on go, go, go, and short on the realization that wherever there is power there is the tendency to corrupt, and thus the need for monitoring and governing. And it is understandable that those whose enterprising requires restraining will feel "harassed."

This is not to cast doubt on Gingrich's assertion that inefficient bureaucracy has invaded governmental agencies. But if he is really concerned with environmental protection, as he says he is in his Chapter 21, then one would expect him to suggest ways to make the monitoring and governing roles of these agencies *more* "efficient" and *more* "effective," rather than cutting down on their authority, which is what, under his leadership, the House of Representatives has done.

Turning to consider what reforms might come out of Corrections Day, one might be surprised (in view of how strongly he has urged sending power back to the states) to read the following:

> What are the possible solutions [to federal bureaucracy]? Decentralizing power from Washington back to state and local government would obviously help. However, all too often the city, county, and state bureaucracies are worse than their federal counterparts.

Before ending his Chapter 26, Gingrich considers how Corrections Day might be utilized by any person or group frustrated by the existing bureaucracy.

> First, any citizen, government, or business stuck in negotiations with a recalcitrant bureaucracy can say, "If you are going to be unreasonable, we will ask our Congressman [sic] or Senator to bring it up at Corrections Day. . . ."

> Second, having an option overturned on Corrections Day will be a psychological as well as a legal defeat for the bureaucracy. No one likes to have dumb mistakes pointed out or be repudiated by the legislators who provide their statutory authority and budget.

> Third, if a department or agency comes up too often on Corrections Day, its oversight subcommittee may decide to hold hearings on the agency's activities. . .

> Fourth, if all this fails, Congress can zero out an agency and bring in new people with new attitudes.

In general, I can only applaud the *concept* of Corrections Day. But I cannot applaud Gingrich's not-so-hidden agenda motivating its establishment.

# IX-27: *Unfunded Mandate Reform*

Again, Gingrich is siding with those at the state level who are complaining that the federal government is mandating them to clean up environmental pollution of some kind. The controversy reduces to a question of fairness. If the standards which a state is mandated to live up to are ones which have been around for a while and have been accepted by the state as reasonable, then it is not unreasonable nor unfair for the state to carry the entire expense of coming up to the standards it should have maintained right along.

On the other hand, if the federal government raises the standards beyond what they were, then it seems only fair that it provide funds sufficient to close the gap between the old standards and the new.

# IX-28: *Term Limits, Defeat of House Democratic Leadership*

After complaining that incumbent Democrats ruled Congress, and especially the House of Representatives, for many years, Gingrich still couldn't generate an argument for or against term limits. He finally came to the following conclusion:

> The twelve-year term limit provides enough limitation to ensure a constant flow of new blood into the House and Senate and at the same time allows enough continuity to ensure the system can retain its institutional knowledge. I support it, and I will continue to work to pass it.

Lacking a principle by which to decide the issue, this seems like a compromise it would be difficult to argue against. However, the ideal would be to have election rules and Congressional rules such that one need not be afraid of someone's building so much power base that s/he had an automatic advantage by virtue of incumbency alone. If that situation could be achieved, and it ought to be, then it would seem best to permit experienced and qualified members of Congress to run for office as often as they liked. However, as we will see in Part II, the problems with the American political structure run far deeper than those dealt with here.

The notion of making a strong commitment at voting time
and then living up to it
is indeed honorable, *provided*
that to which one is thereby committed
is itself honorable.

# Chapter X

# *Evaluating Gingrich's "Conclusion"*

## X-1: *How This Chapter Is Structured*

Gingrich has divided his book into five Parts. The fifth Part is called "Conclusion." It consists of a single chapter, which he names "A New Beginning: The America We Will Create." This would seem to imply that he is going to give us some kind of picture of the America he would like to see created. I was disappointed, however, that such a "picture" never quite emerged. Nor are we ever clearly told why he feels we Americans are faced with a crisis of sorts. Also, what we are encouraged to do about it is painted in extremely vague, and in fairly trivial, terms. He speaks of challenge, and the need for initiative, energy, commitment, and enthusiasm — but the agenda, the great crusade we are to join in order "to renew America," remains largely unstated other than in vague and seemingly trivial form.

For this reason, this is the most amazing and puzzling chapter in the entire book. Here he has put so much effort into persuading us that we face some exciting challenge; yet, from what we read in Gingrich's Chapter 10, all it seems to amount to is devoting "a few hours a month."

In order to justify this brief evaluation to my readers, and because I believe that this chapter can reveal a telling insight into Newt Gingrich and what motivates him, I undertake a rather fine-tuned dissection of Gingrich's thinking as revealed here. My evaluation is divided into four Parts.

*The First Part* is my evaluations of a list of the things that he says concerns him about life in America today, with some hint of why he thinks America's ills have reached a crisis. I call it a "list," but its items are somewhat strewn throughout his final chapter, rather than being neatly gathered together into a focus on some particular page or part of a page. I will call it *The Crisis List*.

*The Second Part* is also a list, a list of what he reveals about the kind of America he would have us work toward achieving. I will call this *The Wish List*.

*The Third Part* is a list of his suggestions for how to achieve the "Wish List." I will call this the *How-To List*.

*The Fourth Part* is an evaluation of what is revealed about how he sees his personal role in relation to the First, Second, and Third parts. I will call this *The Gingrich Fantasy*.

## X-2: *The Crisis List*

**CL-1:** On page 245 Gingrich wonders "how much the world will change" before his eight-year-old nephew grows up. "He already faces dangers from drugs and violence that I never imagined as a child. He certainly cannot walk around Youngstown the way I once wandered the streets of Harrisburg." The implication is that America's streets are not safe, nor free from the contaminating influence of drugs, the way they once were.

**CL-2:** Next he remarks how much two other nephews, both boys, are loved, and how their parents "worry about their college education and what the future holds for them."

**CL-3:** He reports that his mother-in-law "is concerned about the reports that Medicare will go bankrupt by 2002 and worries that her children will face a more difficult life than she had."

**CL-4:** Gingrich takes the above as evidence of "how much a sense of anxiety has increased in America."

**CL-5:** "Nor are these anxieties groundless. How can any American watch the local television news and not have a sense of alarm? Children being abused or killed, mothers being murdered in carjackings, innocent customers shot in robberies. Young men are without education, without jobs, without hope for their own or their younger brothers' futures."

**CL-6:** "When basketball players can die of drug overdoses, when Olympic ice skaters can be injured in ruthless attacks, when the most honored football player of our time ends up on trial for the brutal killing of his ex-wife and a casual friend (while the children were asleep upstairs) what rational person would not feel a little anxious?"

**CL-7:** "On the economic front, everyone from the hard-pressed small business owner to the worker in a gigantic international corporation feels the brutal pressures of the Information Age and the world market."

**CL-8:** "One day you can be doing remarkably well and the next day you are downsized out of a job. Middle-aged managers who have done everything right all their lives suddenly find themselves obsolete."

**CL-9:** From which evidence Gingrich concludes that "Anxiety is a *rational* response to this world of rapid economic change."

**CL-10:** "When people turn toward political leaders and government for help, all too often they encounter meaningless platitudes. Politicians seem to have few skills for positive leadership and many more for negative campaigning and partisan bickering."

**CL-11:** "Any reasonable citizen would feel anxiety looking at the current political scene."

**CL-12:** Gingrich then concludes that all of the above is evidence that America faces what he is building up to calling "a crisis." He says, "I wrote this book to convince you that you should be worried. I want you to understand that your future, your children's future, and your country's future is at a crossroads."

This, then, is the evidence given in his Chapter 29 for his conclusion that America is in a kind of crisis. My judgment is that, even on his incomplete evidence, he has justified his conclusion: America is indeed in a crisis. I do, however, feel that the list is missing its most important items, some of which are suggested below. I will largely limit my additions to those which pertain to the United States, while realizing that the crisis we face is worldwide. Thus, to his list of twelve, I suggest the following:

**CL-13:** The rich are getting very much richer while the poor are getting much poorer, in both America and the rest of the world.

**CL-14:** Homelessness in American streets, and homeless refugees in the world, have been increasing over the past two decades.

**CL-15:** Environmental, even ecological, damage has reached the point where The Worldwatch Institute is warning of the possibility of widespread ecological collapse. And, yet, the Republican Congress is reducing standards and reducing funds to the agencies authorized to uphold them.

**CL-16:** The health hazards from water, air, and food pollution and contamination are substantial.

**CL-17:** There remains the danger of nuclear or bacteriological warfare, especially if one or more nations feel themselves driven to it by being pushed to the wall in the global economic war that is mounting, and in which corporate America is striving, with Gingrich's support and encouragement, to achieve a position of dominance over the entire global marketplace.

**CL-18:** There remains the danger of meltdowns and other nuclear disasters from human and mechanical failure in nuclear power plants still in operation in America and the rest of the world. This danger also exists from malfunction in abandoned or shut-down nuclear facilities.

**CL-19:** The health hazards from diseases which come from unknown sources, such as AIDS, and for which there is no known cure, are ominous.

**CL-20:** Women's rights are not yet fully protected in America, as was emphatically underscored during the recent U.N. Women's Conference in Beijing, China.

**CL-21:** Prejudice on account of race, religious orientation, sexual orientation, and ethnic origin continues in America.

**CL-22:** There are gross economic and other forms of injustice in America, and the rest of the world, especially among those who are not favored by corporate America and multinational corporations generally.

**CL-23:** Justice in American courts depends heavily on one's ability to afford legal counsel. For this reason, there is gross injustice in the treatment of the poor and marginalized.

**CL-24:** The possibility of uprisings seems to be growing: by militant groups from the Right, by the poverty-stricken and marginalized, and by Native Americans seeking truly just remedy for the rape, plunder, and genocide of their people and culture which began with Christopher Columbus's "discovery" of their homeland.[1]

**CL-25:** The injustices which minorities of all kinds constantly suffer as the result of determining justice by a winner-take-all majority-vote process of counting what most people want rather than by somehow determining what is fair. For instance, as Loni Guinier suggests and every parent knows, the most basic rule in fairness is that which says "take turns." Yet, in the simplistic, majority-vote, winner-take-all decision-making process there seems to be no place for this and other devices for determining fairness. (This problem is addressed in Chapters XI and XII.)

**CL-26:** Finally, and perhaps most important, the financial and other bene-fits from our common heritage continue to be monopolized by the most aggressive and acquisitive among us (roughly, those who comprise corpor-ate America), *thus denying a fair share to the rest of the population.* This basic, structural injustice is largely responsible for all the other economic ills, including those mentioned by Gingrich.

What, then, with this larger perspective, are we to say about what Gingrich picks out as evidence of a crisis in America? It seems to me very significant what he mentions and what he leaves out. Personally, I have little problem with what he includes. And if he would have adequately addressed those which he mentioned, many of the others would be much easier to remedy.

---

1. See *A People's History of the United States,* by Howard Zinn, Harpers and Row, NY, NY, 1980

But, this he did not do. We shall see that a major reason for this is to be found in the inadequacies of his Wish List.

## X-3: *The Wish List*

**WL-1:** The first indication we have in his Chapter 29 of what Gingrich would value in a renewed America appears on page 247 when he refers to "the purpose of pursuing happiness and the American Dream." The implication seems to be that an America which would permit the pursuit of "happiness and the American Dream" would be a definite improvement over what we now have.

He doesn't define "happiness," and he doesn't specify *who* is to be permitted to pursue it; but, presumably, he means everybody. However, more importantly, he doesn't state here what he means by "the American Dream." The conjunction "and" suggests that he means it to include more than "the pursuit of happiness." And we shall see that such is indeed the case.

**WL-2:** The next hint we get of what Gingrich would include in the American Dream is farther down the same page when he refers to the "excitement and progress" we will find in the twenty-first century — presumably, only if we pull out of the present "crisis."

**WL-3:** In the very next sentence we are told that "if we do our job right the twenty-first century could be an age of freedom," . . .

**WL-4:** . . . "of exploration,"

**WL-5:** . . . "of discovery,"

**WL-6:** . . . "of prosperity."

**WL-7:** He then seems to imply that the above will not come automatically, but that "*More people* will have *more opportunities* to pursue happiness in more different ways than at any time in human history."

**WL-8:** On page 248 he adds *"invention"* to the list of things (included in WL-3 to WL-6 above) which he hopes we will have the "opportunity" to do if we really do "renew America."

**WL-9:** On page 248 he implies that the opportunity "to learn to read," presumably for everyone, is also something which would exist in an America renewed according to his wish list.

**WL-10:** The opportunity to make money, and

**WL-11:** to help other people. (page 248)

What, then, are we to say about the adequacy of such an American Dream? First, there is no mention of "justice for all" as essential, nor of injustice as something to be prevented and remedied. Because he expresses no concern about injustice, it is not surprising that there is no mention of the fair sharing of our common heritage. Again, as has been pointed out many times, the omission of concern for injustice constitutes a moral flaw throughout his entire book.

In fact, his wish list doesn't even address his own crisis list. He doesn't address the problem of street safety or drug use (CL-1); nor the problem of an uncertain future for our youth (CL-2); of the insolvency of Medicare (CL-3); the multiple evils listed in CL-5; moral decline in sports and among sports heroes (CL-6); nor the problem of downsizing and job loss generally; nor that very great problem to be addressed below, of "the brutal pressures of the Information Age and the world market (CL-7);" nor of being cast aside at middle age by a company one has served well all one's life thus far (CL-8); nor the problem of unhelpful politicians (CL-10). Nor does he address in any substantive way the general problem of resulting anxiety (CL-4, CL-9, and CL-11).

In short, in Gingrich's Wish-List offering we find little more than generalities, and these unrelated to either of his other lists. Almost all of the items in his Wish-List relate to freedom of opportunity of some kind: to explore, to discover, to make money, to achieve prosperity, and to invent. Virtually all are values of corporate America pure and simple! And even the single example of "helping other people" was one of helping someone to use a computer.

Gingrich here reveals that he is so locked into the materialistic, high-tech, aggressive, competitive values of corporate America that he doesn't even notice that he hasn't addressed the crisis issues which even he himself identifies! But, let's give him a full hearing. On to the list of How-To items.

# X-4: *The How-To List*

**HT-1:** The first suggestion Gingrich has for addressing the crisis before us is that readers "be a little anxious, . . . decide [translated, admit] that there is a problem." Only as "enough people decide there is a problem" can they "do something about it."

**HT-2:** His second suggestion is "to turn that anxiety into energy."

**HT-3:** Third, "take the energy aroused by danger and opportunity and channel it into useful efforts."

**HT-4:** More specifically, remember the "opportunity" that's waiting to be tapped in "technology;"

**HT-5:** . . ."in entrepreneurship";

**HT-6:** . . . "in the sheer level of human talent we can attract."

**HT-7:** Then on page 247 he lists several How-To items. The first of these is "courage."

**HT-8:** The next is "creativity."

**HT-9:** The next is "commitment."

**HT-10:** At the bottom of page 247 he says, "Democracies rely only on the unique spark of each person's God-given talent. It may be a far less orderly society [i.e., than a dictatorship], but it is a vastly superior one." Then comes a typical indication of what Gingrich considers a true test of the value of a society: "It was the secret of our ability to defeat Nazi Germany and Imperial Japan."

**HT-11:** On Page 248, he says that he wrote *To Renew America* "because I believe that an aroused, informed, inspired American citizenry is the most powerful force [again, we note the metaphor] on earth. I am convinced that if each of us does a little bit we can remake the world. If each of us plays a small part we can launch our children into a new adventure of freedom, invention, and opportunity."

**HT-12**: He ends the book with the following appeal to his readers to make "a little extra effort." That's all it will take, Newt, to "renew America," and to meet this momentous civilization crisis which we are justified in being anxious about? No world restructuring? No new "contract with America"? No joining together to decentralize a big, bad governmental bureaucracy, or to put the counter-culture in its place, or "elite intellectuals" in their place? All we have to do is exert "a little extra effort" at helping out in our local communities?

Apparently we are to leave to Mr. Gingrich and his colleagues in government the big issues. We are not being asked to participate in the revolutionary restructuring that he has convinced us needs to take place. Here, then, in his own words, is his summary challenge to us:

> To renew America, we simply have to convince ourselves that our country, our freedom, and our children's future are worth a little extra effort.
>
> To renew or to decay, that is the choice that each of us makes, one at a time, day by day.
>
> For me the choice of renewal is clear. I know that at journey's end there must come a Monday morning when we will wake to find that not a single child has been killed over the weekend; that not one single child is forced to attend a school where no learning is possible, that not a single child is trapped in a heartless culture of poverty and violence; that none of our children must face a national debt that is destined to destroy his or her future safety and security.
>
> To renew or to decay. At no time in the history of our great nation has the choice been clearer.

And so, Gingrich gives us his final words regarding how to meet the crisis which he says looms before us. In these final pages we learn that we are not really to worry. All each of has to do is to exert "a little extra effort." And the effort doesn't have to be on any global scale; nor even on a national scale. "Look around you," he writes. "Who could you help to learn to read or to work with a computer? Who is currently ill and needs just a phone call or a visit to raise his or her morale? What local project could ten or twenty families undertake that would improve your community? We have only to be "a little bit heroic." And all he is asking of us is "a few hours a month."

These are all very nice things to do, but they don't speak to the kind of American and global crisis we have been told we should be anxious about. It's as if he wants to convince us at the end that he has a soft heart; that he is just an ordinary guy wanting to be a good neighbor and community activist. Fine. But it doesn't speak to the crisis before us. To speak plainly, it smacks of a cop-out. If we are to address even the limited Crisis List he set before us earlier in his final chapter we must have a vision of economic and political structures which are designed for the task. He simply doesn't offer any. It's as simple as that.

Yet, there may be a hidden-agenda explanation for his getting so chummy and neighborly in these final pages. We take a closer look at his How-To list. We note again that virtually every one is designed to give corporate America what it is calling for in order to *compete* in the global marketplace, all toward the end of dominating it and making all other economic entities in the world accept its dominance.

Our part, as spelled out in the final statement quoted above, is simply to be one of obediently working hard, being good neighbors in our local communities, and leaving the larger picture in the hands of corporate America and its champions like Newt Gingrich. Again, in a very subtle and somewhat manipulative way, we are simply to exert that "little extra effort" to keep peace at the home front, dutifully cleaning up and glossing over any social wounds corporate America might inflict, and thereby, as in the World-War-II war effort, help corporate America fulfill what Gingrich has told us is America's destined role to again be #1 in the world, and as perfectly befits "God's chosen people."

## X-5: *The Gingrich Fantasy*

Gingrich seems to attribute his lifelong interest in what he calls "public life" to an extremely moving experience of his childhood at the age of 10 years.

By an unusual series of happenstance incidents, he was asked to present his request for a city zoo to the city council in Harrisburg, Pennsylvania.

> It was a slow day at city hall and a ten-year-old making an appeal for a municipal zoo made a nice story. When it appeared in the paper the next day, I was hooked forever on public life. The idea that you could make an impact if you worked hard enough was impressed upon me permanently.
>
> Forty-one and a half years later I became Speaker of the United States House of Representatives. Just before I took office, Marianne and I visited her mother in Leetonia, Ohio. The town made quite an event of our arrival. The newspapers printed a half page of Marianne's high school pictures (some of which I had never seen before). When CBS News covered my talk to a group of Leetonia High School students, I knew our lives would never be the same.

The picture I get is of a person who most of his life has hungered for what would be equivalent at the adult level to the exhilarating experience of being at such a public center of attention.

Corporate America has given him that opportunity in his adult life. The multinational corporations which comprise corporate America naturally welcome his support. They welcome his not focusing on the injustices of our present economic and political system, but only on the few remaining barriers it presents to corporate America's having virtually complete control of the monitoring and governing institutions and agencies which stand in its way, or possibly might in the future.

Newt Gingrich has told us why he wrote his book. Now it may be clearer why I am writing mine. I see the values Gingrich stands for, and the position of power he now has to implement them, as constituting a menace on today's economic, political, and, yes, social landscape. It must now be clear that implementing his agenda would lead to ever more riches for the already rich, ever more power for the already powerful, and ever more in-justice for those who are already victims of today's dominant economic and political structures — and not only in America, but in every part of the world dominated by an aggressive and acquisitive corporate America.

One can easily get the impression that Gingrich is "not a bad egg" at heart. He himself says he's really just a kid at heart, "still a happy four-year-old who gets up every morning hoping to find a cookie that friends or relatives may have left for me somewhere."

Well, Newt, that's fine for a kid. But you have maneuvered your way into a world of power brokers who, I believe, will use you and the rest of us for their power-seeking ends if we don't reject your present complicity with them and find a way to truly "renew America" in the direction of "justice for all," not only in America, but in the world as a whole.

And, after indicating, in Chapters XI and XII, what went wrong during that period between the winning of American independence and the coup-like maneuver which established the present U.S. Constitution, I will suggest, in Chapter XIII the direction we are called upon to take for renewing America toward that end of justice for all. Then, in Appendix A, I indicate how I arrived at the estimate of an average of $36,000/year for a family of four as their fair share of the financial benefits from our common heritage, and as a major step toward assuring the right to "life, liberty, and the pursuit of happiness" which the American Declaration of Independence said was the right of "all men" (sic).

Before we can deal with a crisis

we must know

what brought it about,

and what can be done to change whatever that is

into something which will bring about

"justice for all."

In Part II

we shall explore

the structural roots of today's global crisis,

and what might be done

to build a truly just world order

here in earth.

# Part II

## Envisioning
## Economic & Political Structures
## Which Would Assure
## "Justice for All"
## Local to Global

# Chapter XI

# The U.S. Constitution Product of a Coup?

## XI-1: *A Brief Orientation*

In this chapter we trace the political maneuverings which brought the U.S. Constitution into being perhaps the most effective power-conveying political document ever devised. As already indicated, the argument of this volume is not that the U.S. Constitution has no moral merit; indeed, it may still be unexcelled in overall moral quality among modern, industrialized states. We shall see, however, that its moral quality is incidental to its power-legitimating quality. In this respect it was no different from the European states at the time of its founding. Its moral quality consists primarily in its Bill of Rights and in certain safeguards against governmental use of power stated in its various Articles. And it may be largely because of its moral quality that the government founded upon it has become the most powerful in the world.

## XI-2: *After "The Declaration"*

After the 1776 Declaration of Independence the political elite in most of the colonies abandoned their royal charters and established the former colonies as "sovereign states." Their new constitutions varied greatly in moral quality. That is, the mix between idealism and power-seeking was different in each case.

The constitution of Pennsylvania, formulated by William Penn almost a century earlier with the help of John Locke, the famous British philosopher, served as a kind of idealistic model for some of the other states. Also, a century and a half of experimenting with alternative political structures, even as colonies, served as valuable experience for them as future states.

Some state constitutions had a Bill of Rights, and some did not. Some had a single legislature, and some had two houses, but each formed a representative government of some kind. All states limited voting privileges to property-holding white males, and limited office-holding (in effect) to the most financially independent among them. The governments of the southern states were largely controlled by the large plantation owners, with slavery the "lynch pin" of their economy. The New England states had more mixed economies, with bankers, traders, and land speculators having the dominant political influence, and with the slave trade a major contributor to their economies also.

Throughout the thirteen states it is estimated that about 90% of transplanted European households were subsistence farmers, with most getting some income from a small cash crop. In all states the small farmers and small business people were the ones who were most devastated by the war years which followed. They were the ones called to the front lines; they were the ones whose farms and small businesses suffered most by their absence while their very sources of basic sustenance became battle grounds.

The large plantation owners in the South commonly left managers and slaves in charge as they spent their time in financial, military, or political "work" in state or national capitals. During the period of fighting, Thomas Paine spent his time and energy in close contact with Washington's forces in the field, in writing his famous *Crisis Papers* from time to time (designed to build morale both in the field and in the population generally), and in urging politicians and bankers to resist the temptation to take undue advantage of their new-found freedom from Britain's legal restraints. That, roughly, was the state of affairs in the war years after The American Declaration of Independence in 1776.

## XI-3: *After the War: Power in "Self-Serving" Hands*

If readers will imagine themselves in the roles of political power-seekers in America after the British and their sympathizers had been driven back to England or north into Canada, they will be able to imagine the tremendous economic opportunities that must have been discussed among them. Here, now, was a whole continent of nature's most basic means of production, land and its resources, all but in their grasp. The Native Americans might, of course, present some resistance.

To meet such an eventuality there would have to be a national army. A national army might also be needed in order to fight off Britain again, or either France or Spain (both of whom still had claims on the continent). There would no doubt be opposition to forming such an army, considering the war weariness that prevailed, but if only a strong national government could be established, with power to raise revenue to finance it, then surely the necessary forces could be mustered.

There were also other pressures arguing in favor of a strong national government. The large plantation owners of the South couldn't find anything approaching sufficient markets for their crops in America, nor could they buy in America the technology and luxury goods for which their expanding and increasingly affluent lifestyle hungered. Thus, they were dependent on a steady flow of trade with Europe. Freedom to conduct such trade, they argued, depended on at least a minimum navy to protect American ships. Indeed, Great Britain was already making it difficult for American ships to sail the high seas unmolested.

Then there were those who feared slave revolts, and who wanted a stronger national militia to help them retrieve runaway slaves. Those who had invested in western lands, George Washington being foremost among them, anticipating profitable sales to settlers, sought national military help in making such lands safe from attacks from native American Indians. Those native Americans who were not already resentful at being uprooted and displaced, could be expected to become so as they became increasingly victimized by the further maneuvers of the "pale faced" power-seekers.

Indeed, all those who had invested financially in all such commercial operations had a definite economic interest in a strong national government, especially one structured to protect their investments in all these areas, and in one which could help them develop a competitive advantage in the growing global markets. And it was this power-seeking group to which Alexander Hamilton, a New York attorney, and Robert Morris, George Washington's New York banker, mostly appealed. They were successful because, as we shall see, they were ultimately able to outmaneuver the politically unsophisticated 90% living in small rural communities.

## XI-4: *Sovereignty Versus Justice*

In the very same year that the spirit of the American Declaration of Independence was injected into the political bloodstream of the western world, a spirit of comparable potency was injected into its economic bloodstream. I refer, of course, to the economic ideas "triggered" by Adam Smith's *Wealth of Nations*. This is understandable, because by the last quarter of the 18th century the political body most capable of building and wielding power in the world was no longer, as had been the case in a large part of the Middle Ages, the Rome-dominated church, but that thoroughly secular entity so taken for granted by us today: the sovereignty-claiming territorial state.

These dominant political bodies were called "*nation* states" (rather than just "states") because of their *original* divisions among Europeans on the basis of nationality. But, for self-serving power seekers, ever since the 16th century the practical importance of forming themselves into "nation states" has **not** been the feature of common nationality; rather, it has been the opportunity which such a classification affords for making a global claim of *sovereignty* within a given prescribed *territory*. And because of the import-ance of this sovereignty claim, universally made among what I will henceforth call "*territorial* states," we turn now to outline very briefly how the self-serving power-seekers in 18th century America took advantage of this extremely significant mutation in political structure.

Even before its collapse, the Roman Empire had for centuries had little effect on the daily life of the towns and villages on the European continent. As the Roman Empire collapsed, and its protection over its far-flung terri-tories became unreliable, the threat from raiding Germanic and other tribes made it necessary for small landholders to enter into agreements with the larger ones for protection, in return for which they pledged services of one kind or another. During this period, from about the fifth century to the twelfth, the Roman church, especially after its collaboration with Charle-magne at the turn of the ninth century, had substantial political influence. Thus, no king had complete unquestioned obedience from subjects; that is, no king claimed absolute "sovereignty" over any territory and its occupants. Indeed, kings shared political power not only with church officials but with lesser landholders, lords, knights, etc. The way this set of circumstances began to change in England is interesting and significant for the purposes of this volume.

With territorial and other disputes rampant all over Europe there was a crying need for peacemakers. So, lords and kings, motivated by mixed motives, set up courts to settle such disputes. One motivation was to produce income to the royal treasury. In fact, next to income from their land claims, the fees they charged for such a service constituted, for many kings, the major source of income, so great was the need for that service in the market place and so eager were the kings to presume to fill it. And out of this offering of a genuine service came an opportunity for building power per se! Here is the way Joseph P. Strayer, the medieval historian, describes the situation:

> Nevertheless, rulers gradually began to see that justice was something more than a source of revenue. It was a way of asserting the authority and increasing the power of the king or greater lords. Therefore, the ablest rulers tried to increase the number of cases that came to their courts. There were several devices by which the jurisdiction of a court could be increased. Serious criminal offenses, such as murder, could be reserved for the court of the king (or a duke or a count). The reservation of these cases (called pleas of the crown or pleas of the sword) allowed the ruler to intervene in the districts where he had no lands and no local rights of justice. In civil cases, special procedures could be developed by which litigants could by-pass the court of the local lord and go directly to a royal (ducal, comital) court [i.e., a king's court]. . . . Thus, rear-vassals could be protected against their immediate lords by the king (duke, count), and their primary loyalty began to go to the man who protected them. Finally, it was the duty of a king to see that justice was done throughout his realm. . . . A lord whose decisions could be overruled was a lord who had lost much of his authority.[1]

The important point to be noted here is that the absolute sovereign power which kings, like the king of England, gradually were able to claim was originally largely built through the good will generated among the populace by their offering courts of justice in the market place. And as kings were thus increasingly perceived as filling Solomon-type roles they were able to develop the perception of their being in some sense sovereign.

---

1. Strayer, Joseph P., *On the Medieval Origins of the Modern State,* p 29, (Princeton, Princeton U. Press, 1970)

Originally, in order to retain the power which such a perception of sovereignty conveyed, the rulers of territories had to maintain at least a modicum of the *perception* of justice in their dealings with underlings. But, since *power tends to corrupt*, kings gradually tended to use their increasing power to simply *claim* sovereignty, and to enforce such claims, rather than be satisfied with whatever effective sovereignty was voluntarily granted to them by virtue of their social service as purveyors of justice.

Then when philosophers like Thomas Hobbes argued that it was necessary for practical and security reasons to *grant* kings absolute sovereignty, entirely independent of the extent to which they served the cause of justice, the original justice-credentials tended to become as irrelevant in theory as they seemed to be practice.

By this route, then, kings gradually tended to claim sovereignty either as a claimed *natural* right or as a "divine right," depending on whether they chose to appeal to religious beliefs or Hobbsean-type beliefs. Thus, the kings of Europe, including the English and French kings, eventually became very corrupt indeed; so much so that by the middle of the 17th century a British king had been dethroned and executed, and in the 18th century a French king suffered the same fate.

*In view of the above, the thesis I wish to set forth for consideration at this juncture is that (1) the power of the territorial state was originally built, and accepted, by way of "administering justice" in a reasonably sincere way — presumably with great variation from monarch to monarch — that (2) precisely because coercive force is morally justified in order to prevent or remedy injustice (and only for that purpose), genuine and lasting political power remains with those (and only those) who undertake the maintenance of justice as their major commitment and responsibility, and that (3) claims to absolute sovereignty, those which place perceived "national security interests" ahead of genuine justice in determining state policies, are not only morally untenable but constitute a political stance which spells constant military and economic conflict among the territorial states who are making such claims, and will, if persisted in, bring about the ultimate collapse of the civilization comprising such states.*

In the case of England, by the time of the American Revolution a *share* of this sovereignty, at one time claimed by the king alone, was claimed by the British Parliament by way of the Magna Carta. This first of modern parliaments was composed of lesser royalty figures and men of the world who were close enough to the king to know full well the pseudo-nature of his sovereignty claims. In short, by then, sovereignty claims were shifting from the royal family to whatever combination of king, lords, and parliament constituted the make-up of the government of England. In so doing it might be said that sovereignty became more just in being more widely shared, but those left out of the sharing circle were generally not included in any such justice considerations — nor are they in our day.

Thus, today, whenever a group of largely self-serving power-seekers achieves supreme power within a geographic territory (whether by fair means or foul) it is likely to qualify in today's world as the official representatives of all *persons* within that territory, and be accepted as participants in the decision-making processes of the United Nations and other international bodies. And with no nation state having any substantial *moral* claims to sovereignty, moral grounds for requiring any from others are virtually nonexistent. In short, in today's world of nation states, the philosophy of "might makes right" finds few challengers. And this state of affairs, I say, is symptomatic of a very sick civilization, a *morally* sick civilization.

Viewed in this way, with the sovereignty claims of all the "Emperors" of the world (parliamentary or otherwise) seen in all their nakedness, such claims must be considered by us as simply another form of slavery of human *persons*. This is clearly so because, in thus claiming sovereignty in their respective claimed territories, modern territorial states claim a form of limited ownership of all *persons* born within such territories. Out of this territorial claim was derived the claimed right to *charge* persons for utilizing portions of the very common heritage to which each such person *ought* to be granted a fair share as "a natural inalienable right." It was during the deteriorated part of the French Revolution that we see emerging for the first time the claimed right to even conscript into military service the thus-enslaved *persons* residing within such territories.

For several centuries now, such has been the tragic state of affairs for ordinary persons on this earth. In the case of so-called "democracies," such claims are *presumed* to be legitimized by majority vote, with nominal protection of minority rights. But those who effectively manipulate such voting for self-serving ends are as pseudo-sovereign as any king ever was.

Yet they have state *power* at their disposal far greater than any sovereign, pseudo or genuine, of the past.

As Toynbee points out, the conquering of the seas by the European "Christian" states, at the beginning in the 15th century, gave a tremendous impetus to this sovereignty-push on the part of the power-seekers in the various European territorial states. The ease with which the world could then be traversed by ships gave claimants to sovereignty a new source of wealth. They were finding it increasingly difficult to extract money, goods, and services from their exploited subjects at home. But defenseless, primitive peoples in foreign lands were easy prey. Thus began the period of European colonialism.

Nor was it difficult to justify such colonialism once the supposed claim to sovereignty could be "justified," on either Hobbsean, raw-power grounds, divine-right grounds, or some convenient combination of the two.

## XI-5: *The American Power-Seekers Enter the "Big Time"*

Having driven all of the European "sovereign" states from their newly claimed geographical habitat, the American power-seekers sought desperately for a way to *themselves* enter the power-building sovereignty game.[2] The 90% or so small farmers in small rural communities might offer some opposition. But they were pretty much occupied with building community at the grass roots level based on neighborliness and simple fairness in their dealings with each other.

So, with a whole fertile continent of mild climate under their feet and within their political grasp, the power seekers certainly had the territorial makings for becoming a major player in the power-seeking sovereignty game. But, no one of the then-existing thirteen American states was strong enough of itself to compete in such a global, economic, political, and military battlefield. Also, the American power-seekers (except for Hamilton) fully realized that the needed sovereignty could not, in America, take the form of a king. Even a king-plus-parliament government, such as that from which they had just cut themselves loose would be difficult to maneuver. Some other form of territorial sovereignty had to be found.

---

2. Thus, each inner circle in every nation state claiming such sovereignty still has its "power game." The details of this game, as played in the U.S., is spelled by Hedrick Smith in his book of that title: *The Power Game, How Washington Works,* (New York, Random House. 1988. 793pp)

A beginning had, in a sense, been made in the form of the Articles of Confederation. But they were unsatisfactory to the power seekers, for several reasons. First, because they instituted a genuine confederation — no major action could be taken without the consent of each and every member state. This, the power-seekers felt, was a major obstacle to building any substantial claim to sovereignty. One immediate consequence of this provision was that unanimity couldn't be reached on *enforcing* any but the most trivial matters on which they were able to agree. These two structural features of the Articles were a constant frustration to power-seekers like Alexander Hamilton, Robert Morris, and George Washington (See Section VIII-5). How, then, were these major obstacles to be overcome? Historian Vernon Louis Parrington put it this way:

> How the problem was met and the solution achieved by a skillful minority in the face of a hostile majority is a suggestive lesson in political strategy. It is a classic example of the relation of economics to politics; of the struggle between greater property and smaller properties for the control of the state.[3]

There were several circumstances which naturally favored such a plan; and these plus those which the power-seekers manipulated into place proved sufficient for their purposes. For instance, Tom Paine and his mighty pen had left for England and then France soon after American independence was gained (III-2), and no one of sufficient insight and literary skill emerged to discredit their plan enough to defeat it. Might the history of the world have been different if he had remained to see the American revolution through its nonviolent phase as he so faithfully had through its violent one?

Perhaps, but it is unlikely that even Tom Paine would have been able to cope with the political sophistications of men like Alexander Hamilton, Robert Morris, George Washington, and James Madison (VIII-5).

Or would the outcome have been different if Jefferson hadn't been out of the country serving as Minister to France under the new Articles of Confederation? Again, I doubt it. It is true that, as recorded in his *Anas*, Jefferson was horrified at the resulting corruption under the new Constitution, but I suspect that he also would not have been politically astute enough. In any case, both Paine and Jefferson were at a safe distance during the crucial maneuvers. What did happen was that two vigorous young men still in their

---

3. Parrington. Vernon Louis, *Main Currents in American Thought, Book I*, p 274. (New York, Harcourt, Brace, and World. 1927 & 1958)

twenties and early thirties, Hamilton and Madison, with Washington ready to add his prestige when needed, pretty much had the field. Again, Vernon Parrington:

> During these years of unrest [during and after the war] the problem of a new fundamental law [ i.e., a constitution] was carefully studied by the anti-agrarian leaders, and solutions suggested. A remarkable change had come over their thinking. They discarded the revolutionary doctrines that had served their need in the debate with England. They were done with natural rights and the romantic interpretations of politics and were turned realists. They parted company with English liberalism in its desire for a diminished state. Their economic interests were suffering from the lack of a strong centralized government, and they were in a mood to agree with earlier realists who held that men were animals with turbulent passions, and require a government "proper and adequate" for animals . . .
>
> The great obstacle to such a program was the political power of farmers, bred up in the traditional practice of home rule, jealous of local rights, and content with the Articles of Confederation.[4]

So, under Madison's and Hamilton's leadership, the major purpose of the power-seekers became to *replace* (not merely revise) the government of the Articles of Confederation with a strong centralized "sovereign" government. And their big opportunity came on the occasion of a dispute between Maryland and Virginia regarding navigation and fishing rights on the Potomac River.

## XI-6: *Some Madison/Hamilton Preparatory Maneuvers*

It is important to note the sequence of events which led up to "the Constitutional Convention" of May, 1787. It is important because that convention was the key move in a series of moves by the power-seekers which, taken together, constituted perhaps the most skillfully conducted, *almost* completely nonviolent, coup d'etat in the history of the world. And the first step in that sequence was taken on the occasion of the Maryland/Virginia dispute mentioned above.

James Madison initiated this first step. Under his prodding, the Virginia Assembly passed a resolution calling for each state to send five representatives to a meeting at Annapolis, Maryland in the Fall of 1786, ostensibly to

---

4. Ibid., p 278

address the Maryland/Virginia dispute from a broader perspective: "to consider and recommend a Federal Plan for regulating commerce."

That sounded harmless enough, especially since the term "Federal" implied that any proposal would be within the existing confederated structure of the Articles of Confederation. But, as Leonard Levy puts it,

> Those who masterminded the meeting had a much larger agenda in mind: as Madison put it, a "plenipotentiary [i.e., fully empowered] Convention for amending the Confederation."[5]

If Hamilton had called the conference, many would have been very suspicious of his motives, since he had been calling since 1780 for a national convention to establish a new form of government; and many knew that if he had his way it would be a highly centralized monarchy. What emerged was, of course, not a monarchy in name, but we shall see that Hamilton got all the essentials of what he wanted.

Madison's wishes were less well known, and Madison had a generally well-deserved reputation for high integrity. So, even though suspicion was not completely absent, it was manageable. And the Continental Congress addressed whatever suspicion there was *by specifically limiting the mandate of the Annapolis convention to discussing ways to "regulate commerce."*

The convention met at Annapolis September 11-14, 1786. Only five states sent representatives. But the small attendance may also have been expected, and even hoped for, by Madison and Hamilton. After all, the meeting was set at a time of year when most farmers (almost unanimously opposed to having a strong central government over them after having only recently gotten rid of one) would be busy with harvesting their crops. And the fewer small farmers present the less likely would be the opposition to greater centralized power. In any case, those attending were virtually all strong supporters of a much stronger central government. So, the small meeting served quite well as a strategy meeting for laying more carefully the plans for a conference which *would* serve their purpose. Especially significant was the fact that Hamilton was there to support Madison's efforts to plan another such meeting.

---

5. Levy. Leonard, ed., *The Encyclopedia of the American Constitution, vol 1*, p 382. (N.Y., Macmillan Co., 1986)

Readers will not be surprised to learn that no plan for "regulating commerce" came out of the Annapolis meeting, and evidently nothing further was done about the Potomac "problem." But what did come out of it was a proposal formulated by Madison and Hamilton and carried to the Continental Congress the following February 21st as the next "step" in their masterminded overall plan. But this time not only Hamilton but also Madison sought another sponsor. They found their man in John Dickenson. By then there were those in the Congress who suspected what was in the wind. So, in response to the Dickenson request, we find the following in the "Journals of Congress," dated Feb. 21, 1787:

> Whereas there is *provision in the Articles of Confederation and perpetual Union for making alterations therein* [emphasis added] by the Assent of a Congress of the United States and of the legislatures of the several States; and whereas experience hath evinced that there are defects in the present Confederation, as a means to remedy which several states and particularly the State of New York by express instructions of their delegates [mainly Hamilton] in Congress have suggested a Convention for the purposes expressed in the following resolution and such Convention appearing to be the most probable means of establishing in these states a firm national government.
>
> RESOLVED that in the opinion of Congress it is expedient that on the second Monday of May next a Convention of delegates who shall have been appointed by the several States be held at Philadelphia *for the sole and express purpose of revising the Articles of Confederation* [emphasis added] and reporting to Congress and the several legislatures such alterations and provisions therein as shall *when agreed to in Congress* [emphasis added] and confirmed by the States render the federal Constitution adequate to the exigencies of Government and the preservation of the Union.[6]

In short, their mandate specifically limited them to making proposals for "revising" the Articles of Confederation, not replacing them, *and* in accordance with "provisions within the Articles of Confederation." So, it definitely did **not** authorize them to organize an entirely new government to replace the very government that had authorized them to meet in its behalf.

But the Hamilton-Madison coalition was evidently not the least deterred by these limitations on their mandate. In fact, considering the tactics they

---

6. Congress Journals, in *Papers of the Continental Congress*, p 73 (Washington, D.C., National Archives, 1971)

were willing to resort to, they evidently cared very little about what *legal* limitations were placed on them. If we are to judge by the haste with which these Congressional limitations were immediately ignored at the Convention itself they evidently had no intention of being bound by them. In short, all they needed was Congressional authorization to meet at *some* form of Congress-authorized conference. And that's what they got.

Again, it is important to take special note of the time of year set for what turned out to be perhaps the most important meeting ever for the history of not only America but also of the entire world. I refer to the fact that spring-time was again a time of year when their main obstacle, small farmers, would be extremely busy; this time with planting. So, a May meeting would again fit in beautifully with the centralist strategy, as Parrington put it, "to nullify" the effect of the agrarians.

These small farmers (again, composing about 90% of the population and constituting the very moral fibre of the country) had done the bulk of the dying, and sustained the bulk of the injuries, in the just completed revolution. Many came back to neglected or devastated farms. Some had been severely injured. Indeed, for many such small farmers their very economic survival was at stake. Most of the members of Congress repre-senting these agrarians, often themselves small farmers and homesteaders, would likely be busy still salvaging their own or some constituent's farm economies during the very months this crucial meeting was scheduled to take place. Also, any who might have been inclined to attend might have been naively reassured by the explicit restrictions placed on the meeting by Congress — namely, "for the sole express purpose" *of revising the Articles of Confederation.*

A number of small farmers were participants in the now famous Shays's Rebellion. It was already in progress when this convention was being planned, which greatly alarmed the power-seekers. It was a rebellion of small farmers who had lost, or were losing, their farms to bankers and other wealthy investors, largely because of debts incurred during the war and especially high small-farm taxes. (Many small farmers in the present day will readily identify with them.) Yet, while many of these small farmers were fighting and dying (Daniel Shays himself was an officer in the battles of Bunker Hill, Stoney Point, and Saratoga) many power-seekers were anticipating huge profits by the kind of land speculations referred to earlier. So, when bankers callously proceeded to foreclose on small farmers, as if normal times prevailed, the victims of their callousness rebelled. One of the results was Shays's Rebellion. In fact, it was this kind of rebellion that was cited as a justification, if not outright mandate, for a central government strong enough to put them down if necessary.

As the result of all of these factors, those favoring a stronger and more centralized government had very little opposition at Philadelphia. And the power-seekers were there in force.

## XI-7: *The Convention's "End Run" Strategy*

With this much introduction, then, we now turn our full attention to that historic Philadelphia meeting. It finally opened May 25, 1787, eleven days behind schedule because of late arrivals. Madison, however, was reportedly there 10 days before anyone else, and weeks before it got started. He reportedly used the time for talking to Franklin and others about his hopes for the Convention.[7] Madison was just 36 years old at the time, Hamilton was barely 30, and most others who came were young men; Washington and Franklin were the old timers. Sixty-five had been appointed by their respective states, with those able to afford the trip and to be away from their farms or businesses obviously most available to make the then difficult journey, which had to be either by foot or by horse-power. Fifty-five eventually arrived, many of them late. Many of these came and went as personal business permitted and required, and 42 were there at the end.

Both Hamilton and Madison were extremely intelligent, well educated, and well-read young men. Both were college graduates. Hamilton's sharp mind is evident from his many contributions to the later-published Federalist Papers, and Madison was so brilliant that he completed the four-year curriculum at what is now Princeton University in about three quarters the allotted time. Even though Hamilton attended the Convention only enough to deliver an occasional long speech, he ultimately became the major force behind the new Constitution after it was "ratified." He was a New York lawyer and banker, and a royalist at heart. Later, as we shall see, as George Washington's Treasury Secretary, he vigorously manipulated the power-seekers' economic and political interests, facilitated, as later reported in Jefferson's *Anas*, by his admitted willingness to use corrupt means to achieve his ends.

---

7. Incidentally, Franklin was one of the largest of the land speculators.

James Madison was a slave plantation owner from Virginia. He inherited a plantation of several thousand acres and left an estate of about 5,000 acres at his death. When we remember that today's midwest farmers have an average of about 300 acres, we begin to appreciate that Madison was a very wealthy man all his life. Nevertheless, in contrast to Hamilton, he was highly respected by many. In fact, I would not include Madison among "the power-seekers." As revealed in his Federalist Paper #10, his support for not only a strong central government, but a top-down one, was largely due to (1) an evidently genuine concern about what Alexis de Tocqueville was later to call "the tyranny of the majority" and (2) his inability to resist the lure of the tremendous intellectual challenge of forming an entirely new form of government.

Nevertheless, he was thoroughly entrenched in a very elite and wealthy class of owners of large slave-run plantations, and with presumably no experience of what it was like to survive at small-scale farming or trade. Thus, his social status, his superior intellect, and the seductive challenge posed by the opportunity to frame an entirely new governmental structure constituted in toto crucial support for the usurping manipulations of Hamilton and the other power-seekers.

Incidentally, it is significant to note that, whereas in Madison's notes about discussions in the Convention, the term `federal' was used to characterize the *truly* "federating" Articles of Confederation, the promoters of that new constitution did another bit of political manipulating by way of calling themselves by the misnomer term "Federalists." Thus, the title of the document setting forth their major arguments in support of the Constitution: was "The Federalist Papers." Such inappropriate terminology was just one more way of misleading the unsophisticated regarding the nature of what they really were advocating: namely, to *replace a truly federated* system with a sovereignty-seeking, highly centralized, top-down, elite-serving one.

## XI-8: *The Constitutional Convention Itself*

The Convention lasted through a typical, hot and sticky Philadelphia summer (no air conditioning, of course). Anyone who knows what a Philadelphia summer can be like will appreciate that there must have been a strong motivation to accept Madison's very first draft as the basis for the final document (which they did) and to "get out of there" as fast as they reasonably could.

Significantly, one of the very first actions was to decide to hold their meetings in secret, *and to pledge themselves to secrecy* regarding what was transpiring in those meetings! Thus, we need not be surprised that those in our day who are still ostensibly governing according to the Constitution which emerged are also operating by "cover up" maneuvers. Indeed, modern power-seekers might very well claim that they are merely following the example of their "Founding Fathers."

And so, the only relatively complete record we have to this day is that recorded by Madison (with only bits and pieces from others). Furthermore, his notes were not published until 53 years later, in 1840, four years after his death.  In short, it seems that the power-seekers who framed the U.S. Constitution may also have "framed" the American people. They certainly took elaborate measures to assure that no official word would get out about what had actually transpired in those meetings until a politically-safe number of years later. Nevertheless, their actual, ultimate goals were revealed immediately upon adjournment. Here, again, is Leonard Levy:

> The Constitutional Convention of 1787, which formally organized itself on May 25th, lasted almost four months, yet reached its most singular decision almost at the outset. The first order of business was the *nationalistic* Virginia Plan [emphasis added because "nationalistic" was meant to be in contrast to the federated form currently in force under the Articles of Confederation], and the first vote of the Convention, acting as a Committee of the Whole, was the adoption of a resolution "that a *national* Government [italicized in the original] ought to be established consisting of a *supreme* [italicized in original] Legislative, Executive and Judiciary" (May 30th). Thus the Convention immediately agreed on abandoning, rather than amending, the Articles; on writing a new Constitution; on creating a national government that would be supreme; and on having it consist of three branches.[8]

On the very next day, May 31, the Committee of the Whole made other crucial decisions with little or no debate. One, reflecting the nationalist bias of the Convention, was the decision to establish a bicameral system whose larger house was to be elected directly by the people rather than by the state legislatures. And this was by far the most significant change from the Articles, as we shall see in the discussion below. By itself, it may not seem significant; indeed, those who think of "democracy" as simply majority-vote

---

8. Ibid., Levy

directly by "the people" might be disarmed by it. But by-passing the state legislatures was part of the power-seekers' basic strategy to generate a national government of *individuals* (as distinct from *states*), from whom (as subjects of the "sovereign") tax and military "obligations" could then be claimed *without any approval from the state governments in which their existing political loyalties were primarily based.*

Consider, then, what the existing state governments would thus be asked to do. They would be asked to literally turn over their respective individual citizens to an entirely new political structure! And in Federalist Paper #15, published later as part of a campaign to get support for the proposed new constitution, Hamilton makes it clear how important this change was to his basic strategy:

> The great radical vice in the construction of the existing Confederation is in the principle of LEGISLATION for STATES or GOVERNMENTS in their CORPORATE CAPACITIES, and as contradistinguished from the INDI-VIDUALS of which they consist.

The upper case emphasis is his. Obviously Hamilton felt *very* strongly about these few words. They are the key to the basic "Federalist" strategy at the time, a strategy designed to build a modern, *sovereign*, territorial state where the role of assuring *justice* for residents of the territory isn't even mentioned in the following statement of the "principal purposes" of the state Hamilton sought to establish:

> The principal purposes to be answered by union are these: the common defense of the members; the preservation of the public peace, *as well against internal convulsions* [emphasis added because the likely reference here is to things like Shays's Rebellion] as against external attacks; the regulation of commerce with other nations and between states; the superintendence of our intercourse, political and commercial, with foreign countries. (Federalist Paper #23)

Keeping these sovereignty-like purposes in mind, what, then, do Hamilton's emphasized words reveal about the "Federalist" *structural* goal? When placed alongside many other statements (and subsequent actions to be noted in Jefferson's *Anas*) they reveal the basic goal of this aggressive leader of the "Federalists." Hamilton was so frustrated with dealing with a *truly* federal form of government that he was determined to maneuver an "end run" around the existing state governments in order to get at the

"INDIVIDUALS" who, at the time, were in some sense citizens of one or another of the thirteen existing, semi-autonomous, and fully established governments.

As has been noted, these state governments were by no means perfect. There were disputes yet to be worked out among them and things needing radical reform within them. For one thing, some of them were also caught in the "sovereignty" illusions of grandeur. But the needed reforms within the states would understandably take time, especially considering the hardships and devastation of the recently ended war. The power-seekers were not willing to take the necessary time, nor would the outcome of such "taking time" be serving of their agenda of a strong "national" government as distinct from a genuine *federation*.

We keep in mind that these thirteen states were the culmination of a gradual and continuous groping toward what I have called "The *Early American Dream*" over a period of a century and a half. Despite their many moral faults, these thirteen states were perhaps the most humane and equitable political structures in the entire Western world. And they were already genuinely "federated." They were federated into a government which reflected the ideals of The Declaration of Independence much more than would the proposed new national government.

For instance, most states had a Bill of Rights (for which there was no provision in the new constitution as originally "ratified"), and they had agreed among themselves not to split into factions. Rather, they had agreed to proceed rationally and carefully into this new unknown. Again, as an important safeguard against hasty actions, they had agreed (XI-5) to change their federal structure *only as each and every one of them agreed to do so after careful debate.*

But the power seekers of 1787 really didn't want "careful debate" as much as they wanted a means to build a powerful central government which could claim "sovereignty" sufficient to compete with other such claims in the world.

We see now how Hamilton's emphasis on a government of INDIVIDUALS rather than of federated states was the key to realizing their basic strategy. By generating a government of individual members they could circumvent those troublesome states, so difficult to control and manipulate, while concurrently gaining much easier control over largely unsuspecting "INDIVIDUALS."

Thus became possible the power and resulting claims to sovereignty which they so eagerly sought. The funds they were able to extract from the states were piddling. But, taxes on individuals they could enforce. Individuals could be either conscripted (this to come later) or lured with patriotic propaganda. Most basically of all, individuals could be kept in the dark about what was really going on, and lured into supporting things they couldn't possibly fully understand. And the skills needed to do such manipulating have been perfected into an art form by master strategists like Newt Gingrich in our own day.

Thus, individual Americans and their largely rural farming communities — through whose influence over time the states might gradually have become able to really assure "justice for all" — became unwilling captives of a new, much more aggressive, and more sovereign-claiming *national* government. It was truly a tragic "turning point" in the history of America. It was, in fact, the beginning of the full-blown corporate America of our own day. And now we can see how, with the establishment of the *non*-federating U.S. Constitution, today's corporate America was all but inevitable.

What basically happened was this: instead of helping this *Early* American Dream to a wholesome rate of growth to maturity, the so-called "Federalists" took advantage of a temporary confusion, weakness, and naive vulnerability in the general unsuspecting population in order to make their coup d'etat power-move. The methods they used were many and varied. But among the most ingenious and despicable was their modification of the classical political maneuver of "divide and conquer." For they were well aware that the national government could much more easily manipulate and coerce "INDIVIDUALS" than it could any of the thirteen states, *as states*.

They were already exploiting the Native Americans and the enslaved Africans. Their new, more powerful, centralized government was, as we now know, destined to exploit still further these unfortunate victims of the white European power-seekers as the latter expanded their claims of sovereignty into the vast lands westward and as their slave plantations and trade and banking interests received a mutation in prosperity under the protection of their new constitution.

Yes, they could find substantive arguments in support of their centralizing designs. There was general agreement that changes in the Articles were needed. This is why Congress authorized a convention to recommend *amendments*. There was no argument about that. There was no objection to the thesis that the individual states would have to yield some of their sovereignty in the course of such changes.

And it was also the case, as so often happens in revolutions, even in so-called nonviolent ones, that there were those former heroes of the revolution who were misusing their new-found freedom under the Articles. In doing so they were giving those power-seekers who wished to impose an iron hand the excuse to do so. Thus, in the years immediately after the war, before each of the various states could recover their composure, there was a certain amount of "mob rule." It played right into the "Federalists" agenda. For instance, some in the Shays's Rebellion camp were reputedly often crude, drunk, and cocky, the discipline among them being quite loose.

But the power-seekers had brought much of it on themselves. For much of the rash behavior that manifested itself was energized by pent-up resentment on the part of those who had been victimized by the royalists and near-royalists in the "Federalist" camp. Nevertheless, it still must be granted to the "Federalists" that there did exist among some radicals a simplistic concept of "democracy," one which led them to rash actions at times. But, again, the corrective needed was not top-down centralization, but a truly federalized one, federated all the way from the local community level to the national.. The coup which established the U.S. Constitution stopped this process in its tracks. One day, however, it will have to be given a rebirth. The kind of token and politically-motivated "decentralization" which Gingrich advocates will not do the job, however. His approach will only entrench further the top-down form of centralization already ominously advanced.

If the delegates to the May convention had stayed with their mandate as prescribed by Congress, there would have been less to criticize about their maneuvers. They might even have made an important contribution to improving the federalism that already existed. But, again, what they did instead was to come forth with a document which effectively skirted the existing Congress as if it hadn't existed, and then they proceeded to intimidate the states into ratifying the new political structure. This latter they did by the following maneuvers.

As noted above, the Articles of Confederation represented a commitment on the part of its member states to a certain political structure. Included was the commitment on the part of each member state to not join with others in any structural change without the consent of each and every other member state. But the 1787 power seekers wanted no part of a ratification process that required the approval of all 13 states. *True, they had all participated in the commitment at the heart of the Articles which required such unanimity.* But violating that commitment didn't seem to bother them. So, in specifying what was to be required for ratification of the new Constitution they decreed that it would be considered ratified as soon as only nine of the thirteen did so.

That meant that, as soon as nine states ratified, there immediately would be a new government *in which the remaining states would have no place.* The government in which they formerly were participants would have been thus simply replaced. And considering that it was all done in several quite illegal steps it doesn't seem unfair to describe the total process as a coup d'etat.

This ratification provision put pressure on each state to act quickly, and, many felt, hastily, in order not to be left out of what would be the only remaining national affiliation. But haste was, as we shall see, a part of the basic strategy. Here is what Charles Beard says about the pressure on Rhode Island, for instance:

> It was not until May, 29, 1790, that Rhode Island ratified the Constitution, and this action was brought about by the immediate prospect of coercion on the part of the government of the United States, combined with the threat of the city of Providence to join with the other towns which were Federalist in opinion in a movement to secede from the state and seek the protection of the federal [sic] government. Without these material considerations pressing on them, the agrarians of that commonwealth would have delayed ratification indefinitely; but they could not contend against a great nation and a domestic insurrection.[9]

Rhode Island and Pennsylvania were unique among the original colonies. First, they were unique in having been founded by persons, Roger Williams and William Penn respectively, who made a deliberate effort to enter into agreements with native Americans about sharing the continent in ways which were agreeable to all parties. Second, unlike Massachusetts, they invited all comers who would honor these agreements. There were no

---

9. Beard, Charles, *An Economic Interpretation of the Constitution,* p 237 (New York, The Macmillan Co., 1913 and 1935)

hangings of religious dissidents, as in Massachusetts, where Mary Dyer and other Quakers were hung. Third, their governments were the most participatory by far of all the colonies. And this was what was most disturbing to the power brokers, because it took discussion, it took the working out of differences, it took *time*. Again, the power brokers were impatient to get their agenda for this resource-rich continent underway as quickly as possible.

This helps to explain why the people of Rhode Island were so resistant to being conscripted, intimidated, and finally forced to participate in the new coup-established government. In the case of Pennsylvania, there was resistance, as we shall see; but the reasons for it, as in almost all the other states, were much more complicated.

## XI-9: *The Coup d'Etat Strategy*

One clear evidence of the power-seekers' strategy of haste is revealed in a decision at the Constitutional Convention made near the end of the nearly four months of meetings. Edmund Randolph, then Governor of Virginia, was one who became increasingly apprehensive about the way the proposed constitution was developing. Others who had come to feel this way had simply walked out; but he stayed. He may have felt an obligation to do so because he had officially introduced the original "nationalizing" proposal which became the basis for all subsequent discussion — though it was actually Madison's proposal placed in Randolph's hands for presentation in order to be less identified with Madison's known bias at the time toward a much more centralized government. Randolph's concern was noted in Madison's notes of the Convention as follows (as noted above, made public four decades later):

> Mr. Randolph animadverting on the indefinite and dangerous power given by the Constitution to Congress, expressing the pain he felt at differing from the body of the Convention, on the close of the great & awful subject of their labours, and anxiously wishing for some accommodating expedient which would relieve him from his embarrassments, made a motion importing "that amendments to the plan might be offered by the States Conventions, which should be submitted to and finally decided on by another general Convention." Should this proposition be disregarded, it would he said be impossible for him to put his name to the instrument. Col. Mason seconded & followed Mr. Randolph in animadversions on the dangerous power and structure of the

Government, concluding that it would end either in monarchy, or in a tyrannical aristocracy; which he was in doubt, but one or other, he was sure. This Constitution had been formed without the knowledge or idea of the people. A second Convention will know more of the sense of the people, and be able to provide a system more consonant to it. It was improper to say to the people, take this or nothing. As the Constitution now stands, he could neither give it his support nor vote in Virginia; and he could not sign here what he could not support there. With the expedient of another Convention as proposed, he could sign.[10]

But Mason's and Randolph's efforts to rescue some modicum of the lost integrity from this Convention were deliberately rejected. Behind the prestige of Washington and Madison, who were also in the Virginia delegation, a majority in that delegation outvoted him. And a majority in the eleven (not the full thirteen) other delegations voted to present their new document on a "no amendments" basis. Subsequently, many in the general public were to roundly criticize the signers of the Constitution for the same rigidity and impatient haste which disturbed Randolph, and also Mason, at the time.

But, as we shall see, the power-seekers had manipulative political skills sufficient to meet all challenges from the caught-unawares and less politically sophisticated general population. The power-seekers had already begun to learn what politicians like Newt Gingrich have since perfected into a fine-tuned manipulative art form — namely, that if a population can be separated out into individuals having little genuine *community* relations with one another that they can (though within limits, to be sure) be maneuvered in directions carefully orchestrated and energized.

Still another example of such political manipulation was in evidence at the end of the Constitutional Convention. After less than four months a *majority* in each of the twelve delegations present (Rhode Island had refused to send a delegation) had approved a final version. There were

---

10. Ferrard, Max, ed. *Records of the Federal Convention of 1787* (New Haven, Yale U. Press, 1911)  James Madison took the most complete notes at the Constitutional Convention of 1787, though others have been gradually added. Madison revised some of his notes later, and, as noted above, after being kept secret for 53 years they were published in 1840.  Ferrard attempted to reconcile all notes to each other in these volumes.  The Madison notes quoted from here are all from the last day or so of the Convention as the delegates were anxious to leave a very hot and humid Philadelphia.

dissenters in each delegation. So, either there would be a single signer for each delegation, or only the agreeable members of each delegation would sign. But the supporters wanted more signatures on the document than either of those procedures would yield. They especially wanted the signatures of people like Randolph and Mason, both of whom voted against in their delegations.

Also, they wanted to create the impression that support was unanimous among all *representatives,* and not only among the state delegations represented, each of whom had dissenters from the majority vote. How, then, could those who opposed the document in their various delegations still be persuaded to sign the final document? The strategists had a solution ready at hand:

> He [Benjamin Franklin] then moved that the Constitution be signed by the members and offered as a convenient form viz. "Done at Convention by the unanimous consent of THE STATES present the 17th of September etc., In Witness thereof we have thereto subscribed our names.
>
> This ambiguous form had been drawn up by Mr. Gouveneur Morris in order to gain the dissenting members, and put into the hands of Doctor Franklin that it might have the better chance of success.[11]

The key words in this statement were, of course, "the States" and "in Witness thereof." Taken *literally,* the dissenting representatives were merely being asked to agree *that* a majority of delegates in each attending state delegation had in fact approved the document, which was literally true even though it was hoped that the impression left would be that it had been approved by every *individual* signer.

But, most of the dissenting members didn't take the bait; they would not put their names to a statement which, though *literally* true, would give the impression to readers that all signers, including themselves, had approved of the *substance.* It is of some consolation to know that some delegates at the convention retained some personal integrity.

Significantly, the man who engineered this particular maneuver, Gouveneur Morris, became Minister to France under Washington's subsequent Presidency, and in that capacity was instrumental in retaining Tom Paine in the Paris Luxemburg castle-become-prison along with others awaiting the

---

11. Ibid.

guillotine under Robespierre's rule when the French Revolution turned sour. It was only when Morris was replaced by James Monroe that the Tom Paine who had inspired the idealistic part of The Declaration with his crucial *Common Sense* pamphlet, and who had kept up morale throughout the Revolution by his *Crisis Papers*, finally escaped France "by the skin of his teeth."

This report of the events at the Convention is getting long, and it could go on for much longer. I hope readers will bear with me a bit longer considering how important it is that the truth about how the Constitution came about be well known at this 20th century time of "crisis" for America and the world. For instance, the account must not be ended before reporting on what happened when George Mason raised his concern about the lack of a Bill of Rights in the new Constitution.

There was plenty of precedent for a Bill of Rights. A Bill of Rights had been incorporated in most of the state constitutions, and was being pressed for in the others. In view of this, and of the centrality of concern about "inalienable rights" in The Declaration, it may seem puzzling that the framers of a *national* Constitution would neglect to include one, especially since human rights might be in much greater jeopardy under the much more powerful national government than under any of the states. But the explanation is that the omission was quite deliberate. Here is Madison's cryptic reference to that crucial issue when it was raised by Mr. Mason in one of the closing sessions.

> He wished the plan had been prefaced with a Bill of Rights, & would second a Motion if made for the purpose. It would give great quiet to the people; and with the aid of the State declarations, a bill might be prepared in a few hours. Mr. Gerry concurred in the idea & moved for a Committee to prepare a Bill of Rights. Col. Mason seconded the motion. Mr. Sherman was for securing the rights of the people where requisite: The State Declarations of Rights are not repealed by this Constitution; and being in force are sufficient. The legislature may be safely trusted. Col. Mason: The Laws of the U.S. are to be paramount to State Bills of Rights. On the question of a Committee to prepare a Bill of Rights. . . [Here Madison simply listed the votes of the states. A majority in ten state delegations voted "no", one abstained, and the rest were absent.][12]

---

12. Ibid.

The cryptic way in which Madison, without comment, simply listed the state votes on this important issue may be one of the most amazing and revealing indications of the motivations of a majority of the representatives at this Convention. And the fact that a majority in ten state delegations deliberately rejected the inclusion of a Bill of Rights is further evidence of the extent to which state delegations were comprised of those who wanted no more restraints on their power than absolutely necessary. Nor is this surprising, considering the fact that those favoring a more sovereign state generally made a deliberate effort to get appointed to the Convention.

The telling note by Madison is the one reporting Mason as saying "The Laws of the U.S. are paramount to State Bills of Rights." He was, of course, reminding the other delegates that the new Constitution was structured top-down in such a way that its laws could *over-ride* the Bills of Rights of all of the states, and therefore the Bills of Rights of the states were not safe unless the national Constitution had a Bill of Rights of its own. And yet, this telling and relevant statement was ignored to the point of rejection by the majority, including by Madison. Their preferring to accept Sherman's statement that "The legislature may be safely trusted" is clear evidence, it seems to me, of the climate of either arrogance or power-seeking (or both) which prevailed at this historic Convention.

## XI-10: *Maneuvers Within the Congress Itself*

The delegates to the Constitutional Convention must have felt very timid in returning to the Continental Congress with an "amendment" which was not an amendment at all, and which therefore was a clear indication that they not only hadn't fulfilled the mandate they were given, but that they had deliberately violated it. Indeed, they had done so realizing that their mandate had been *deliberately* limited by Congress *precisely* in order to prevent what took place at Philadelphia. We remember that Congress had only authorized suggested *amendments* to the Articles, not a document *replacing* them. *Indeed, all who participated in the Convention, especially those who signed the final document, violated their own commitments of support for the Continental Congress.*

Thus, the evidence mounts, and could be strengthened still more by further documentation, that not only did the participants in the Constitutional Convention participate in a coup d'etat, they did so in a manipulative way that undermined their own moral integrity. Furthermore, constitutional loopholes permitted forms of corruption which began immediately after its first President, Washington, took office and his Treasury Secretary, Hamilton, continued, while in office, the same manipulative quality of political maneuvering which got him what he wanted in the Constitution, and got him his government post. Jefferson's later account of Hamilton's maneuvering is given at the end of this chapter.

The arrogance with which the self-serving power-seekers had immediately abandoned their mandate at the Convention itself, and their daring to return with their coup d'etat alternative to the very Congress they were maneuvering to skirt, is largely explained by the fact that they had *George Washington* in their midst, and most especially because he had presided over the Constitutional Convention itself. He made almost no contribution himself. He was there for show, dressed in a new military uniform for the occasion, the only one so attired. It served as a constant reminder of his role in achieving the Independence which made possible all that was transpiring there. It might also have served to set a military-like tone for the gathering, one conducive to outmaneuvering those who would oppose them in their cleverly orchestrated coup.

Even so, there were enough members of Congress who rejected the full wishes of the Convention power-seekers. They didn't act with the courage one might have hoped, but we do find in the Continental Congress Minutes of September 27th, 1787, approval of the following "motion of Mr. Dane on the new constitution":

Whereas Congress sensible that there were defects in the present Confederation; and that several of the States were desirous that a Convention of Delegates should be formed to consider the same, and to propose necessary alterations in the federal Constitution; in February last resolved that it was (in their opinion) expedient that a Convention of the States should be held for the sole and express purpose of <u>revising</u> [emphasis added] the Articles of Confederation, and reporting to Congress and the several legislatures such alterations and provisions therein. as should when agreed to in Congress, and be confirmed by the States. render the federal Constitution adequate to the exigencies of Government. and preservation of the Union; And whereas it appears by Credentials laid before Congress that twelve States appointed Delegates who assembled in Convention accordingly, and who did on the 17th instant by the unanimous consent of the States then present in Convention agreed upon. and afterwards laid before Congress a Constitution for the United

States, to be submitted to a convention of Delegates, chosen in each State by the people thereof, under the recommendation of its legislature, for their Assent and ratification which constitution appears to be intended as an entire system in itself, and not as any part of or alteration in the Articles of Confederation; to alterations in which Articles, the deliberations and powers of Congress are, in this case, constitutionally confined and whereas Congress cannot with propriety proceed to examine and alter the said Constitution proposed unless it be with a view so essentially to change the principles and forms of it, as to make it an additional part in the said Confederation, and the members of Congress not feeling themselves authorized by the form of Government under which they are assembled to express an opinion respecting a System of Government no way connected with those forms; but conceiving the respect they owe their constituents and the importance of the subject require that the report of the Convention should, with all convenient dispatch, be transmitted to the several States to be laid before the respective legislatures thereof.

Therefore, RESOLVED that there be transmitted to the supreme executive of each State a copy of the report of the Convention of the States lately Assembled in the City of Philadelphia signed by their deputies the 17th instant including their resolutions, and their letter directed to the President of Congress.

We note, therefore, that Congress did not specifically endorse sending the proposed Constitution to the states for *ratification*, as called for in the "Federalist" proposal, but only that the documents from the Convention be "transmitted to the supreme executive," etc. In short, the majority in Congress didn't themselves literally join the conspiracy, but they also didn't expose it to the public. Rather, they participated in its furtherance by a further kind of sleight of hand. And that was all the power-seekers needed for their next "move," which was now to proceed to the legislatures of the various states as if Congress had approved the states' proceeding with the formation of the state constitutional conventions, as called for in the proposed new constitution.

There followed cries of outrage, especially from Virginia's Richard Henry Lee, who wrote extremely telling criticisms in various journals. Patrick Henry was also extremely outspoken against ratification. And in many states the debates were bitter and long and the power-seekers' manipulations outrageous. Perhaps the most notorious of those reported, because of its overt violent nature, was the behavior of the "Federalists" in the Philadelphia legislature. That legislature was in session when word was momentarily expected that Congress had sent the proposed Constitution to the states for consideration. When the hour became late, the anti-Constitutionalists went home. When word finally did come about the Congressional action the anti-Constitutionalists were still absent. Here is an account of how the Constitution got sent on its way by the Pennsylvania Legislature.

> Hoping that the opposition of the minority would now be removed, the sergeant-at-arms and the assistant clerk were dispatched to hunt up the malcontents, show them the resolution, and summon them to attend. The two officers went first to Major Boyd's, where were James McCalmont, who sat for Franklin, and Jacob Miley, from Dauphin. They were shown the resolution, [We remember that Congress had not approved to have the Constitution sent to the states "for ratification," only for discussion.] and stoutly said they would not go. The people [there is suspicion that "the people" were hired], however, decided that they should; broke into their lodgings, seized them, dragged them through the streets to the State House, and thrust them into the assembly room, with clothes torn and faces white with rage. The quorum was now complete.[13]

The two states that were most crucial and most in danger of upsetting the "Federalist" strategy were New York and Virginia. So Hamilton and Madison recruited John Jay to join with them in writing what have come to be known as "The Federalist Papers." These Papers contained by far the most influential of the arguments urging state legislatures to ratify the new Constitution. The two most important ones are Federalist Paper #15, by Hamilton, already referred to above, and #10 by Madison.

In the next chapter of this volume I conduct an in-depth analysis of this attempt by Madison to justify a top-down as against a federal-type national government.

My conclusion from this chapter, then, is that the power-seekers, championed by the "Federalists," sought a more powerful centralized national government not only in order to have more power to implement their

---

13. *Pennsylvania and the Federal Constitution, vol. 1,* 1787-88, ed. by Bach McMaster and Frederick Stone, pub. by Historical Society of Pennsylvania, 1970, page 4

*domestic* agendas, but also in order to have a more credible claim to *sovereignty* in the international club of territorial-states making similar claims. Thus, their main purpose in forming the Constitution was *not* primarily in order to be better able to administer *justice* — in fact, that was an agenda item far down their list. As we have seen (XI-8), Hamilton's stated purpose in promoting the adoption of the new Constitution made no mention of justice. Rather, the emphasis was on *utility, political prosperity, republican government*, and *liberty*. The "liberty" which he had in mind, or course, was liberty to pursue the Federalist agenda. And in Jefferson's *Anas* one can read of the outrageous manipulations Hamilton was willing to resort to, *and which the new Constitution permitted*, in order to fulfill that agenda. An account of one aspect of such manipulations is given by Jefferson upon his return from France, where he had been serving as Ambassador during all the manipulations which installed the new Constitution:

> The courtesies of the dinner parties given me, as a stranger newly arrived among them placed me in familiar society. But I cannot describe the wonder and mortification with which the table conversation filled me.
>
> Politics was the chief topic, and the preference for kingly over republican government was evidently the favorite sentiment. An apostate I could not be, nor yet a hypocrite; and I found myself, for the most part, the only advocate on the republican side of the question, unless among the guests there chanced to be some member of that party from the legislative houses. Hamilton's financial system had been passed. It had two objects; first as a puzzle, to exclude popular understanding and inquiry; second, as a machine for the corruption of the legislature. For he avowed the opinion that man could be governed by one of two motives only, force or interest; force, he observed, in this country was out of the question, and the interests, therefore, of the members must be laid hold of to keep the legislature in unison with the executive. And with grief and shame it must be acknowledged that his machine was not without effect; that even in this, the birth of our government, some members were found sordid enough to bend their duty to their interest, and to look after personal rather than public good.
>
> It was well known that during the war the greatest difficulty we encountered was the want of money or means to pay our soldiers who fought, or our farmers, manufacturers, and merchants who furnished the necessary supplies of food and clothing for them. After the expedient of paper money had

exhausted itself, certificates of debt were given to individual creditors, with the assurance of payment so soon as the United States should be able. But the distress of these people often obliged them to part with these for the half, the fifth, even the tenth of their value; and speculators had made a trade of cozening them from the holders by the most fraudulent practices and persuasions that they would never be paid.

In the bill for funding and paying these, Hamilton made no difference between the original holders and the fraudulent purchasers of this paper. Great and just repugnance arose at putting these two classes of creditors on the same footing, and great exertions were used to pay the former the full value, and to the latter, the price only which they had paid, with interest. But this would have prevented the game which was to be played, and for which the minds of greedy members [of the legislature] were already tutored and prepared.

When the trial of strength on these several efforts had indicated the form in which the bill would pass, this being known within doors sooner than without, and especially than to those who were in distant parts of the Union, the base scramble began. Couriers and relay horses by land, and swift sailing pilot boats by sea, were flying in all directions. Active partners and agents were associated and employed in every state, town and country neighborhood, and this paper was bought up at 5s., and even as low as 2s. in the pound [20 shillings made up a pound], before the holder knew that Congress had already provided the redemption at par. Immense sums were thus filched from the poor and ignorant, and fortunes accumulated by those who had themselves been poor enough before.

It was, of course, the members of Congress, and their friends, who thus reaped huge profits. And Jefferson goes on to report how Hamilton planned it that way, in order to make the members of Congress indebted to him personally. The "leader" and "chief" referred to in the following continuation of the quotation from Jefferson was, of course, Hamilton:

Men thus enriched by the dexterity of a leader would follow of course the chief who was leading them to fortune and become the zealous instruments of all his enterprises. This game was over, and another was on the carpet at the moment of my arrival; and to this I was most ignorantly and innocently made to hold a candle. . . .

Jefferson goes on to relate another of Hamilton's schemes to bring power to himself by appealing to the corruptible side of the members of Congress he needed for support at crucial points in his power moves. He then goes on to show that Hamilton was not the only one who considered top-down, even monarchical, government the best form:

> After the cloth was removed, and our question agreed and dismissed [Jefferson had been asked by Washington to bring some business before the others.], conversation began on other matters, and, by some circumstance was led to the British Constitution, on which Mr. Adams observed, "Purge that constitution of its corruption and give to its popular branch equal representation, and it would be the most perfect constitution ever devised by the wit of man." Hamilton paused and said, "Purge it of its corruption, and give to its popular branch equality of representation, and it would become an impractical government; as it stands at present, with all its supposed defects, it is the most perfect government that ever existed."

This is the man whom Gingrich's hero, George Washington, knew extremely well from many years of close association, and yet chose as his right-hand man both during the war and within the new government. One can only assume that Washington shared his views on government and his manner of wielding governmental power. So, we need not be surprised at the political power plays we see going on in Washington these days. They are quite in keeping with those of "our Founding Fathers," and with the top-down, power-promoting Constitution which they established as a means of pursuing their power-brokering purposes.

It's rather disconcerting to realize
that the constitution
of the government one has been living under
is the result of a kind of coup,
undertaken as the first of the political maneuvers
designed to serve the interests
of power brokers.
But,
that does seem
to have been the case.

# Chapter XII

# *James Madison's False Reasoning*

## XII-1: *The Purpose of This Chapter*

The main purpose of this Chapter is to indicate the basic rationale for establishing the U.S. Constitution. This rationale was presented by Alexander Hamilton, James Madison, and John Jay in that series of 85 newspaper articles which became known as "The Federalist Papers." Although the articles were originally addressed "To the people of the State of New York," they were read, and greatly influenced opinions, throughout the entire country. Hamilton initiated the series, and 49 of the total have been definitely attributed to him. Jay wrote only four. Fourteen have definitely been attributed to Madison, and the authorship of each of the others is in dispute.

Because Hamilton began the series, wrote the last 21, and the majority of the total, he is definitely considered the major author. And in that first "Paper" Hamilton states *his* purpose clearly:

I propose, in a series of papers, to discuss the following interesting particulars: *The utility of the UNION to your political prosperity; The insufficiency of the present Confederation to preserve that Union; The necessity of a government at least equally energetic with the one proposed, to the attainment of this object; The conformity of the proposed Constitution to the true principles of republican government; Its analogy to your State constitution; and lastly, The additional security which its adoption will afford to the preservation of that species of government, to liberty, and to prosperity.* [1]

The general tone of the entire first paper, and, indeed, of all the papers attributed to Hamilton, is well represented in the above quotation. We note that (as in the XI-8 quotation) there is no mention of what in this volume we are assuming to be the main role and responsibility of any coercive agency such as a government: i.e., there is no mention of anything which could be interpreted as *"preventing and remedying injustice."* In virtually every paper written by Hamilton, his main concern centers around the preservation of "liberty" and property. Except for the last two papers, the closest he comes to addressing concerns about justice is in arguing that the Constitution preserves "a republican form of government," by which he means one where decisions in its various branches and departments are made by majority vote among representatives elected by majority vote, and where the powers granted **to** each branch and department are prescribed by the Constitution itself. Indeed, his arguments in the last two Papers against a Bill of Rights are based on such a conception of a "republican government."

The inadequacy of simple majority-vote as a determiner of what is humane and equitable has already been alluded to in this volume, and will be discussed in more detail in the next chapter. Indeed, we shall see that finding a corrective to simplistic majority-vote was one of Madison's main concerns in his Federalist Paper #10, which we shall thoroughly analyze in this Chapter.

As already hinted at above, Madison, in sharp contrast to Hamilton, did display a sincere concern about justice, though his perception of it was from the perspective of an owner of a large slave plantation and a member of a

---

1. Hamilton, Alexander, *Federalist Paper #1*, There are many sources for these "Papers." The index in any good library will indicate several.

very privileged class of southern squires. We have seen that Madison was in many ways the most influential architect of the new Constitution. Even though others arrived so late for the Convention that it didn't start until eleven days after the scheduled date (XI-7) Madison was there several days ahead of the scheduled time. He had prepared for this day for several years. He had done extensive research in Greek philosophy of government. He had been active in the government of Virginia and a representative under the Articles of Confederation. He came with a Constitutional draft already prepared, and it became the basis for all discussion and for the final document.

So, it has been truly said that Madison was the father of the U.S. Constitution, and that he was more familiar with its details, its essential structure, and its rational basis than anyone else. Add to this his outstanding intellectual competence, bordering on genius, and we begin to appreciate why the Federalist Paper #10, the Paper which was designed to justify the Constitution and its structure, is so crucial in understanding what it was structured to accomplish and what even today are its inherent moral merits and flaws.

How, then, given his *apparently* genuine concern about justice, do we explain Madison's refusal to support the move for a Bill of Rights in the original Constitution (XI-9)? Also, how do we explain the false reasoning displayed in his Federalist Paper #10 and evidenced in the pages to follow?

In the next Section I will attempt a partial answer to these questions. It still is not clear to me whether his flawed reasoning was part of a deliberate attempt to manipulate his readers into accepting the new constitution, or whether he really believed that his reasoning was sound. In either case, it unfortunately contributed greatly to the discrediting of the Articles of Confederation in the eyes of many then and since, and to support for the Constitution. Our task in the following pages is not only to reveal the flaws in Madison's thinking, and thus in the structure of the U.S. Constitution, but also to show that truly sound reasoning, truly in search of justice for all, would lead to quite a different outcome. Then, in Chapter XIII, we will see that "different outcome" spelled out in considerable detail. That is, the purpose of that final chapter will be, first, to envision, and then to suggest how to achieve economic and political structures specifically designed to assure what has been the goal throughout this volume: *justice for all, local to global.*

## XII-2: *James Madison, an Enigma*

I refer to Madison as an enigma for many reasons, but mainly for the following. First, he joined wholeheartedly with Hamilton in promoting a strong, impersonal, centralist government, and, as noted, in deliberately refusing to support those championing a Bill of Rights in the original Constitution (See XI-9). Then, four years later, influenced by Jefferson and others in Virginia (notably Richard Henry Lee), and disenchanted with Hamilton, he became the main promoter of a Bill of Rights as Amendments to the Constitution. Perhaps a brief biographical sketch will help us to understand.

Madison was born in Montpelier, Virginia, March, 1751. A quick calculation shows him to be a young bachelor, barely 36 years, at the time of the Constitutional Convention. Considering the influence he and his thinking have had on life in America for the past two centuries, and thus on that in the whole world, this in itself is amazing.

His father was the owner of a several-thousand-acres, slave-run plantation, which Madison eventually inherited and drew income from the rest of his 85 years. He was, however, more liberal than most Southern country squires and most politicians of his day. He favored Unitarianism as a religious orientation, and seven years later, at 43, married a member of the Religious Society of Friends (Quaker). As noted (XI-7) his intellect was so superior that he completed the normal 4 years at Princeton (then the College of New Jersey) in less than three years while still having time to be very active in a literary debating society. He had a reputation for being a very sharp debater, something to be kept in mind as we check out his arguments in the pages that follow!

I am no specialist as a Madison scholar. From what I have gleaned, however, my explanation for his enigmatic behavior from time to time is that he thoroughly enjoyed intellectual challenges, especially political ones, and at *winning* at them even if it took a bit of intellectual sleight of hand to do so—a tactic not uncommon in debating societies, where cleverness is often rewarded as much as sound reasoning. Perhaps his later life was somewhat influenced by the tricks he learned in confounding his debating opponents during his college years at Princeton. This theory fits with what was sometimes said of him: that his greatest fault was "not admitting his mistakes." On the other hand, by later leaving the "Federalist" camp to join with Jefferson in opposing Hamilton it might be said that he somewhat admitted, by implication, his earlier mistake.

There is no doubt, however, that his interest in promoting the new Constitution at the time went far beyond his fascination with intellectual challenges. Since at least 1780 he had been frustrated in his efforts to get member states in the new Continental Congress to abide by their commitments to support the new government, financially and otherwise. It may be that it was the combination of this frustration plus the lure of an intellectual challenge, which partially explains his temporarily joining with Hamilton in promoting the power-seekers' cause in the form of the new top-down constitution. In any case, that is what he did.

Was he, then, "used" by supporters of a top-down government somewhat as Tom Paine may have been "used" in support of the revolution, and as Jefferson may have been "used" in his being urged to write the first draft to The Declaration as a public relations document? Were each of these men, each in his own way a man of unusual moral integrity, lured into complicity with the power-seekers by that hunger for "community" which we all experience and which few of us satisfy without some degree of moral compromise? For instance, did his not having a wife and family of his own at the time contribute to his placing a high value on "community" with other young and eager power-seekers, like Hamilton?

Fortunately, we need not have answers to such questions in order to evaluate the merits of Madison's arguments in support of the Constitution. But it may be important to keep these various observations in mind as a way of maintaining our alertness to any debating "sleights of hand" which might otherwise catch us unaware of clever manipulations.

One more relevant comment before proceeding. We keep in mind that when Madison wrote this Federalist Paper #10 he had already been through his lengthy preparations for all that led up to the Constitutional Convention, through the Convention itself, and had time to think about what happened there. In short, we have every reason to believe that the reasoning Madison displays here had been matured and refined over several years. We also keep in mind that this was primarily a political document, designed to win support not only in the crucial state of New York, but also in his home state of Virginia, each of which was full of doubters and skeptics; and with good reason. Hamilton and his tactics were well known in New York, and

Madison's vested interests in having the new constitution ratified was well known in his home state of Virginia. We have here, therefore, the most skillfully crafted arguments for the U.S. Constitution that existed at the time, and perhaps even that exist today.

## XII-3: *Madison Defines the Problem*

The approach in analyzing this "Paper" by Madison will be to scrutinize each point in his argument in turn. He reveals his main concern in its opening lines. They revolve around his concern about "factions," which he defines as "a number of citizens, whether amounting to a majority or minority of the whole, who are united and actuated by some common impulse of passion, or of interest, adverse to the rights of other citizens, or to the permanent and aggregate interests of the community."

His concern to eliminate the influence of factions might be considered a part of that basic and *only* justification for all governing: namely to prevent and remedy injustice in all its forms. Though Madison's concern was relevant, it was, nevertheless, only a small part of the concern which a government must address in order to justify its claim to a near-monopoly of coercive power. Therefore, even if Madison had been successful in addressing his concern about factions, he would still have fallen far short of what would have been required to justify the Constitution. With this much preparation, then, we keep our wits about us as we hear Madison's best effort to justify the basic principles upon which the structure of the U.S. Constitution is based.

> Among the numerous advantages promised by a well constructed Union, none deserves to be more accurately developed than its tendency to break and control the violence of faction. The friend of popular governments never finds himself so much alarmed for its character and fate as when he contemplates their propensity to this dangerous vice. He will not fail, therefore, to set a due value on any plan which, without violating the principles to which he is attached, provides a proper cure for it. The instability, injustice, and confusion introduced into public councils, have, in truth, been the mortal diseases under which popular governments have everywhere perished; as they continue to be the favorite and fruitful topics from which the adversaries to liberty derive their most precious declamations. The valuable contributions made by the American constitutions on the popular models, both ancient and modern,

cannot certainly be too much admired; but it would be an unwarranted partiality to contend that they have as effectually obviated the danger on this side as was wished and expected. Complaints are everywhere heard from our most considerate and virtuous citizens, equally the friends of public and private faith, and of public and personal liberty, that our governments are too unstable, that the public good is disregarded in the conflicts of rival parties, and that measures are too often decided, not according to the rules of justice and the rights of the minor party, but by the superior force of an interested and overbearing majority. However anxiously we may wish that these complaints had no foundation, the evidence of known facts will not permit us to deny that they are in some degree true. It will be found, indeed, on a candid review of our situation, that some of the distresses under which we labor have been erroneously charged on the operations of our governments; but it will be found, at the same time, that other causes will not alone account for many of our heaviest misfortunes; and, in particular, for that prevailing and increasing distrust of public engagements, and the alarm for private rights, which are echoed from one end of the continent to the other. These must be chiefly, if not wholly, effects of the unsteadiness and injustice with which factious spirit has tainted our public administrations.[2]

## XII-4: *Madison's Missed Opportunity*

We must grant Madison his initial point that "factions," as he defines them, are a problem with which governments are challenged to cope. But, as we do so, we maintain a distinction between factions and "interest groups," the latter being often tagged with the same pejorative connotation of being "adverse to the rights of others." Interest groups can also serve as safeguards against oppression wherever there is concentration of power. With this tangential commentary in mind we turn to Madison's next step in his reasoning process:

> If a faction consists of less than a majority, relief is supplied by the republican principle, which enables the majority to defeat its sinister views by regular vote. It [the minority "faction"] may clog the administration, it may convulse the society; but it will be unable to execute and mask its violence under the forms of the Constitution. When a majority is included in a faction the form

---

2. Madison, James, *Federalist Paper #10*

of popular government, on the other hand, enables it to sacrifice to its ruling passion or interest both the public good and the rights of other citizens. To secure the public good and private rights against the danger of such a faction, and at the same time to preserve the spirit and the form of popular government, is then the great object to which our inquiries are directed.[3]

Again, it is difficult to understand how a person making such a succinct statement of the problem (a problem inherent in that simplistic form of "democracy" which gives all ultimate power to those who can get a majority to vote for them) could have missed the opportunity so clearly presented to him at the Constitutional Convention to at least partially solve it. I refer, of course, to Madison's missed opportunity to support the move by Mason and Gerry to insert a Bill of Rights into the original Constitution, and to thereby place legal limits on what would-be manipulators of majority vote could legislate.

The traditional role for a Bill of Rights is precisely to prevent the misuse of majority vote, for which misuse Madison here claims to be seeking a cure. Yet, at the Philadelphia Constitutional Convention he joined in *opposing* Mason and Gerry when they argued for its inclusion (again, see XI-9). In short, Madison deliberately signed a constitution which, in being without a Bill of Rights, was devoid of an important form of the very protection of "both the public good and the rights of other citizens" which, in the above quotation, Madison says is lacking in the simple majority-vote process.

Madison's concerns about factions with majority support were not without foundation. There evidently were, in fact, "town meeting" gatherings, where charismatic figures could get their privileged ways by manipulating the most gullible and most easily bought-off to generate a majority vote in favor of their personal interests. A complementary part of the problem was undisciplined mob action, which also was subject to being generated by political manipulators. A Bill of Rights serves to cut off at the point of legislation some of the most serious violations of human rights that might otherwise be inflicted by such manipulations.

Perhaps it is important to remind ourselves how easy it is to become so enthusiastic about one's cause that one fails to consider how it might go astray. Enthusiasts about the majority-vote process, so seemingly idealistic,

---

3. *Ibid.*

especially in regard to the principle of equality, seem especially vulnerable in this regard. Indeed, even Tom Paine, the author of *Common Sense* and *The Rights of Man*, seems to have fallen prey to such vulnerability when he declared that "what a nation chuses to do it has a right to do." Paine was, of course, merely stating more bluntly the position affirmed in the Declaration of Independence, that a government "derives its just powers from the consent of the governed."

These words sound unanswerable until they are analyzed. In doing so, we see that they imply that whatever a majority "consents" to will necessarily be "for the common good," even though such consent may have been secured by withholding information, by bribery, by giving misinformation, or by any one of countless other manipulated or morally insensitive means. Consent may, in short, have been given by the most gullible and most easily bought off by appealing to their personal self-interests rather than to what is truly justice for all.

Even in the unlikely eventuality that no such manipulations take place, a majority vote has a very strong tendency, by its very nature, to represent what a majority *wants* out of self-interest rather than what the voters sincerely *feel* is "justice for all." In any case, what a *majority* wants may be far different, as we well know, from what any of several minorities want. In short, the majority-vote process evades completely the justice process of balancing wants against each other in a truly just mix. One way to approach such a just-mix is, of course, to "take turns," but there is little or no provision for this or any other justice consideration in most voting. In the next chapter we shall see how this problem might be addressed in ways designed to supplement and strengthen the partial solution provided by the Bill of Rights.

It was John Quincy Adams, son of John Adams, just three years out of Harvard, and only recently set up in law practice, who, at the time, most effectively answered Tom Paine's simplistic statement. He did so long after the Constitution was adopted and functioning, but his point is nevertheless valid, and as valid today as it was then.

> This principle, that a whole nation has a right to do whatever it pleases, cannot in any sense whatever be admitted as true. The eternal and immutable laws of justice and morality are paramount to all human legislation. The violation of those laws is certainly within the power, but it is not among the

rights of nations. The power of a nation is the collected power of all the individuals which compose it. . . If, therefore, a majority . . . are bound by no law human or divine, and have no other rule but their sovereign will and pleasure to direct them, what possible security can any citizen of the nation have for the protection of his unalienable rights? The principle of liberty must still be the sport of arbitrary power, and the hideous form of despotism must lay aside the diadem and scepter, only to assume the party-colored garments of democracy.[4]

It is indeed ironic that a "Federalist," of all people, should be the one reprimanding Tom Paine, the very author of *The Rights of Man*, for his implied disregard for those rights, especially since, just a few years before John Quincy Adams made this statement, the "Federalists" had proposed a constitution without any reference at all to inalienable rights and without even a Bill of Rights. But it must be said in Adams' defense that he was not a hard-nosed "Federalist," and that he later pretty much dissociated himself from the Hamiltonian camp. In any case, credit must be given where truth is spoken, especially as vital and important moral truth as John Quincy Adams has proclaimed.

## XII-5: *Madison's Reasoning Begins to Break Down*

We proceed, then, to hear Madison's next point in his supposed effort to justify the Constitution on the grounds that it solves the problem of "factions."

> There are two methods of curing the mischiefs of faction: the one, by remov-ing its causes; the other by controlling its effects.
>
> There are, again, two methods of removing the causes of faction: [1] the one by destroying the liberty which is essential to its existence; [2] the other, by giving every citizen the same opinions, the same passions, and the same interests.[5]

Madison quickly concludes that both these alternatives for removing the *causes* of factions (as distinct from "controlling its effects") are unsatisfac-tory. His arguments for rejecting them are as follows:

---

4. Adams, John Quincy, *The Writings of John Quincy Adams*, ed. by W. C. Ford (Westport, Conn., Greenwood Press, 1968, reprint of 1917)
5. *Ibid.*, Madison

It could never be more truly said than of the first remedy, that it was worse than the disease. Liberty is to faction what air is to fire, an aliment [sustenance] without which it instantly expires. But it could not be less folly to abolish liberty, which is essential to political life, because it nourishes faction, than it would be to wish the annihilation of air, which is essential to animal life, because it imparts to fire its destructive agency.

The second expedient is as impracticable as the first would be unwise. As long as the reason of man continues fallible, and he is at liberty to exercise it, different opinions will be formed. As long as the connection subsists between reason and his self-love, his opinions and his passions will have a reciprocal influence on each other; and the former will be objects to which the latter will attach themselves.[6]

Taking his arguments in order, surely we are morally justified in curtailing the liberty of that faction which insists on driving while drunk, on polluting the rivers, or that insists on claiming as private property all that its members have the power to seize of our common heritage of land and resources. Granted, that any curtailment of liberties requires moral justification. But surely, many such curtailments can be morally justified under some circumstances. To put the matter generally, it is surely morally justifiable to curtail — in a humane way, to be sure — liberty which is being used to inflict gross injustice. (We remember that the same issue was addressed in IX-13.)

In short, Madison fails to consider the option of curtailing only certain *kinds* of liberty, namely those which a Bill of Rights, or certain laws, would curtail. If he had considered that option he would naturally have been led to consider what should be included in such curtailment, and to consider how to assure that laws curtailed *only* those liberties which perpetrated injustice on others. Unfortunately, Madison considered only the option of curtailing *all* liberty, which option can, of course, be readily dismissed in the way he effectively does dismiss it. Criticism of Madison's position in this regard is of such crucial importance because *what* liberty is justifiably curtailed, and what is not, is precisely the kind of distinction which must be provided for in a constitution designed to assure justice for all.

---

6. *Ibid.*

As for Madison's second point (still on removal of causes), regarding the "giving" of interests and passions, he says it is "impracticable." But, surely it is *not*. Governments and ad-men do it all the time with their propaganda and advertising. And surely it is not only practicable but is sometimes morally justified — even morally required — as in the case of curtailing the distribution and consumption of destructive drugs, or curtailing alcohol consumption among those who tend to become violent and uncontrollable when under its influence. Indeed, isn't part of the purpose of educating the young in order to develop in them socially responsible "interests and passions" rather than socially irresponsible ones? Granted, great care must be taken in doing so. And thereby we are again reminded of the need for guiding *principles* and decision-making *processes* appropriate to determining what guidance in this respect is morally responsible, and what is not.

Therefore, it must be said of Madison's analysis of the *causes* of factions that not only can the causes of factions be controlled, not only would it at times be wise to do so, but that at least some of them *ought* to be.

Madison's argument for the impracticability of eliminating all differences among interests and passions is more persuasive. But it is not clear from the above quotation why it would be necessary to do so. Again, we would only be justified in removing (or modifying) those which would inflict injustice on someone, either directly or indirectly.

> The diversity in the faculties of men, from which the rights of property originate, is not less an insuperable obstacle to an uniformity of interests. *The protection of these faculties is the first object of government* [emphasis added]. From the protection of different and unequal faculties of acquiring property, the possession of different degrees and kinds of property immediately results [granted]; and from the influence of these on the sentiments and views of the respective proprietors ensues a division of the society into different interests and parties.[7]

Granted, there are differences among human beings regarding what Madison calls "faculties of acquiring property," and that these differences result in differences in the actual kinds and amounts of property which persons acquire, even when no one takes **unfair** advantage of others (which, unfortunately, the Constitution does permit the most aggressive and acquisi-

---

7. *Ibid.*

tive to do). What is not to be granted, however, is that "the protection of these faculties" is the *first* object of government." As I have argued several times in the previous pages, the first and only object of government (because governing involves coercing) is to "prevent and remedy injustice;" there is no other justification, I would argue, for one or more persons "governing" the activities of one or more other persons.

Indeed my concern about the kind of government which Madison is here advocating derives partly from the fact that it seems designed *primarily* to protect the "faculty for acquiring property," and to protect it outright, *without sufficiently distinguishing between just and unjust acquisition.* Thus, a government based on the principles Madison is here advocating would, as its "first object," defend the ostensible "right" of the most aggressive and acquisitive to accumulate a virtual monopoly of our *common* heritage, such as of land and resources. *No wonder, then, that this is precisely what has happened under the Constitution based on such Madisonian principles!*

Therefore, as we proceed further with an analysis of Madison's defense of the Constitution we are thereby alerted to possibly uncovering further evidence that he is defending a constitution whose main object is to protect "faculties for acquiring property." It is in this alerted frame of mind, then, that we proceed to hear the next point in Madison's argument.

Having reached (through false reasoning) the conclusion that the *causes* of factions either could not or ought not to be controlled, he turns his attention to how one might control what he calls their *effects*.

> By what means is this object obtainable? Evidently by one of two only. Either the existence of the same passion or interest in a majority at the same time must be prevented [A form of restricting "liberty"], or the majority, having such co-existent passion or interest, must be rendered, by their number and local situation, unable to concert and carry into effect schemes of oppression [also a form of restricting "liberty"]. If the impulse [i.e. "passion or interest"] and opportunity [i.e., opportunity to concert and carry into effect schemes of oppression] be suffered to coincide, we well know that neither moral nor religious motives can be relied on as an adequate control. They are not found to be such on the injustice and violence of individuals, and lose their efficacy in proportion to the number combined together [presumably because of the dangerous passions sometimes generated in a mob]; that is, in proportion as

their efficacy becomes needful [presumably because a mob, or those who control it, can do more damage than an individual].

From this view of the subject it may be concluded that a pure democracy, *by which I mean a society consisting of a small number of citizens, who assemble and administer the government in person* [emphasis added], can admit of no cure for the mischiefs of faction. A common passion or interest will, in almost every case, be felt by a majority of the whole; a common communication and concert result from the form of government itself, and there is nothing to check the inducements to sacrifice the weaker party or an obnoxious individual [But there might be, at least partially, with an adequate and enforced Bill of Rights]. Hence it is that such democracies have ever been spectacles of turbulence and contention, have ever been found incompatible with personal security or the rights of property, and have in general been as short in their lives as they have been violent in their opinions and their passions.[8]

We note that, though he has said that he will now turn to deal with "effects," he is still dealing with "causes": essentially causes in the form of a common passion "felt by a majority of the whole." This confusion between causes and effects seems of little substantive importance, however, except as a further indication of the fallibility of Madison's reasoning in this quotation. Keeping this in mind, there are several points to be noted here.

First, we note that he is assuming that all decisions in such town meeting groups are made by majority vote, *and without any restraints on such votes.* But this need not be the case. Again, small groups as well as large groups can be restrained by enforced rules of order, and by incorporating into such rules certain restrictions on coercive measures. Also, some groups, notably Quakers, make all their decisions by some form of consensus approaching unanimity. But Madison doesn't consider any of these. Nor does he consider any other ways of preventing the evils which might be perpetuated by factions, whether small or large. And we shall see that the reason he doesn't consider these options is evidently because he has an alternative method to propose. He has a "hidden agenda."

Before going on to his own agenda, it is important to point out some of the ways in which groups of a great variety of sizes have protected against "destructive" factions. The common element in all such methods is *commit-*

---

*ment*. That is, a condition for participating in the decision-making process in well ordered groups is a commitment to abide by certain procedures and certain courtesies. In many bodies using the majority-vote decision-making process the commitment is to Roberts Rules of Order. The U.S. Congress uses a variation of these rules. They have been perfected many times since Henry M. Robert first published them in "Pocket-Manual" form in 1876. Among other things, such rules are designed to generate full discussion of an issue before any vote is taken. They are only one of the ways in which the influence of "factions" can be minimized.

Another is by simply refusing to admit to decision-making participation those who will not commit themselves to certain safeguarding procedures. One way is to give the chairperson of the meeting the authority to call for the eviction of anyone who severely violates the rules.

Still another is the consensus method of decision-making, where no decision is made until every participant agrees.

But Madison considers none of these protective measures. He hastily jumps to the conclusion that there are none such. This, evidently gives him justification in his mind for proceeding with his own agenda. Here, then is the beginning of his proposal for eliminating the destructive influence of factions:

A republic, by which I mean a government in which the scheme of representation takes place, opens a different prospect, and promises the cure for
which we are seeking. Let us examine the points in which it varies from pure
democracy, and we shall comprehend both the nature of the cure and the efficacy which it must derive from the Union.

The two great points of difference between a democracy and a republic
are: [1] first, the delegation of the government, in the latter, to a small number of citizens elected by the rest; [2] secondly, the greater number of citizens,
and greater sphere of the country, over which the latter may be extended.

The effect of the first difference is, on the one hand, to refine and enlarge
the public views, by passing them through the medium of a chosen body of
citizens, whose wisdom may [!] best discern the true interest of their country,
and whose patriotism and love of justice will be least likely to sacrifice it to
temporary or partial considerations [provided such representatives truly **do**
love justice, and are more committed to it than those who elected them].
Under such a regulation it may well happen that the public voice, pronounced

by the representatives of people, will be more consonant to the public good than if pronounced by the people themselves, convened for the purpose. *On the other hand, the effect may be inverted. Men of factious tempers, of local prejudices, or of sinister designs, may, by intrigue, by corruption, or by other means, first obtain the suffrages, and then betray the interests of the people* [emphasis added].[9]

Precisely; and, as we shall see, Madison doesn't offer a satisfactory way to assure against the latter. In the next section we shall see what he does propose in this regard, and then go on to see why he arrives at his conclusion by false reasoning.

## XII-6: *The Nub of Madison's Argument*

I have no substantial disagreement with Madison's arguments for representative government as superior to "pure democracy" where the bodies of persons at issue are of the size of states or nations, or even of counties and cities. But, serious flaws in his thinking creep in when he tries to persuade us that representatives from the larger the republics (such as nations) are likely to be "more consonant to the public good" than those from smaller republics (such as one of the then 13 states).

Perhaps imagining himself back in his debating society at Princeton, what he evidently hoped to do was to persuade us that representatives elected into national office by the general population of the entire nation would necessarily be more socially responsible than those elected into state office by the smaller population of one of the states. If he could persuade his readers of this, then he presumably could justify the coup by which the citizens of the various state governments were, in effect, conscripted into national citizenship so that they could directly elect people to national office rather than, as in the Articles of Confederation, have the national offices filled by representatives from the state legislatures in true federation fashion. Here, then, is the beginning of his argument in this regard.

The question resulting is, whether small or extensive republics are more favorable to the election of proper guardians of the public weal; and it is clearly decided in favour of the latter by two obvious considerations.

---

9. *Ibid.*

In the first place, it is to be remarked that, however small the republic may be, the representatives must be raised to a certain number, in order to guard against the cabals of a few; and that, however large it may be, they must be limited to a certain number, in order to guard against the confusion of the multitude. Hence, the number of representatives in the two cases not being in proportion to that of the two constituents, and being proportionally greater in the small republic, it follows that, if the proportion of fit characters be not less in the large than in the small republic, the former will present a greater option and consequently a greater probability of a fit choice.[10]

Here Madison's argument has moved very quickly, and become very complicated. So, we must look at it closely. First, we summarize his argument by giving an example.

**Point #1:** There is an optimum number of representatives forming a legislative body; less than that would leave some unrepresented; more would make the body unwieldy (for ease in discussion, assume 100 members as that optimum number).

**Point #2:** We assume, therefore, that both a national body of representatives and a smaller one (such as in one of the states) would ideally have this optimum number of (100) representatives.

**Point #3:** the optimum number (100) of representatives at the state level would constitute a larger *percentage* of the total state population (perhaps 100 out of ten to twenty million, which would be one out of 100,000 to 200,000) than would be constituted by the 100 at the national level of the total national population (perhaps 100 out of 150 million, which would be one out of 1,500,000).

**Point #4:** Therefore, there would be a "greater number of people to choose from in forming the national body [7-1/2 times as many] as in forming the state body."

This is fairly acceptable reasoning thus far. But now comes that incredible step into glaringly false reasoning:

**Point #5:** *"If the proportion of fit characters be not less in the large [i.e., national] than in the small [i.e., one of the states] republic, the former will present a greater option, and consequently a greater probability of a fit choice."*

---

10. *Ibid.*

First we note that his conclusion depends on there being as great a proportion of "fit characters" in the large as in the small. And we can agree that this would likely be the case, or close enough to it for the argument which follows.

But, then he goes on to state that "the former" (the national population in our example) "will present a greater option, and consequently a greater probability of a fit choice" than would the population of the small (in our example, than the state population).

We note that there are two parts to his concluding argument here. First, he is saying that there will naturally be a greater number of "fit" persons in the large population than in the small. This we can grant. But, then he also states that there will be a greater *probability* "of a fit choice" in the large than in the small. We note here that he has jumped from "greater number" to "greater probability." Because there is a greater *number* of "fit candidates" in the large body, he concludes that there is a greater *probability* that one will be chosen.

This simply doesn't follow. Apart from considering the choosing process, what he overlooks is the fact that there will not only be a greater number of "fit characters" in the large population, but also a greater number of "unfit characters"!

Therefore, it cannot be logically said that there would be a larger *probability* in the large than in the small that the fit would be chosen rather than the unfit. Stated another way, since the proportion of fit to unfit is the same in large as in small, the likelihood of fit being chosen over unfit is logically the same in the large as in the small.

Furthermore, as will be argued more fully below, since offices in the larger body are more powerful than in the small they will be more likely to attract those who are essentially power-seekers, and who are therefore more likely to resort to manipulative tactics in order to get elected. For this reason alone it seems logical to expect more *moral* fitness among the representatives in the small than in the large.

In short, the linchpin of Madison's whole complex argument falls to the ground, and he has lost one more debate. But this is not just another loss for his debating team. This is a loss for the credibility of the entire U.S. Constitution, for the coup which established it, and for the whole foundation of what might be called the modern conception of top-down "democracy."

If we really want to address the issue of reducing the influence of "factions" and of assuring as best we can the "justice for all" which we seek, then we must address the question which Madison raises in a more fundamental way, such as by addressing the following question:

*At what level — the small town, with perhaps 500 inhabitants; or the average city, with perhaps a hundred times that number (i.e., 50,000); or the state, with perhaps a hundred times the number in the average city (i.e., 5,000,000); or the nation, with perhaps 50 times the number in the average state — are the voters more likely to (1) be motivated to and (2) be able to select those in the population who are most "fit" in the best sense of the word?*

Clearly, voters in today's small towns and small cities are *considerably* more able to select out the socially responsible candidates from the manipulating ones than voters in today's large cities, states, or nation. I say "today's" because it is conceivable that we will someday learn how to develop the kind of "caring community" in our larger political bodies that we now have in some (though not all) small towns and cities. In any case, all other things being equal, it is certainly easier to distinguish between the genuine and the fake in a living situation where one knows candidates in face-to-face relations, where one saw them "growing up," going through school, taking a bit of responsibility here, a bit there (or usually ducking it), failing and recovering (or not), admitting mistakes (or not), making good on failed promises (or not), and generally being a responsible member of a "caring community" (or *not*).

In short, we must conclude that voters in small towns will, and **do** (though with exceptions), select out the *truly* "fit" from the unfit with much more accuracy than voters in large cities, states, and nations. And the basic reason seems to be that we haven't learned yet how to build genuine "caring community" in populations beyond the small town and small city level. Nor had they learned to do so in Madison's day, when primitive communication and transportation facilities made it very difficult for any but the rich slave plantation owners, bankers, large traders, real estate speculators, and professional politicians to know very much about anything beyond one's immediate region or town except by hearsay and occasional travelling speakers.

As for whether voters in the large political unit or the small will be more "motivated" to *select* the socially responsible candidate, again both my reasoning and my substantial personal experience give me the same answer: voters in the small towns are *much more* motivated to do a responsible job of voting than in large cities, states, and nations. But, again, the difference doesn't consist only in difference in size, but also as difference in the *quality of community life*.

When people relate to each other in a truly caring way they *think and act* in terms of "social responsibility." They do so partly because they see from personal experience that when people relate to each other in a caring way, everyone experiences "a win-win situation." In such a true community, most people think in terms of which candidate would do the most responsible job in building and maintaining that *quality* of life that I have called "caring community." It's a quality of life which is difficult to describe in expository writing. It is easier to describe in poetry or in the form of a novel. In this day of television dominance, I am reminded of the TV series called "The Waltons." The play, "Our Town," by Thornton Wilder also captures some of it. Most readers will have had a sufficient amount of either direct or vicarious experience of "caring community" to know what I mean. It is a quality of life which emerges in time of tragedy. As this is being written we are seeing it emerging in the various efforts to bring relief to the victims of a devastating hurricane.

Caring community is a quality of life which we all recognize when we see it, but which is very difficult to bring about today (except in an occasional small town) because of the hectic *pace* of life in the super-technological civilization which presently dominates life on this earth and which is so desperately in need of "healing."

Yet Madison seems to take an almost exactly opposite position, as follows:

> In the next place, as each representative will be chosen by a greater number of citizens in the large than in the small republic, it will be more difficult for un-worthy candidates to practice with success the vicious arts by which elections are too often carried; and the suffrages of the people being more <u>free</u>, will be more likely to center in men who possess the most attractive merit and most

diffusive and established characters [emphasis added because below we will note that the <u>sense</u> in which he uses the term "free" is crucial].[11]

What Madison seems to be saying here is that in a national election it will be more difficult for candidates to deceive the electorate than in a local election. His reasoning is based on the assumption that as part of a large amorphous mass "the suffrages of the people" will be "more free." It is not completely clear in the above quotation in what sense he means "more free," nor what they will be more free *from*. But in the following quotation it becomes clear that what he feels they would be more free from is a faction which would constitute a majority.

> The smaller the society, the fewer probably will be the distinct parties and interests composing it [point #1]; the fewer the distinct parties and interests, the more frequently will a majority be found of the same party [point #2]; and the smaller the number of individuals composing a majority, and the smaller the compass within which they are placed, the more easily will they concert and execute their plans of oppression [point #3]. Extend the sphere, and you take in a greater variety of parties and interests [point #4]; you make it less probable that a majority of the whole will have a common motive to invade the rights of other citizens [point #5]; or if such a common motive exists, it will be more difficult for all who feel it to discover their own strength, and to act in unison with each other [point #6]. Besides other impediments, it may be remarked that, where there is a consciousness of unjust or dishonorable purposes, communication is always checked by distrust in proportion to the number whose concurrence is necessary [point #7].[12]

Taking Madison's "points" in turn, points #1 and #2 may or may not be so, depending on the extent to which people in a region have been "brainwashed." For instance, I would guess that there is a greater variety of *political* opinion in a small college town like Yellow Springs, Ohio (when I lived there, a town of less than 5,000 people), than in most totalitarian countries, whether of "left" or "right," or even, perhaps, than in most big cities in the United States, considering the extent to which the mass media generates mass mentalities.

---

11. *Ibid.*
12. *Ibid.*

And this reminds us that the degree of variety in thoughts and interests among a people depends largely on the extent to which they **are** influenced by the mass media. And people in large cities tend to be much more influenced than those in small towns, because residents of the former generally don't have the degree of *community life* experienced by the latter, whose daily life tends to be much richer in terms of meaningful human relations, and thus much more stimulating of a variety of ideas, than in a mass society.

A related factor is the tendency for majority-takes-all politics in a mass society to favor those candidates who can devise a "platform" which appeals to the self-serving interests (as against justice-serving interests) of those most likely to vote, and then to use those mass-psychology techniques which appeal to self-serving motivations. Such techniques are likely to be resented in a "caring community" where people are more committed to justice (in the sense of neighborliness), and where they have seen how destructive the simplistic self-serving motives can be of what is most worthwhile in life.

It is true that there are enclaves of feverish intellectual activity in most large cities, but the overwhelming majority of citizens are media-manipulated into a *political* majority by the advertisements and political maneuvers of corporate interests, including by professional politicians (called by Madison "factious leaders") who do the bidding of those who finance their campaigns and swell their personal bank accounts.

As for Madison's points #3 to #6, it is true that like-minded people communicate more easily in a republic of small, as against large, geographical area. But we need not assume, as Madison does, that such uniting is always for the purposes of "oppression." In fact, as noted above, in a small town people are less likely to *want* to act irresponsibly toward their neighbors, whereas in mass impersonal societies the mass manipulators are the ones who are most likely to "concert and execute their plans of oppression," and to have all the techniques of modern technology and manipulation at their disposal for doing so. Even in Madison's day, without even a telephone, and with horse-drawn travel the fastest means, Hamilton, Madison, Washington, and a few others (like Sherman, who argued at the Constitutional Convention against a Bill of Rights) managed to "concert and execute their plans of oppression" in what may have been the most ingenious coup ever implemented.

Turning to Madison's point #7, I confess that I am not clear enough on his meaning here to comment intelligently. But **if** he was saying that the "concurrence" necessary to muster an oppressive majority is difficult to achieve "in proportion to the number whose concurrence is necessary" then I would suggest that getting a majority doesn't depend on getting a certain *number* of votes, only on getting a certain *percentage*. Again, how much "distrust" or questioning of authority there is in a society (or needs to be in order to check oppression) depends crucially on how much genuine "caring community" exists; and how *effective* any such distrust is in checking oppression depends on the extent to which people in the population are free of mass manipulation.

As a general comment, Madison betrays his ignorance of what it is like to live in genuine caring community. He and Hamilton operated on the assumption that everyone is out for personal gain and in almost bitter competition with everyone else. Thus, in their way of thinking, the only basis for joining together is in order to form a faction to compete with other factions. Thus, they were apparently completely ignorant of the social phenomenon of a community of people joining together for a life together of mutual caring for each other and of genuine social responsibility toward those outside their own group or community. Because they thought in these competitive terms, they twisted their reasoning in such a way as to present *their* aggressiveness in forming a powerful centralized government as the solution to the self-centered aggressiveness of others. In fact, Hamilton and his fellow power-seekers were by far the greatest menace extant at the time they were ostensibly warning people about others.

Thus, because Madison and his co-manipulators discounted the value of small caring communities, they likely had no regrets about the fact that these were excluded from both participation and consideration in the formation of the new constitution even though their residents would likely be most impacted by it. I say this because persons in outlying areas, as noted earlier, were largely free from the impositions of governments of any kind until the drive for big-time national sovereignty extended its conscripting arm to claim them as a kind of political "property." Thus, when Madison spoke of the Government's main task being the protection of individual and governmental property, he may not have realized that, in effect, if not in conscious intention, the new Constitution was extending such governmental "property" to include each and every "INDIVIDUAL" living within the claimed territory of the territorial state by means of which they were hoping to achieve a greater status of sovereignty in the world.

So, today we need not wonder at some of the bitter fruits which have resulted from the seeds planted by the slave plantation owners, the land speculators, the international merchants, and the investment bankers and their clients who pushed through that centralizing document two centuries ago. The political manipulators we see today are simply the more sophisticated and ominous inheritors of the political machinery which lends itself to such manipulation, and which was designed to so lend itself by the political manipulators of an earlier day.

## XII-7: *A Summary Analysis of Madison's Argument*

Madison summarizes his conclusions as follows at the end of Federalist Paper #10:

> Hence it clearly appears, that the same advantage which a republic has over a democracy[13] in controlling the effects of a faction, is enjoyed by a large over a small republic, [and] is enjoyed by the Union over the States composing it. Does the advantage consist in the substitution of representatives whose enlightened views and virtuous[14] sentiments render them superior to local prejudices and to schemes of injustice? It will not be denied that the representation of the Union will be most likely to possess these requisite endowments. Does it consist in the greater security afforded by a greater variety of parties, against the event of any one party being able to outnumber and oppress the rest? In an equal degree does the increased variety of parties comprised within the Union increase this security. Does it, in fine, consist in the greater obstacles opposed to the concert and accomplishment of the secret wishes of an unjust and interested majority? Here, again, the extent of the Union gives it the most palpable advantage.

---

13. The distinction being, we recall, that, in the former, decisions are made by elected representatives, whereas, in the latter, citizens participate directly in "Town Meeting" style.

14. Madison has not spoken to the issue of how to assure virtue in representatives!

The influence of factious leaders may kindle a flame within their particular States, but will be unable to spread a general conflagration through the other States. A religious sect may degenerate into a political faction in a part of the Confederacy; but the variety of sects dispersed over the entire face of it must secure the national councils against any danger from that source. A rage for paper money, *for an abolition of debts, for an equal division of property*, or for any other improper or wicked project,[15] will be less apt to pervade the whole body of the Union than a particular member of it; in the same proportion as such a malady is more likely to taint a particular county or district, than an entire State.

In the extent and proper structure of the Union, therefore, we behold a republican remedy for the diseases most incident to republican government. And according to the degree of pleasure and pride we feel in being republicans, ought to be our zeal in cherishing the spirit and supporting the character of the Federalists. [signed always with a pseudonym] PUBLIUS

First, he is saying "it will not be denied" that control over factions can more easily be achieved at the national level than at the state level. The first reason he gives (point #1) is that the representatives at the national level are "most likely to possess "enlightened views and virtuous sentiments" which "render them superior to local prejudices and to schemes of injustice" I have already commented on this outrageous claim. I would claim just the opposite, and believe that much evidence could be mounted to refute his position. But it is clear that he claims it in order to presume support for the top-down form of government which he ultimately succeeded in getting established in these United States.

In point #2, he is claiming that the increased variety of parties at the national as against the state level makes it less likely that a majority faction will form at the national than at the state level. First, in the issue of generating power that will have a tendency to corrupt, that is more likely to take place at the mass-society atmosphere of national politics. What happens at that level is not so much that a majority faction forms among people who know each other and have the same views. Rather, a small

---

15. Emphasis added to call attention to the kinds of things Madison considered "wicked," the very things which some of those in Shays Rebellion were seeking as partial remedy for the harm done to them (they who had done the fighting in the war) by the power-seekers.

clique of political manipulators who — having access to money from large power brokers in corporate America — artificially seduce people into such majority factions.

And this is essentially what the Hamilton-Madison-Washington faction did in their time. In a local community, however, any "faction" sufficiently large to form a majority is more likely to represent a kind of community conscience guided by a community sense of justice. When people live close enough together to have to relate to each other day in and day out they show their true colors, and the manipulators are rapidly shown up for what they are.

I regret to observe, however, that both state and local politics have become increasingly corrupted over the past two centuries by national politics. In a top-down government, any corruption at the top tends to spread all the way to the very local. I have felt this in living in a small community. The manipulators at the national level seek out those at the state level who can "be bought," and so they are supported in state politics. The same thing happens down the line, all the way to the local level. Now we see that the seeds for this corrupting process were laid when the top-down form of republicanism was established in the form of the U.S. Constitution two long centuries ago.

Points #3 through #8 are all proceeding on the premise that all corruption comes from below, by way of local factions. What Madison is saying is that the great variety of these at the state and local levels will tend to cancel each other out at the national level, and thus be "controlled." Again, his thesis hangs on the assertion that corruption is more likely at the local than the national level. Thus, his argument for a strong national government, organized at the top, and applying moral discipline to factions as they develop, supposedly from the bottom.

The truth is that many of the local factions which Madison wanted to cancel each other out were, in his day, legitimate protests against the mini-corporate America forming at that time. That's a major reason the Madison-Hamilton combination wanted to set up a strong national power structure for keeping them in line, once and for all. These two young men were very savvy politically. They knew that would provide them with a far more effective and lasting method of dealing with dissenters — especially if they could keep a Bill of Rights out of the Constitution — than by trying to put down individual rebellions here and there and now and then, especially since they seemed to be mounting.

The result was what we see today — power brokers at the top dishing out power to the other levels to the extent that they will "play the game." By now the corruption has penetrated so deeply into our social fabric that it will take a major cultural, social, economic, and political metamorphosis to bring us back to where America was when the original coup took place. I am not suggesting a revolution as a means of accomplishing this, nor another constitutional convention. What I will be suggesting, with more detail in Chapter XIII, is a gradual taking back of the Early American Dream that was beginning to take form under the Articles of Confederation. But, more of this later.

As a summary comment on Madison's argument, I would suggest that the advantages he cites for political awareness and consideration beyond the local and provincial can best be achieved by a *federation* of caring communities rather than by a top-down national government which distrusts the local input and seeks to circumvent it.

When I first read Federalist Paper #10 it seemed to me incredible that Madison, whom I had always thought of as an intelligent and basically well-meaning person, should set forth arguments so insensitive to the values of genuine community life, and so obviously faulty in other respects. But, when we remember his aristocratic background we realize, as suggested above, that he probably never himself experienced genuine caring community. Certainly he couldn't have had it with his slaves; and I doubt if elitist slave owners could have genuine caring community with each other. In general, his way of life, and that of all those at that clandestine and secretive Constitutional Convention, must have been radically different from the lives of persons in the backwoods New England's small towns.

In any case, at this stage of his life, a young 36 years of age, before he distanced himself from the "Federalist" agenda, this much seems clear from both his and Hamilton's contributions to the Federalist Papers: that, however well-meaning Madison's motives may have been in relation to his values and cultural orientation, he was arguing for a constitution which did in fact serve the power-seekers' goal of *sovereignty* and their mass manipulation methods in achieving not only that goal but also their goals of political power and economic prosperity for themselves and their kind. And we still have that constitution with us today as a major obstacle to a truly humane and equitable society.

In contrast to Madison's conclusions, therefore, in the next chapter I suggest that the foundation for assuring "justice for all" must be mini-societies which *are* based on caring community, and therefore on a high degree of personal integrity, and which are joined together in a truly *voluntary* federation. Such caring communities must include *persons* who know each other well enough to judge true integrity from manipulative insincerity, because people give constant feed-back to each other regarding vital social issues. It is such communities that must form the foundation for a truly federated national government, and ultimately for a truly just world government, one which makes claims to power over member states or individuals *only* to the extent that it is used to truly administer justice for all.

Again, the most basic reason the U.S. Constitution just isn't good enough is because it was designed primarily to promote sovereignty and only incidentally to promote justice, and that any efforts on behalf of the latter were therefore largely undermined by those in behalf of the former.

It's even more disconcerting
to realize
that the constitution
which emerged from the 1787 coup
is going to be a problem for us
for a long time to come,
because
as long as it is in effect in its present form
it will be very difficult
to maintain corporate America
within the moral bounds of justice for all.

# Chapter XIII

# How to Assure Justice for All Local to Global

## XIII-1: *Common Sense for Our Day*

Two centuries and two decades ago, on January 10, 1776, one Thomas Paine, having arrived in America from England just 10 months earlier, electrified the inhabitants of his new-found country with a pamphlet called *Common Sense*. It called on Britain's American colonies to declare independence from the British crown. And it succeeded dramatically. It brought together in one articulate and inspiring document all the arguments which had been festering. It placed them in a larger perspective, one which made a crucial distinction between government and society as a whole. As Paine's biographer put it, its effect "has never been paralleled in literary history." Within six months Jefferson had written *The Declaration of Independence* and gotten it accepted by a new and still fragile revolutionary government. Paine opened his pamphlet with the following statement:

> Some writers have so confounded society with government as to leave little or no distinction between them; whereas they are not only different, but have different origins. Society is produced by our wants, and government by our

wickedness; the former promotes our happiness *positively* by uniting our affections, the latter *negatively* by restraining our vices.[1]

And that's about right. Farther on in this chapter we will see that when we identify government with society the head of government tends to become a parental figure, to whom is then granted power over our lives far in excess of what is wholesome or appropriate — we dare never forget that "power tends to corrupt." Paine then goes on to persuade the residents of the American colonies at the time that this was what had happened to the British government, which he had experienced first-hand for the first 38 years of his life.

Paine's *Common Sense* is not a flawless document, nor is The Declaration of Independence which it inspired. But they both implied that government is only justified to the extent that it promotes justice-for-all, whereas the U.S. Constitution, which followed just over a decade later was designed, as we have seen, to promote power-seeking. and power seekers. Therefore, what we face today, and not only in America but worldwide, is a situation comparable to that of Thomas Paine's day. We face governmental structures from which human *societies* all over the world are hereby called upon to seek their rightful independence, in the sense of limiting them to their appropriate, limited role of "preventing and remedying injustice."

Let it be clear, however, that this is not a call for the violent overthrow of any existing government. This is a call for what I call "radical evolution" as against disruptive revolution. If Thomas Paine and his fellow patriots had considered more carefully the *means* by which their admittedly worthy goals might be achieved they might not have given the American power seekers the foothold they needed to bring America right back into the sovereignty-seeking mold from which its residents had so recently escaped. The Philadelphia Quakers immediately took issue with their fellow Quaker from oversees. They rejected Paine's implicit call for military resistance to the British crown. Unfortunately for the future of America and the world, the Philadelphia Quakers were vulnerable to Paine's counter-attack, for they didn't reject the British military adventures and misadventures with the same logic or forthrightness. Indeed, they reaffirmed their loyalty in the following unfortunate way:

---

1. *Writings of Thomas Paine*, page 69, edited by Moncure Daniel Conway. pub. by AMS Press. Inc., NY 1967

May we therefore firmly unite in abhorrence of all such Writings [referring to Paine's *Common Sense*] and measures, as evidence and design to break off the happy connection we have heretofore enjoyed with the Kingdom of Great Britain, and our just and necessary subordination to the king, and those who are lawfully placed in authority under him. . . .

As I wrote in an earlier volume,[2] "In defense of the Quakers, they were at the time living under a charter (for the entire state of Pennsylvania) which was secured by William Penn during the previous century from the then British king, and which had resulted in the most liberal of any of the state constitutions for almost a century. . . . Also, they feared that a break with Britain would mean an end to their beautiful constitution and a 'mob rule' government in its place." History has proven them partly right, perhaps. In any case, I still feel as I wrote then:

> Rebel Quaker Tom Paine and the more conservative Philadelphia Quakers had, I believe, the possibility of coming up with a position which both reconciled and transcended their two positions.

If they had meditated together, and thereby sought out in each other "that of God" in traditional Quaker fashion, they might have emerged with a way to bring about a relatively nonviolent transition to a far better kind of independence. A less violent struggle might left them much more able to resist any power-seeker's coup, such as actually took place about a decade later. Perhaps this would have been too much to ask. But Canadians were able over the years to bring about Canadian independence for all practical purposes, while still giving only token acknowledgement of their roots. And, under Gandhi's leadership, a considerably less violent revolution has brought about Indian independence.

What I am suggesting here is that we still face in our day the challenge to bring about governments which truly do assure "justice for all," and to do so in ways which are themselves just. Fortunately, we now have the advantage of not only historical perspective, but of considerable experience with how to bring about change nonviolently in the modern world.[3] The

---

2. *Liberating the Early American Dream*, pps 132-133
3. Gene Sharp has recorded the history of the successes of nonviolent struggle in several of his books, beginning with his *The Politics of Nonviolent Action*, pub. by Porter Sargent Publisher, 11 Beacon St., Boston, 1973. See also, *The Power of the People*, an impressive and thoroughly authentic pictorial history of nonvio-

prolonged civil rights movement has provided much of the needed experience. And this has been made possible largely because of that saving-grace part of the U.S. Constitution, the Bill of Rights. Thus, even though we have seen that the Constitution has basic moral flaws, a widespread commitment to the Bill of Rights, so specifically designed to protect us from the misuse of governmental power, truly is our saving grace (See VI-3). It provides for the kind of criticism here being presented. It provides protection for those being critical. And it provides protection for proposing alternative governmental structures, and for those doing the proposing.

The various struggles for justice-for-all in the United States during this century, largely inspired by Mahatma Gandhi's example in India, have mostly focused on *resistance* to isolated injustices. They have not generally focused on alternative governmental *structure* as such. The exception has been the extent to which there has been participation by communists and communist sympathizers. Now that the communist ideology of state ownership of means of production has been largely discredited, and rightly so, that influence is no longer of any practical consequence. What is still lacking, however, is a vision of the essential ingredients of a truly justice-assuring political structure. In this regard, there has, up to now, been no serious challenge to the Western-type political structure notably exemplified by the U.S. Constitution.

This volume, however, does constitute such a challenge. The two previous chapters have given the argument for the moral inadequacies inherent in that historic document. This chapter now offers the broad outlines of an alternative structure, while envisioning its gradual implementation over the next few years or decades. But it also anticipates substantial help from those features of the U.S. Constitution which **do** have moral merit; notably the Bill of Rights, and especially from those Americans who are committed to join with others in following their individual and consensual senses of justice in the difficult times ahead.

Karl Marx was correct in pointing to the injustices implicit in the near-monopoly ownership of means of production that existed in his time, and which continues today in the United States in the form of corporate America. His proposed solution, that all but the most trivial means of production be owned collectively, and operated collectively, was bound to lead to some

---

lent struggle in the United States during recent decades; edited by Robert Cooney and Helen Michalowski, pub. by New Society Publishers, Philadelphia, 1987

form of totalitarianism. What I am suggesting, on the other hand, as noted throughout this volume, is that the near-monopoly ownership of means of production be remedied in quite another way.

Let us acknowledge that all persons and groups have a right to "private" ownership of, and income from, that capital which they generate, produce, innovate, etc. over and beyond, and quite distinct from, that common-heritage capital which is our generation's gift from Nature's God and from previous generations. Let us, then, as has been suggested, hold our common-heritage capital in Trust. Let us arrange to lease it out to anyone who will pay the market price for it — *though only for environmentally and socially responsible uses.* And let us limit the role of government to assuring "justice-for-all," notably in those other areas of our lives which do, or might, impact on others unjustly if not monitored and governed.

We need the coercive power of government in order to keep that natural and legitimate drive for initiative, for private enterprise, and for power generally well within what I have called "the moral bounds of justice for all." But the coercive power of government must be restricted to this limited, though essential, role.

## XIII-2: *Let Our Senses of Justice Be Our Guides*

In what follows I will suggest in broad outline a vision of such a governmental structure, and how governments thus structured might be truly federated with each other, from local to global. In doing so, I propose to consult my personal sense of justice every step of the way. And I invite you, my reader, to check everything here set forth with your own sense of justice. The only way we have, after all, to know whether an action, a principle, a political structure, a law, or a government promotes justice or not is by consulting these ultimate moral judges.

In personal relations, our personal senses of justice are often sufficient unto themselves. Daily, even hourly, they are called upon to answer questions like the following: What should I offer to pay the person who stopped to help me replace my flat tire? What tip should I leave for the waitress? Should I reprimand my son for coming home late for dinner? Should I tell my hostess that I can't stomach the dish set before me, or should I eat it and chance getting sick later?

However, government officials to whom we grant near-monopoly coercive power, and who must be able to deal with justice-injustice issues which extend their tentacles far beyond the personal, must be able to draw on much more sophisticated spiritual resources. These must include the senses of justice of others in addition to their own. Here is a suggested list of the most important qualifications to be met by candidates for governmental positions in any political structure designed to assure justice for all:

*Candidates Qualification #1:* First, we want to have assurance of their deep and sincere commitment to be true to their personal senses of justice in making governmental decisions. The stronger that commitment, the less likely they are to let decisions be influenced by self-interest, intimidation, seduction, bullying, manipulation, attempts to confuse, paranoid tendencies, or partiality of one kind or another.

*Candidates Qualification #2:* Second, we would want assurance that their senses of justice have successfully dealt with a great variety of justice issues of the kind they would be called upon to confront in their governing roles.

*Candidates Qualification #3:* Third, we want assurance that their senses of justice take into account *facts and beliefs* which are relevant to justice for all. Our senses of justice, as with intelligence generally, can only function in relation to information fed to us. Sound information and realistic beliefs are essential input for truly just decisions.

*Candidates Qualification #4:* Fourth, we want to be assured that the senses of justice they draw on are being guided by *principles* of justice and other "considerations" which have been checked out by mature senses of justice, in both the past and the present. To some extent, the Bill of Rights serves this function within the U.S. Constitution. Utilizing principles of justice which have stood the test of time is absolutely essential in achieving justice *for all* in the face of complex social dilemmas.

I am not suggesting that there are any principles of justice which will substitute for on-the-spot *sense* of justice. What I am suggesting is that those which have stood the test of time can serve as important moral reminders and guides. Each has its special area of relevance. Each has its limitations. In each concrete situation justice is achieved by noting the relevance and limitations of each, and then giving the appropriate weight to each — along with other on-the-spot "considerations" — in an overall, reconciling "just-mix." And only morally mature, sensitized, and alert senses of justice can perform this reconciling function.

For instance, a principle of justice which has widespread approval, and which most senses of justice would affirm, is that against lying. It may be severely found wanting, however, when a member of a Salvadoran death squad calls at your door inquiring about a person to whom you have given shelter. But it serves us well in all but the most unusual circumstances.

A still more sweeping moral principle is The Golden Rule, in either its positive or negative form. Again, there are many situations, especially where many persons are involved, where it is too crude. But it reminds us of justice "considerations" which we might otherwise overlook. For instance, recalling the scenarios mentioned above, it might alert one's sense of justice to ask: "How would I feel if I were in my son's situation, or that of the waitress, or of the person who helped with my flat tire?" But when faced with our most difficult justice decisions, no already established rule will alone suffice. Relevant also are not only other principles of justice but more specific, personal "considerations."

For instance, in many situations, some of the more common considerations are the following: who has been unjustly discriminated against, what has been agreed to, who has honored and who has defaulted on an agreement, what past injustices deserve remedy, what will serve the common good, what will assure "peace and tranquillity," or what will assure least restriction on freedom. These are the kinds of on-the-spot considerations, along with relevant principles of justice, which must be weighted against each other to achieve a kind of "just-mix" which, at its best, constitutes what I call "overall, objective justice."

What follows is a list of those Principles of Justice which I would especially want to be given substantial "weight" in such a just-mix.

*Principle of Justice #1: The power given governments must be limited to that necessary to prevent and remedy injustice.*

Because coercion is a major source of injustice, there must be *limitations* placed on the coercive measures which governments are empowered to employ. As has been noted, even when governments' uses of coercion are specifically designed to prevent or remedy injustice, there is the danger that such use will generate more injustice than it prevents or remedies.

For this reason we dare not give them power to perform any coercive measures beyond this limited role. We must not empower them, for instance, to operate educational institutions beyond that needed to inform people about the circumstances under which specific coercive measures will be used. They must not be given power to institute what are called "transfer payments" except as these are a part of remedy for past injustices, *such as in lieu of people's getting a fair share of the financial and other benefits from our common heritage.* Until such benefits are obtained, existing (and even added) transfer payments are likely justified.

A special case of this *Principle* regards using governmental coercive powers to collect taxes to meet the cost of governing. As noted in the Preface, my sense of justice declares that governments are justified in forcing people to pay for governing only to the extent that they behave in ways that require governing (See P-5, VII-4, IX-24).

This limited and precisely defined role for governments is in sharp contrast to the present-day image of government as a kind of father figure. The image of the father as head of the family (itself finally being questioned) got historically transformed into that of the chief, a sort of father of the tribe; and then of the king as the father of the nation. In a republic, the president tends to be called upon to fill this role. That is a major mistake.

Whereas the role of government, as an institution with near-monopoly coercive power, must be limited to preventing and remedying injustice, that of a parent goes far beyond this. The parent has played a decisive role in bringing a child into this world, or in adopting it. And therewith go incalculable responsibilities and rights. Neither the government as a whole, nor its executive head, has such broad responsibilities.

This is not to say that there isn't a need for persons other than biological parents to assume parental-like responsibilities. Indeed there is. But such persons must be able to have much more intimate relations with their adopted extended-family members than the head of a governing body can possibly have. Indeed, in today's break-up of biological families there is a crying need for extended families, in which parental-like responsibilities are shared among several persons, many of whom serve as parents to each other. The communes of the sixties and seventies, and the far more mature and highly promising "intentional communities" of today, have been sociological and spiritual developments designed to meet a hunger which traditional families have increasingly neglected and left unmet. Indeed, the more socially responsible of today's intentional communities may be either the catalysts or the seeds of the kind of caring communities which will gradually federate, locally to globally, into forming the truly just and wholesome world order for which there is such a crying need today.

*Principle of Justice #2: Each person born into this earthly life has a natural right to a fair share of the financial and other benefits of our common heritage.* The basis for this provision has been stated several times in the previous pages, including in the Preface (See P-4).

**Principle of Justice #3:** Any departure from treating each person on this earth as *equal* in rights must be justified by reference to one or more previously approved principles of justice or justice considerations.

**Principle of Justice #4:** Any departure from forcing a person to live up to any *agreement or contract* freely entered into must be justified with reference to one or more previously approved principles of justice or justice considerations.

*Principle of Justice #5: Most important of all, in determining what is truly just in a given situation, the senses of justice of governmental officials must give appropriate moral weight (1) to previously approved principles of justice, especially those listed above, and (2) to those justice "considerations" unique to the situation at hand.*

# XIII-3: *Underscoring the Challenge We Face*

We turn now to a proposed candidate for Principle of Justice which deserves special mention only because of the extent to which it has become incorporated into the U.S. Constitution, and thus into the political structures of the democracies of the world generally. I refer to what is known as *utilitarianism.*

Utilitarianism has been rejected by most moral philosophers of our day as anything other than a moral "consideration," along with many others, such as those mentioned above. But it is still widely employed in political decision-making far beyond its moral merit. In my opinion, we cannot fully understand today's civilization crisis apart from understanding the inordinate influence that utilitarianism has had on modern life.

Roughly put, but not unfairly, the founders of utilitarianism proposed that all social, economic, and political decisions be designed to achieve "the greatest good for the greatest number [of persons]." It is important to realize at the start that this is not a proposal for achieving justice. How much weight is given to justice as one of the "goods" to be maximized varies considerably from disciple to disciple. But what is clear is that justice is counted as only one of many "goods." In fact, as we shall see, as incorporated into the U.S. Constitution and other political documents which call for virtually all decisions by majority-vote, justice is neglected almost entirely. That's why social conscience steps in at some point to call for things like a Bill of Rights, a Declaration of Human Rights, social safety nets, welfare programs, and other programs designed to remedy, at least to some extent, the injustices which inevitably result from the strict application of strict, majority-vote utilitarianism.

By "good" is meant something valued by some person — stated less anthropomorphically, something valued by some sentient being. The more something is valued, the more someone will make sacrifices, or exert effort, in order to achieve it, the greater is that "good" *for that person.*

Thus far the principle has a certain amount of merit, though limited, especially if it extends to non-human sentient beings. If no sentient being capable of conscious experience existed anywhere, there couldn't be anything either good or bad. All measures of good and bad must be in terms of conscious experiences of sentient beings. In ancient philosophy, the principle was stated more narrowly as "man is the measure of all things." Advertisers have come to realize this. Rather than put all their emphasis on the product, they emphasize also the pleasure it will bring to our conscious awareness: that sensation, that thrill. And usually the ultimate thrill appealed to, however subtly, is the sexual one. It is also intended that we experience a certain amount of pleasure in anticipation of the promised thrill, just enough to keep us reminded of what we are missing until we avail ourselves of "the real thing." Thus, ads are designed to instill in us desires, desires which will make us restless until we have satisfied them.

But advertisers are only taking advantage of a natural tendency in all of us. Many kinds of desires were there "naturally" long before Madison Avenue advertisers came along. In fact, desires are what give us our basic information about what experiences are promised to be "good" once they are achieved. Thus, again, it is "natural" that we humans are driven by desires of various kinds.

However, there are major problems with basing one's judgment of good and bad on desires as such. For one thing, the satisfaction one is expecting from fulfillment may not take place. For another, it may be accompanied by unexpected side-effects which are devastating to oneself and others. One may have a strong desire to see a certain film, but be greatly disappointed upon seeing it. One may have a strong desire to have a love affair with a particular person and not only be disappointed with the results but bring ruin upon one's own family relationship, lose the respect of friends, find oneself out of a job, and lose self-respect in the bargain. As this is being written, teenage pregnancies are greatly complicating the lives of countless young people and their families because the desires which were satisfied didn't carry with them the full information about consequences.

*In short, desires usually do not tell the whole story about what is in store at their fulfillment — not only for oneself but for others impacted by one's decisions. Therefore, they are not a reliable indicator of the total picture of what "good," if any, will actually be realized.*

Utilitarians are generally too sophisticated to count on either natural or instilled desires as measures of goods which will actually be realized. Nor are their "goods" limited to the more crass and "sexy" kind. Included are aesthetic and intellectual satisfactions; perhaps even moral satisfactions. To devoted utilitarians, a good is a good, no matter what kind. But, in estimating that "greatest good to the greatest number" they do face several problems.

There is the problem of giving weight to the various kinds of good. In considering various options, such weights must be given in order to deter-mine which option yields the greatest total. There is also the problem of weighing, and then subtracting, those unexpected and side-effect negatives. These, also, must be evaluated in order to give a reliable judgment.

But, by far the most serious problem with utilitarianism is that which it poses for our senses of justice when it fails to consider the justice or in-justice of the way the goods and their negatives are distributed among those impacted. By strict utilitarian principles, it might be argued that a rape was justified if the pleasure of the rapist was greater than, and thus canceled out, the pain of his victim.

Even if everyone benefitted equally from the goods and the negatives (which, of course, they seldom do), justice questions would still remain. Those who have been victimized in the past are normally due a larger share of goods as compensation for past injustices, while their oppressors are due a larger share of the negatives. In such a case, equality in distributing each would not be justice.

The next assumption made by most utilitarians — and clearly by pol-itical democracy — is that what one person counts as "good" must be given the same moral "weight" as that of another. That's how we get the demo-cratic principle of giving one person's vote (i.e., desire, want, etc.) the same "weight" as every other. The result is a simple political formula. Each vote is an indicator of something "good," to be counted equally along with other voted "goods" in determining that telling total called majority vote by the politician and "the greatest good to the greatest number" by the philosophical utilitarian. Since the good represented by one vote is equal to every other good represented by every other vote, deciding among options becomes merely a matter of counting votes.

But, what about the saying that "one person's meat is another's poison"? That is, is it possible that satisfying the desires of a majority might result in terrible suffering for at least some of those who fall outside the majority? For instance, suppose a majority "desires" to keep certain people "in their place"? Suppose a majority "desires" slavery, as was the case in the American South for about two centuries? Suppose a majority in one country wants to invade another?

Again, the missing ingredient in all such calculations is that of justice. Justice is not merely a matter of adding goods going to some people and subtracting the negatives going to others. Justice relates to the manner of *distributing* both goods and negatives. The fact is that no amount of good to one or more persons can justify harm done to others. *Justice requires that in evaluating an option, the goods and negatives balanced against each other must be experienced by the same person.*

The proponents of utilitarianism are constantly seeking ways to meet the objections listed above. But almost none of them are met by the manner in which utilitarian principles are incorporated into the majority-vote political process. Whether these take the form of the U.S. Constitution or some other, it is the most primitive form of utilitarianism that is incorporated.

For instance, in the political process what a vote represents is not some realized, overall good, with unexpected and negative side-effects factored in. Rather, each vote merely represents a desire, a wish, a hoped for outcome. So, it is not only advertisers who appeal to both natural and instilled desires. Politicians become very skilled at both instilling and appealing. Nor is consideration given to what votes might do injustice to others if they were to be implemented. Not at all. Every vote is counted the same as every other, regardless of the positive or negative quality of the desires motivating them. We need not be surprised, therefore, that the majority-vote process results in gross and lasting injustice, especially, as Madison pointed out (his quote in XII-4), when a "faction" constitutes a majority. And such is often the case. For instance, in America, Caucasian whites constitute an overwhelming factional majority in relation to non-whites, as do sexually "straight" persons in relation to homosexuals, as do adults in relation to children, as do homeowners or home renters in relation to homeless persons.

Some argue that "taking turns" (See IX-12) can be an important corrective on "the majority takes all." But this principle also has its limitations. Having Southern blacks and whites "take turns" enslaving each other wouldn't make either enslavement "just." If taking turns is to be a corrective on simplistic, winner-take-all majority vote, then that which each part "takes turns" in doing or experiencing must be a "good" which doesn't inflict injustice on anyone else.

Democracy in practice has not, of course, lived by majority-vote alone. It has usually included social "safety nets" to provide remedy for those victimized by majority vote. Also, democracy in practice has usually included assurance of certain "human rights." One of these is equality under the law. As noted, the Bill of Rights offers a certain amount of protection against some forms of injustice; mainly those which the governments might otherwise inflict. Trial by a jury of one's peers is another supposed corrective, but we have seen that those who can afford the most skillful attorneys have a good chance of escaping any jury.

During colonial times, and in many years after Independence, juries were expected to "nullify" the law when it didn't serve justice. In short, they were to decide what was just overall, with legality being only one consideration among many. Today, juries are increasingly told that they must limit themselves to deciding guilt or innocence as specified by the law; nothing else. There is some justification for this. It's the very unusual jury that is capable of weighing all the relevant "considerations" to produce a just outcome. Many an all-white jury, for instance, refused to convict another white man whom they knew to be guilty.

Thus, today, it is the law, imperfect though it may be, rather than justice, that prevails in most U.S. courts. With heavy court loads, it's a lot simpler that way.

The popularity of utilitarian, majority-vote democracy also stems largely from its simplicity. The simplest way to "solve" any moral issue is to vote on it. No need to struggle with sense of justice or conscience. Just take a vote. Let the majority vote decide everything.

It's simple, yes. But it's no way to determine justice, especially as the issues and dilemmas of modern society become increasingly complex by the day. The tragedy is that the more complex a society becomes, the more justice issues arise, but also the less able a society becomes to determine, let alone bring about, "justice for all." In fact, as we tend to move farther and farther away from it, the more skillful politicians like Newt Gingrich become at working the angles of the Constitution and its majority-vote means of decision-making. One of the major consequences of the political manipulation going on at the present time is the removal of those absolutely essential safety nets, without which majority-vote loses the small amount of moral correctives that have been applied to it over the years. This latest attack on what up to now has been a make-shift system for achieving a modicum of justice in relation to a system designed to favor power-building and power brokers rather than justice is a warning that we dare not depend any longer on such a tokenist approach to a truly just political structure. We dare not postpone any longer assuming the responsibility to envision, and then institute, truly just political structures, local to global. And it is to this challenge that we now turn our full attention.

## XIII-4: *Applying Principles of Justice to Decision-Making*

I do not, therefore, argue that there is no place for majority-vote in a truly just decision-making process. It does have a place, as one of many "considerations" under Principle of Justice #5 noted above. But, when it is used as the sole determiner of what decisions and subsequent actions are to be undertaken, we usually, as we have seen, get one or more forms of injustice.

How, then, are we to employ our senses of justice in determining the appropriate role for simple voting in arriving at what is just? I suggest that we distinguish between two quite different parts of the process of meeting our governing responsibilities.

**First**, there is the part having to do with *selecting* the government officials who are to be empowered to make the decisions regarding how coercive governmental power is to be administered.

**Second** is the part having to do with decision-making among the selected and empowered officials themselves.

Clearly, the ideal way to select the officials to be empowered with governmental coercive power would be by way of a consensus of the senses of justice of all who would be impacted by their decisions. But, this is practically impossible. Even in New England Town Meetings, of both past and present, the norm is decisions by majority vote. Quaker groups have, of course, traditionally arrived at decisions by such a consensus process, though the preferred term is "sense of the meeting." Largely because of contact with Quakers and Quaker groups in human rights movements, many social-change groups have adopted consensus as their method of making decisions. Also, an increasing number of "intentional communities" are making their decisions "by consensus," though what this amounts to in practice varies greatly.[4]

The consensus process is most potent when it includes the provision that any member may "block" a decision which s/he doesn't feel right about. It is expected that s/he will try to explain to the rest as best s/he can the basis for this feeling; and simple preference or self-interest of some kind would not be considered acceptable. So, because of the power to block, a person is advisedly admitted into a consensus decision-making group only after all existing members of the group know that person quite well, and are per-suaded that s/he will not misuse the process, especially the blocking process.

It must be clear, then, largely because of the "blocking" provision, that the consensus decision-making process only "works" to the extent (1) that there is a common commitment among members to substantial (as against trivial) moral values, and (2) that commitment to simple fairness (i.e., to be guided by sense of justice) is included in the commitment they hold in common. The Fellowship for Intentional Communities takes a step in this direction by requiring as a condition for membership a commitment to non-violence and to permitting anyone to leave the member community at any time s/he wishes. This is a deliberate effort, among others, to exclude extremist cults from membership.

In both Quaker and most social-change groups using the consensus pro-cess there is a provision for "standing aside" in cases where a person has reservations about a decision but these are not strong enough to justify "blocking." However, it is important **not** to thus stand aside if a member has

---

4. *The Directory of Intentional Communities* gives information about hundreds of intentional communities from many parts of the world. Its almost 500 pages (8.5" by 11" each) of text and pictures are constantly updated. Pub. by the Fellowship of Intentional Communities; $23 postpaid (as of 1995) from FIC, Rt. #1, Box 151-C, Rutledge, MO, 63563.

serious reservations about the decision at issue. It is especially important that fairness consideration be given to not only group members but to those outside the group who might be impacted by the decision.

Since there isn't anything approaching this quality of common commitment in any general American population, consensus decision-making wouldn't work in any such random body of persons. If America ever becomes organized into intentional communities of sufficient moral quality, and these, in turn, become truly federated "from local to global" we might see an approach to the ideal we seek. Until that day, however, we must look to more immediately practical measures. One such is described below.

Even though it is impractical to use consensus decision-making within the general population, because of little common commitment to the necessary moral values, might it be possible, by some means, to select government officials who themselves shared socially responsible common commitments? If so, then they, presumably, would be able to employ the morally superior consensus process in making their internal, governmental decisions. These, then, would be immeasurably more truly just than those resulting from the present power-brokering methods. We turn, then, to consider more precisely what qualifications we must look for in prospective governmental officials. We then go on to explore how officials meeting such qualifications might be identified and selected.

## XIII-5: *Ideal Qualifications for Government Officials*

Based on the above discussion, truly just governmental decisions are going to be largely dependent on filling governmental positions of power with persons who have the following unusual qualifications:

**Power Qualification #1**: All governmental officials must be committed to following their senses of justice in employing their exceptional power.

**Power Qualification #2:** They must be committed to considering in any decision all relevant justice considerations, such as those listed in XIII-2.

**Power Qualification #3:** They must be of sound mind, be well versed in that knowledge and those facts generally relevant to making justice decisions, remembering that our senses of justice can only make good justice decisions if they have information and understanding which coincides with reality as it must be lived by those over whom they have power.

**Power Qualification #4:** They must be favorably inclined to work with colleagues in a spirit of cooperation and mutual respect and must have substantial skills in this regard.

**Power Qualification #5:** In general, they must have a substantial historical record of having dealt fairly with persons with whom they have associated in the past, and be known in their local communities as exceptionally fair-minded persons in dealing with a great variety of human relations issues.

## XIII-6: *Selecting Qualified Governmental Officials*

Clearly, qualified governmental officials must be selected by persons who would recognize such candidates by virtue of observing them behave toward and relate to others over an extended period of time. They must have been observed in situations which naturally *reveal* the required moral maturity, moral integrity, and commitment to justice for all. It follows from this that they could best be identified and selected by persons sharing with the candidates a neighborhood, community, or region where substantive human relations, including moral dilemmas, had been experienced, confronted, and satisfactorily dealt with by the candidates over an extended period of time. Obviously, this is a requirement which could best be met in selecting officials for local governmental positions. In fact, it would be difficult, if not impossible, to meet these requirements in selecting other-than-local officials by the usual methods of voting. We shall see, however, that there does exist a far better alternative.

We ask next how we could assure that a voter would vote for candidates with the moral qualifications we have identified. Voters could, of course, be *asked* to vote on the basis of such qualifications, but that would give little assurance. The requirement which yields the needed assurance is suggested by recalling the moral force of *commitment*.

I suggest that a basic requirement for voting for government officials should be a *commitment* on the part of each voter to select on the basis of the above-stated qualifications rather than, as tends now to be the case, on the basis of self-interest. I suggest that voters also be required to reaffirm such commitment just prior to entering the voting booth — that is, when voting for candidates with responsibility for "preventing and remedying injustice." They would also be assured that there would be many other opportunities to vote their personal preferences, and even their most egotistical, idiosyncratic self-interests — that is, when voting is among options each one of which has met all the usual justice criteria, and where justice would be still better served by implementing that option which most voters preferred.

But, commitment to vote according to whether candidates meet certain moral standards would not be enough in and of itself. A further requirement would be voter knowledge about these standards and about how the whole political system works. This suggests that an educational program should be offered free of charge to any who would want to participate. It should be one designed to familiarize each voter with the entire governmental structure s/he would be participating in, along with the crucial importance of voting in accordance with the moral standards implicit in it. We dare not call for a testing program, however, remembering how this practice was at one time used to exclude non-whites from voting in the United States.[5]

It would be expected, therefore, that self-interest votes among one or more groups will be called for quite often, but always in the interval between elections for government officials, because they would be called for by government officials as a way of helping them to arrive at overall fairness in their decisions. Self-interest voting would sometimes include the entire population of a region; at other times it would be limited to the elderly, the youth, or some other group which would be especially impacted by the outcome. The only voting requirement in such votes would be evidence of some minimal length of residency. Some residency time would be required, because the precise purpose would be to determine the wants, self-interests, etc. of persons who have shown that they intend to remain in the area.

Votes for the purpose of expressing self-interest might be called for locally, globally, or at any regional level in between, since policies set by administrators at all such levels would, from time to time, require self-interest input from either the entire population or parts of it. Thus, there might be much more voting going on than at present. And electronic devices being constantly perfected would greatly facilitate such self-interest voting with ever-greater ease and ever-reduced cost.

However, again, voting for government administrators is quite another matter. In such voting, the sober commitment requirement for voter eligibility referred to above would continue to apply.

---

5. Who would conduct such an educational program and pass judgment on adequate understanding will be addressed later in this chapter.

Wherever appropriate, voting would be by weighted voting. Every voter should be able to indicate, in order of preference, a number of candidates (perhaps as many as five) for each government position and self-interest preference, each of whom s/he considers acceptable. Each selection of each voter should be weighted in accordance with the priority position in her or his list. In this way, even though a candidate, or a preference, isn't listed first by any voter, s/he (or it) might still be voted into office (or implementation) by getting enough second, third, and fourth preferences. Also, in this way each elected official would have a series of possible alternates who, in order of indicated voter preference, could assume office in case of emergency.

Voters would be free to form political parties, but appeals to self-interests clearly destructive of "justice-for-all" should somehow be discouraged if not restrained. On the other hand, encouragement should be given to offering facts relevant to candidates' qualifications as to fairness, education, experience, etc. as these bear on the likelihood that a candidate would meet the qualifications for a particular administrative position. However, party candidates would receive no special treatment. Presumably, as now, any candidate receiving a specified number of signers on a petition would be listed on the ballot, and write-ins would be permitted. Appeal to the self interests of a voter would not be permitted in voting for administrators, but would be permitted, even encouraged, in voting specifically designed to determine majority self-interest.

Finally, in as many self-interest voting situations as possible, there would be provision for "taking turns." For instance, if a majority voted for having the county fair in July, but quite a few preferred June, it might be held in June every third year. In general, a sober atmosphere should be maintained at the voting places, especially in the case of commitment voting — an atmosphere designed to remind voters of the awesome responsibility associated with the commitment they have made and are reaffirming.

# XIII-7: *Administrative Divisions*

Picture the entire world divided into Regions, Regions into Nations, Nations into States, States into Counties, and Counties into Districts, Districts into local communities or neighborhoods. In many cases, a city would constitute a County in which Districts would be neighborhoods. No doubt, the world will never be divided so neatly, and there might be several more divisions.

But, for our purposes, the above divisions will serve to illustrate basic moral principles and how one likely distribution of semi-autonomous groupings of persons might relate politically.

Picture an above-described County as an area comparable to a county in one of the states in the United States. In my experience, despite the corrupting influences from the "top," government in the United States is best at the local, county level. At that level it is more difficult for clever politicians to fool people. So there are several features of governing at the county level which are worth emulating. For instance, normally, there is no father figure or mother figure. Most are governed by a Board of Supervisors, and they take turns at serving in the role of the chair. This has a wholesome, humbling affect on all Board members, and avoids many evils of major centralization of power in one person. In the following envisioning, this feature will be wholeheartedly emulated.

Also, each supervisor is elected *only* by voters who reside in her or his district, and who therefore have opportunity to know her or him personally over a period of years. We have noted that this is an absolutely essential requirement for our envisioned structure. However, the purpose of having voters and elected officials well known to each other is not primarily so that the latter may better "represent" voters' *interests*, though this can be important in some issues; rather, as noted, so that voters can make an accurate evaluation of the candidate's reliability in the interests of *justice-for-all*, where the "interests" of a constituency is normally only one of countless "considerations" in achieving or maintaining that state of affairs.

For these and other reasons, the easiest level of government at which to begin to change political and economic political structure in the United States will likely be at the existing local or county level.

While noting similarities to present county government in the U.S., we note significant departures. These reflect the above-noted difference between the purpose inherent in our envisioned governments and those presently in existence. For instance, instead of a single Board there will be three: The Board of Overseers, the Policing Board, and the Common Heritage Board.

*The Board of Overseers* would have overall responsibility for assuring justice-for-all in the County. Except for meetings for the purpose of personnel selection or changes, all of its meetings would be open to attendance by qualified voters, but *only* to qualified voters! Its basic responsibility would be to set operational standards for the other Boards, designed to implement the County's political structure. It would conduct research designed to promote justice-for-all in ever more effective ways. Its only power would be in the power of persuasion based on its demonstrated moral maturity and integrity in establishing and constantly updating standards of "good order" required to maintain justice-for-all.

*We have noted several times the importance of pace in such good order. This Board will be mainly responsible for maintaining development of various kinds within a* **pace** *conducive to justice-for-all.*

This Board would have the acknowledged right to inspect all records, to attend all meetings, and to interview all members of either of the other Boards. It would also have the acknowledged right to inspect the activities of any business enterprise in the County. It would perform a much more thorough watchdog role than the most diligent investigative reporter.

It would develop *Procedures* for each Board to follow, and would have sole responsibility for monitoring the other two Boards, *and for constantly updating their findings in reports to the qualified voters.* This would be a very important function. By means of these reports from the Board of Overseers, voters would be constantly informed about what was happening at levels not accessible to the media. It would also have responsibility for *initiating* changes in the commitments required of qualified voters, the various Board members, and of various personnel in the various Boards. In order to fulfill all these responsibilities it would conduct research designed to yield a constant flow of knowledge about how to better achieve justice-for-all.

It would provide courts of justice for the purpose of reaching justice determinations in all justice matters arising in the County. It would not, however, carry out any coercive measures. That task would fall to the Policing Board. It would offer education designed to generate an ever more complete understanding of the political structure upon which the County government is based. This would include the educational program for voters. Thus, it would serve the functions performed in most existing governments by both the legislature and the department of justice, except that it would call on the Policing Board for all coercive measures. Thus, the election to determine members of this Board of Overseers would be the most important of all the elections.

The Board of Overseers would have its income from taxing the other Boards. The amount of the tax would depend on expenses in performing its responsibilities. Each Board would be taxed according to costs of monitoring it and supplying it with oversight. Thus, each of the other Boards would have incentive to perform in ways which would require minimal monitoring.

This would likely be the first Board to come into existence in the transition from the existing government at the local level to the one here being envisioned. It's first function in such transition would be to formulate a written document suggesting commitments for persons to undertake as a basis for our envisioned political structure at the County level. It would be elected by persons who had committed themselves in the manner indicated above.

After formulating a written set of proposed commitments, it would begin monitoring the operations of the existing government, and reporting to committed voters, and somewhat to everyone, comparisons between how the existing government is operating and how a government would operate under the proposed commitment complex. Again, this would require conducting research into how injustices might better be prevented and remedied.

At first, apart from elected Board members, most roles would be filled by volunteers; financing would be by voluntary contributions. The Board would gradually develop stature sufficient to call for elections to name a Common Heritage Board. Electing a Policing Board would likely be a final step in the transition, because of its role in enforcing by means of coercion.

*The Policing Board* would have sole responsibility for *preventing* and remedying various kinds of injustices, and for doing so in accordance with the standards prescribed by the Board of Overseers. In general, its role would be to *enforce* the political structure as set forth and interpreted by the Board of Overseers. More specifically, it would assure, through its enforcement, that all but trivial injustices are prevented, and that appropriate compensation and consolation is given to victims of those injustices which aren't prevented. In general, it would be authorized to use coercive measures within the moral bounds suggested above.

It would conduct tests designed to determine eligibility for various kinds of business licenses, and for operator licenses of various kinds. It would issue licenses to qualified applicants and monitor and police all manner of public behavior and private, licensed behavior in the County *as prescribed by the Board of Overseers*. In this regard it would function very much like police in U.S. counties at the present time. But in a larger sense it would be equivalent to the executive branch of government, though, as indicated above, with a quite different set of responsibilities.

The Policing Board would receive financing from two sources. In its role of preventing injustice it would get income from licensing fees for various kinds of operations. A typical example would be fees for motor vehicle operation in the county. As is presently the case in most U.S. counties, every kind of business would require a business license. The amount of the charge would vary according to costs of testing — such as for driving skills in the case of motor vehicle operation. For instance, an application for practicing medicine or law would require much more testing than one for dressmaking in the home. Counties with heavy industry would have much more elaborate testing programs than those with light industry, and would be charged accordingly.

Testing costs would be charged whether a license was issued or not. The charge for a license after all tests had been passed would depend on administrative expenses in connection with each kind of license, the largest being the cost of policing and incarcerating. In the case of a motor vehicle license, the cost of maintaining traffic police, roads, and traffic regulators generally would have to be covered. Each kind of industry or profession would have special policing requirements. Individuals who were not behaving in any way threatening injustice would be free of any charges, unless s/he had violated a law in the past. In that case, s/he may be required to pay for undergoing tests of some kind, and to contract for some form of "liability insurance."

Thus we are reminded of the second source of income; namely, that from the "remedy" part of the role of the Policing Board. I refer to the income from charging for various kinds of "liability insurance" comparable to that required in motor vehicle operation. In cases where the bulk of the fee is paid to private insurance companies, an additional fee would be paid to the Policing Board to cover administrative costs and to provide back-up for the private insurance companies. The costs of unforeseen costs of compensating victims would also have to be covered by the fees.

Again, liability insurance costs would vary greatly from business to business, profession to profession, and, in the case of prior criminal activity by individuals, person to person.

Individuals posing a threat to justice would be constrained in their activities, even to the point of being incarcerated. A person might be constrained in activities because past behavior showed her or him to be a threat to others in some way. In that case, s/he would be required, if able, to cover the cost of such constraint, either financially or in goods and services, until it is judged that the threat no longer exists. Or, s/he might be constrained solely for the purpose of providing remedy for a perpetrated injustice. Or, s/he might be constrained on both accounts. A person who is incarcerated might be forced to work at producing income in order to compensate someone to whom s/he has done an injustice, or in order to cover the costs of the incarceration if these are not met by other financial means. Normally, those in prison would be encouraged to engage in educational activities designed to encourage commitment to behavior which is at once more socially responsible and less in need of annoying restraints on freedom of movement. In general, as noted several times in previous pages, the cost of governing would be met by persons to the extent that their behavior required governing.

*The Common Heritage Board* would have sole responsibility for (1) identifying the common heritage for a county, (2) holding it in a County Common Heritage Trust, (3) collecting the money from leasing it out for uses which are socially and ecologically responsible, and (4) distributing the income among County residents in keeping with equitable criteria, such as length of residency in the county. It would, however, operate according to standards prescribed by the Board of Overseers. It would call upon the Policing Board to apply any needed coercive measures.

This Board would be financed out of the Common Heritage Fund and be monitored in doing so, as in all other matters, by the Board of Overseers. The largest income to the Fund in most counties would be from leasing land. The leasing charges would, of course, be greatest for urban land, where urban infrastructure and its technological base, both contributed largely by previous generations, would constitute a major part of the lease value. Lease charges for technology generally would be charged by some political body resulting from the federation of a number of Counties, a number of States, or even a number of Nations.

The Overseer Board would also be responsible for distributing to the residents in the county the income from such leasing. In addition to the common-heritage dividend from the county, each resident would receive dividends from each governmental layer. Presumably, most, if not all, of the beyond-county dividends (derived mostly from technology leases) would be collected and paid out by the local Boards. For instance, each local Common Heritage Trust Fund would receive a share of income from patent rights, since all inventions rest on the shoulders of prior technology. And when patent rights ran out for the inventor, the entire amount of all further royalties would be paid to one or more such Funds.

Administrative expenses and expenditures designed to make Our Common Heritage more useful, more income-producing, and more serving of "justice for all" would be borne by the Funds themselves.

Any help anyone might need to deal with personal emergencies, or for some form of "safety net" beyond her or his income from the Common Heritage Right, would have to be covered by insurance policies or be taken care of by voluntary associations (referred to above), caring communities, or friends. Again, to give Board members the power to tax for welfare purposes would give them inappropriate coercive power.

Each Board would hire administrative personnel as needed. But there would be no father figure, or mother figure, in the form of a mayor, governor, or president for either a District or a County. As is common in U.S. counties, the position of chairperson for each Board would rotate rather than be elected. Again, we keep in mind the limited role of each, and of the combination, the latter being to assure that substantial injustices will be prevented or remedied. Thus, none of the Boards will be sponsoring cultural events, athletic events, or anything not specifically for the purpose of preventing or remedying injustice. In addition to the Board of Overseers' educational programs directed toward qualified voters, the other Boards would sponsor educational programs which can be justified in relation to their respective responsibilities — but not beyond that. None will sponsor overall educational programs. These would be sponsored by individual families, groups of families, cultural groups, religious groups, and other non-governmental groups and individuals.

## XIII-8: *Decision-Making Process Within the Various Boards*

We turn next to consider how the various Boards would make their commitment decisions. It wouldn't be appropriate to make them by simple majority vote, because that is not a reliable way to determine what would be "justice for all." We remember that Board members wouldn't be "representing" any "constituents" as such, except in cases of what I have called "preference issues," where justice is served by balancing self-interests.

We need a decision-making process which would give maximum assurance of justice-for-all. In order to meet that high standard we will have to envision a multifaceted process, one in which majority vote is used in some situations and unanimous consensus in others.

Basic to such a multi-faceted process is the role of *commitment*. We remind ourselves of the crucial part played by commitment in establishing voting eligibility and how voters are reminded of this commitment prior to voting. We remember that the various Board members are very aware of their commitments, and that all voters are also very aware of theirs. In short, every Board member is being closely supervised by her or his own conscience, by her or his own sense of personal worth, by fellow Board members, by friends, by fellow members of any caring community s/he may participate in, and by the general public — and especially by members of the Board of Overseers. All these psychological and spiritual forces combine to form a very high level of "assurance" that each and every Board member will seriously consult her or his sense of justice in making commitment decisions, especially those which clearly impact for good or ill on fellow sentient beings.

Nevertheless, they are all human. They all have other *urges* influencing them. Therefore, in order that their joint decisions will give maximum assurance of justice-for-all, unanimity will be required in most situations.

It is important to realize why unanimity assures the highest likelihood that a decision by the Board will be just/fair. It might be argued that since each member is committed to decide in accordance with justice-for-all, they would all presumably vote the same way in any case. But we recall the importance of deliberation, and that checking our senses of justice with one another reveals oversights in each. Thus, if all are required to agree, any initial disagreements will be discussed, reasons given, information sources and opinions checked, and a joint insight gained which would necessarily be wiser and more considered than any one member could muster before such exchange. The same reasoning argues for the requirement of unanimity in the case of an American jury.

There are those whose first impression of this requirement will be that it is unworkable, and that it will make reaching decisions too difficult. But I can testify to its being very workable, especially when backed by the commitments that are a prerequisite. I have had personal experience with decision by unanimity for almost a half century. I lived for ten years in a cooperative community of thirty families in which all decisions were made by unanimity. My experience is that deciding by unanimity what is just/fair is much easier than reaching a unanimous decision in what I call "preference issues," that there is a far greater difference among mature and responsible people regarding *preferences* of one kind or another than about justice issues.

We note the radical difference between the political structure envisioned here and the one commonly employed today under the name of "democracy." Again, as we see below, there is a role for voting in these various Boards, but only within a unanimity context.

I have become persuaded that the workability of unanimity in reaching justice decisions is to be explained by the fact that there is such a thing as *objective* justice, whereas *preferences* and personal interests for which one might seek political "representation" are inherently subjective. Thus, when mature and socially responsible persons have all the relevant information about an issue there tends to be unanimity about what is just and unjust. The fact that the unanimity requirement in the jury system works as well as it does is evidence of this,[6] especially since most juries are composed of people who have made no strong commitment to justice for all. The fact seems to be that one's urge to follow sense of justice emerges with extraordinary and compelling force under certain circumstances. And a strong commitment, in advance, to honor it makes it almost irresistible!

Unanimous decisions which can be reached quickly automatically become one-stage decisions. These would normally be regarding issues with which all are very familiar, and about which no one feels the need for further information.

If any Board member does feel the need for further information, further thought, or further meditation, then decision would be postponed, with a time set for reopening consideration. In the meantime, several Board members might want to introduce variations for consideration. This is done in preparation for a possible vote among several alternatives, *each of which has received unanimous approval.* The reason voting is morally acceptable

---

6. When, however, defendants have the resources to spend millions of dollars on a "dream defense team," then the justice of the outcome is bound to be in doubt. Again we see a manifestation of top-down corruption at work.

among such unanimously-approved options is this: unanimous approval of each has assured that any one of them would be morally acceptable, thus making choice among them a mere *preference* issue. *And in mere preference issues, the option which most people prefer is the most just one — provided there is also provision for "taking turns."*

At first glance it might seem more difficult to get unanimous approval on several options than on just one. But the thing which makes it easier is the prior agreement to vote among the options. That provision introduces the additional ingredient of fairness referred to above; namely, providing a place for favoring that option which most prefer. Fair-minded persons will realize this and will accept it. Without that provision a Board member might feel morally compelled to refuse to accept an option which all other Board members approve, because s/he feels that an option which is also morally acceptable would be preferred by most people. We see, however, that such a hesitancy can be overcome by providing for a preference choice among unanimously approved options. In some cases, if a final decision can be postponed, the agreement might be to place several morally acceptable options before the voters in the general population.

There may be several motives behind a particular Board member's preference for a particular option. The provision for voting among several unanimously approved options leaves open the possibility for each Board member that her or his preferred option will emerge successful. It also gives each Board member an opportunity to persuade the others, or the voters, prior to the final vote. We remember, however, that, in order for a proposal to be accepted as an option to be voted on, it must first be judged to be within the bounds of justice-for-all by each and every member of the Board.

At times a vote might be conducted for information purposes only, with the final decision still to be made by one of the Boards. If the issue is one of primary concern to senior citizens, then they might be the only ones asked to vote. If of primary concern to teenagers, they might be the only voters. And so on. Such voting would be called for when a Board judges that majority preference among either the entire population of voters, or a sub-group, would be an important factor in determining justice-for-all.

I suggest that changes in the required commitments constituting the *political structure* at each level should require a three-step process. First, any proposed change would have to receive unanimous approval from the Board of Overseers. This might require the two-step process described above, of first developing unanimously approved options and then selecting among them by weighted voting. Next, the successful option emerging from weighted voting among the Overseers would require majority-vote approval from the *qualified* voters. And, finally, if approved by the voters, it would require a second unanimous approval by the Board of Overseers. Any change in the required political structure would have to take place over a period of time, so as to permit time for serious discussion and deliberation.

I emphasize again those certain absolutes from which we dare not permit governments to depart. These would include permitting some persons to remain as non-participants in the governing process, henceforth to be called "Independents." This would not be difficult for our envisioned governing body to permit, since Independents would have to meet almost all the requirements voters would have to meet. However, they wouldn't have access to certain information, such as that compiled by the Board of Overseers. There might be other restrictions regarding access to governmental facilities and meetings.

## XIII-9: *Moving from Local to Global*

The Board of Overseers at the County level would organize regular meetings of all three Boards, for the purpose of feed-back and general sharing. It would also join with Boards of Overseers in other Counties in organizing meetings of Boards statewide. The purpose would be multiple. One purpose, again, would be to share experiences and information.

*But, a more important purpose would be to get familiar with one another as **persons**, and with her or his qualifications (including, especially, depth of commitment to justice-for-all). In this way it is hoped that the body of County Board members across the State would form a kind of "community" of persons with a shared commitment to implementing justice for all. Board members in each County would develop a sense of which of their colleagues would operate best at the County level, and which best at the State level.*

Thus, what we are envisioning is the following: The body of Board members in each County would elect a member to each Board at the State level. And the body of Board members at each State level would elect a member to each Board at the Nation level. And so on to the Global level.

It seems important to take special note of what is accomplished by this structure. Not only are Board members at each level, from local to global,

elected by persons who have opportunity to observe the depth and effectiveness of commitment to justice-for-all on the part of each candidate, but the
closer the process gets to the global level the more qualified become not
only the candidates, but those who do the voting!

In some ways, the most precarious selection is that for the Board members in the various Counties, because these are elected by voters whose
qualifications for evaluating depth of commitment in candidates, and whose
personal depth of commitment to vote by that standard, cannot be well
tested. As noted, an educational program can be offered, a sober atmosphere can be maintained at the voting places, and a personal *statement* of
commitment can be required. But that's the extent of the assurance that can
be achieved among voters in each County. However, in electing delegates to
the State level, each voter, being a Board member in some County, has been
picked out from among thousands as exceptionally committed. Therefore,
each voter for Board members at the State level will be not only exceptionally committed to justice-for-all at the County level, but also exceptionally
qualified to vote for candidates at the State level.

And the closer one gets to the Global level the more the voters for Board
members, and the more the Board members themselves, will have been
evaluated, tested, and passed by knowing colleagues. On the other hand, in
the *present* system of having each level of government official elected by
individuals in the general population, the closer one gets to the global level
the more precarious is the assurance we can feel about either the qualifications of the candidates to undertake such awesome responsibility or the
ability of the voter to judge such qualifications.

We can see more clearly now the importance of the area-wide meetings
among Board members at the various levels, beginning with meetings
among Board members in the various Counties. And meetings among the
Boards members in the various States would be important in preparation for
careful and responsible election of Board members at the level of the
Nation. In each case, because of many meetings for sharing experiences and
noting each other's qualifications, election would be with knowledge of the
depth and effectiveness of each candidate's commitment to justice-for-all.

*We note that each candidate elected at the Nation level will have been
elected at some previous time at some local level.* Each and every one will
have had such humble beginnings. And each will have been elected to
subsequent levels by persons who were themselves thus elected and were

well acquainted with all candidates. Thus, no one would arrive at the Global level without having at some point been elected at each of the lower levels in turn: District, County, State, Nation, and Regional. And everyone elected at every level above the District level would be elected by persons judged to be of exceptional moral maturity and integrity, and sincerely committed to justice-for-all.

*Thus, what is being envisioned here is a genuine federation of governments, from local to global.* It may not take the precise form suggested above. It probably will not. But it is hoped that the importance of the federated concept is apparent. The key feature in this envisioned federated structure is the assurance that government officials in positions of responsibility, and with tremendous coercive power, are selected by persons in a position to know them personally, and to know their true moral qualities.

To get some sense of the size of the governing bodies at each level, we take the United States as an example. Assume an average of ten Districts in each County. Thus, each County, on the average, would have ten Board members on each of its three Boards; a total of 30 Board members. Assume an average of 50 Counties per State. With each County sending three delegates to the State Boards, this would make about 50 members on each Board, or a total of 150 Board members. And at the level of the Nation, assuming our envisioned States would correspond to the existing 50 states, the numbers would be the same — three Boards of 50 members each.

These would seem to be workable numbers for decision-making bodies. If unanimity proved too difficult among 50 members, smaller committees could be authorized to come up with options to be voted on by the larger body. The total number of Board members at all levels across the country would then be about 80,000. This would not be too great a number to meet together on special occasions, though it would take a large sports arena to hold them all. In any given State, the total Board members at all levels would be less than 2,000. These could quite easily meet together for special occasions.

A major reason we have such oppressive economic and political structures regionally and globally is that their foundations in local caring community have crumbled. So, reconstituting both caring communities and their political structures at the local level must be among the first steps we take after personal commitments. Basically, it is caring community that must do the empowering, set the limits, monitor those limits, and pull back the power to the extent that it is misused. So, in order to keep political structures "in their place," caring communities must become and remain vital and vibrant. How we might take steps in that direction is a matter which should concern all of us, but dealing with it must be for another time.

It must now be apparent that what is being offered here is a vision of a radically new and different *economic* structure — radical in access to, and in sharing the economic benefits of, our common-heritage environment. It is a vision which is not only being offered, but advocated!

It also must be apparent to many readers that what is being offered and advocated here is a still more radical *political* structure. This must not be overlooked, for two reasons: it is political structure which must legitimate *and enforce* economic structure; and that which is thereby legitimated and enforced extends far beyond economic matters into all areas of our lives where there is a need to "prevent and remedy injustice." In short, the political structure we have sought to envision is the one which yields the maximum assurance of justice-for-all for all sentient beings on this earth for the foreseeable future.

## XIII-10: *Some Transition Considerations*

There are several transition considerations which remain to be addressed. There is the transition from (1) the present top-down, father-figure kind of government we generally have today, in one form or another, all over the world, to (2) the limited, truly just, local-to-global, community-based governmental forms so desperately needed.

There is the transition from the existing economic structures in which the most aggressive and acquisitive receive almost all the financial and other benefits from that common heritage capital to which each resident of this earth has a right to a fair share.

Then there are the transitions which individuals and groups will have to make in their personal lives in order both to meet personal needs and contribute to the larger transitions to truly just economic and political structures.

First, we consider the transition to a just economic structure, whereby each resident of this earth receives a fair share of income from our common heritage. The existing income from taxing land could be gradually shifted to "the Fund" while costs of governing are covered by increasing taxes on individuals and corporate entities "to the extent that they behave in ways that require governing." Also, taxes on land could be gradually increased to the point where they are in keeping with actual market value. In regard to income from technology, when existing patents to the inventors run out, they could be taken over by the Fund for collecting royalties from then on. Also, charges could gradually be increased for using technology clearly contributed by previous generations. How this could be done had best be determined by the senses of justice being employed in emerging, truly just political structures.

Regarding transition to truly federated political structures, this calls for revitalizing local communities. So many small towns and cities have become mere suburbs of metropolitan centers, with the corruption at the upper levels of government seeping down to the local regions. In a sense, the small community movement and the intentional community movement are efforts to reverse this process.[7]

As local communities regain their moral integrity they will tend to federate (as intentional communities are already doing), and thereby will be laying the foundation for more just political structures "local to global."

As for individual contributions to the needed transition, it is hoped that the vision presented here will encourage those who choose to commit themselves to justice for all "from local to global" to explore practical ways to shift their commitments, and thereby find one another in the process. When they do, they will begin joining together to form the kind of caring communities which are absolutely essential to realizing that vision.

It is not expected that our envisioned commitment complexes either could or should become a reality worldwide in the near future. But it is expected that if our vision proves inspiring, it can serve to guide us to countless satisfactions in step-by-step achievements along the way, and to full realization eventually. The first of such achievements must be at the local level, gradually reaching the global level within the next few decades. Again, what is advocated is radical *evolution*, not disruptive revolution.

---

7. Arthur Morgan, reviver of Antioch College in the twenties, and former Chairman of the Tennessee Valley Authority (TVA) saw this breakdown in local community coming over seventy years ago. So he founded Community Service, Inc., still operating in Yellow Springs, Ohio. He sets forth his concern in his *The Small Community*, pub. by Community Service Inc., P.O. Box 243. Yellow Springs. OH, 45387

Though the realization of that vision in its full, local-to-global blooming is still far off, the sprouts and buds which result from our initial, groping "steps" will so regenerate the social climate as to constitute the most difficult and essential level of achievement: that of being well underway. An old adage says, "A job well begun is half done." That's not literally true, but it contains a kernel of truth which is crucial to ultimate success.

The first steps in that commitment-building will necessarily be of a very personal nature for each of us, having to do with commitment shifts which we must make personally. The decisions which you and I will be called upon to make at this initial level will emerge from private consultations with your and my very personal senses of justice and conscience. And every personal commitment to justice-for-all constitutes a part of the total fabric of commitments comprising any political structure worthy of support.

So, let us not minimize the importance of such personal commitments. These really are the necessary first steps. Since our most fundamental commitment must be to justice for all, any step taken in keeping with one's sense of justice, even though it may not have any immediate structural implications, is a step in the right direction.

## XIII-11: *A Summary Challenge to Newt Gingrich*

Whereas, Gingrich would have us strengthen still more the economic, political, and thus social and cultural grip which corporate America has on the people of this country and the world, I would work toward containing it within the moral bounds of justice for all.

Whereas, what he advocates is a world of aggressive and competing power structures destined to continue to clash not only economically and politically, but also militarily, this volume envisions economic and political structures designed to assure that all aggressiveness and acquisitiveness is restrained and contained within the moral bounds of "justice for all"; this would tend to encourage mutual appreciation rather than constant competition to see who can win over others and become "#1."

Whereas, the kind of decentralizing he advocates is mere tokenism, sending back to the states only the most difficult, inadequately funded justice-for-all issues, this volume suggests a radical decentralizing of the existing top-down structure, a structure legitimated by a U.S. Constitution which was established by a manipulating coup just over two centuries ago.

Whereas, the governmental structure which he would essentially continue is primarily designed to generate economic, political and military power for corporate America in relation to other power centers in the world, what is here proposed is designed to assure justice for all residents of not only the United States but of the entire earth.

Whereas, his proposal for speeding up the growth of high-tech and Third Wave technology will inevitably bring about a global environmental collapse as well as social, psychological, cultural, and general social deterioration, the proposal contained herein suggests a pace which will rebuild the joys of meaningful community life from local to global, and thereby assure interesting cultural diversity all over the world.

Whereas, his proposal is so confused and disjointed that he was unable to pull it together into an integrated, rational, and inspiring conclusion in his final chapter, what is here proposed is designed to leave the reader inspired and energized to begin immediately to rebuild local economic, political, and community life.

Whereas, his proposal is built on the assumption that Americans are God's chosen people, this proposal takes the position that all sentient beings have Divine blessing and support so long as they remain within the moral bounds of justice for all.

Whereas, his proposals would continue the near-monopoly ownership of and financial and other benefits from our common heritage, the proposal here set forth would provide for a fair sharing of all benefits from our common heritage, and thereby bring about a new sense of fairness throughout all aspects of life.

Whereas, his proposal would continue the process of rich getting richer and poor getting poorer, this proposal would not only end poverty, but would do so without having to continue any of the dehumanizing aspects of the present welfare programs.

Whereas, his proposal puts increasing power over the lives of ordinary people in the hands of an aggressive and acquisitive elite constituting corporate America, this proposal would put increasing and rightful power into the hands of ordinary people all over the world, and thereby control over their own lives again.

Whereas, what he proposes would continue the empowerment of the descendants of those who virtually stole, and almost destroyed, that Early American Dream of building society from the ground up by way of justice for all, what is here proposed will contribute to Liberating the Early American Dream.

## XIII-12: *A Challenge to the Knowledge Industry*

I end this volume with a challenge to what Clark Kerr, former president of the University of California, has called "the knowledge industry." As we read what he wrote over three decades ago, and then note what is happening today in The Information Age, we cannot but marvel at his prophesy:

> Knowledge has certainly never in history been so central to the conduct of an entire society. What the railroads did for the second half of the last century and the automobile for the first half of this century may be done for the second half of this century by the knowledge industry: that is, to serve as the focal point for national growth. And the university is at the center of the knowledge process.[8]

At present this knowledge industry is feeding that most fundamental of all power for us humans, knowledge-power, into a society, an economy, a political climate, a military-industrial complex at an unprecedented pace. It is the technical knowledge being constantly fed into the corporate world of power brokers that is setting the hectic pace of modern life. All over the world, economic and military power of all kinds is being generated faster than we can institute humane and equitable control sufficient to assure that it is contained within the moral bounds of justice. Power tends to corrupt. And unless safeguards designed to prevent such corruptions are instituted at a pace comparable to the pace of power generation, it will corrupt. Presently, the pace at which knowledge-power is being generated at our major research universities, and then fed into the military-industrial complexes of the world, assures the corruption which is so widespread these days.

What is urgently needed, therefore, is for the major universities of the world to stop turning out knowledge-power *indiscriminately*, or to the highest bidder, and, instead, to direct their research toward how we can bring about a truly just world order. The best educators know that young people can be overwhelmed by their being permitted freedoms, and faced with options, at a pace greater than one with which they can cope in a good way. It is the same with a society. We don't turn college-level chemistry sets over to kindergarten children. But something equivalent to that is being done by universities in our day. They are turning over to a very immature and confused world civilization very potent knowledge-power at a pace with which our civilization cannot cope in a good way.

---

8. *The Uses of the University*, by Clark Kerr, pub. by Harper & Row, NY, 1963

A major obstacle to accepting such social responsibility in the past has been the belief among the intellectuals of Western civilization, especially those at our major universities, that the universe is just one big impersonal machine, and that there is no place in that paradigm for the human spirit beyond the inevitable death of the physical body. The good news is, however, that this discouraging, mechanistic conception of reality has now been discredited by quantum physics.[9]

This belief that human values, and humans themselves, have nothing but a very temporary existence in the larger scheme of things has been especially disconcerting to the most intellectually astute among us for about three centuries now — ever since mechanistic, Newtonian physics began dominating all serious attempts at understanding the world of the physical sciences.

This has now all changed. As yet, no new paradigm has been generally accepted as replacement for the mechanistic one. But, in a very real sense, the human spirit has been set free. There now exists a solid, scientific basis for a return to sanity. And, as our spirits begin to feel the new lease on life which is on the horizon, our finest minds will again begin to take heart. And as this happens I predict a turning away from indiscriminately feeding the power brokers of the world. As this happens we shall again see the universities of the world assume the kind of social responsibility which they at one time did assume, and of which they still are capable.

My conclusion is, then,
that Newt Gingrich's agenda for America
is not nearly radical enough,
would head us in exactly the wrong direction:
toward a more violent society,
toward the rich getting even richer
on the backs of the poor getting even poorer,
all the while damaging still further
an already endangered environment and ecosystem.
But our problem and our challenge
extends far beyond Newt Gingrich and his agenda.

---

9. See, for instance, a book by one of the main architects of this physics, Werner Heisenberg, *Physics and Philosophy*, Harper & Row, NY. 1958

It extends to the very structure
of the United States Government itself,
and to the Constitution upon which it is founded.
Dedication to that Constitution
has been heading us in the wrong direction.
It was founded by power-seekers,
and it is designed to serve the self-interests of power seekers.
But,
thanks to James Madison and a few others,
it has a "saving grace":
The Bill of Rights.
By means of that belated addition to the Constitution
it may still be possible to rescue it,
and all the residents of this planet,
from an otherwise tragic future of economic and other wars
among the power seekers of the world.
So, in this volume
I suggest that rescue is possible
by way of establishing caring communities
which,
if they are sufficiently committed to justice for all
can gradually,
by joining together in true federations,
from the bottom up rather than from the top down,
serve as the foundation
for building truly federated political structures, local to global.
Only then will we be assured
that the very much needed initiatives
and "free enterprises"
which we humans seem to be capable of dreaming up
will be at all times contained
well within
*the moral bounds of justice for all.*

# Appendix A

# *Calculating*

# *Common Heritage*

# *Dividends*

## A-1: *Contributions from Nature and Private Enterprise*

In this Appendix, I will conduct the calculations designed to determine what a fair share of income from our common heritage would have been in the United States for an average family of four if the proposal suggested here had been in effect for the past several decades. As in the rest of this volume, our senses of justice will be our main guide. More specifically, we seek a calculation of Common Heritage Dividend of which our senses of justice can approve.

We humans are constantly noting changes in what we consciously experience, and in what we then try to "make sense of." With each new experience we grope for concepts in terms of which we can "make sense" of it. This must be especially the case for a baby. Until we have developed adequate concepts and conceptual systems in terms of which ever new experiences can be organized, they tend to be disjointed and confusing. Until then, we vaguely experience objects moving about, sounds coming and going, various colors and shades of light brightening and fading, a sense of other persons approaching and leaving; emotions rising and falling, and pleasures and pains intensifying and subsiding.

With the help of these concepts and conceptual systems (which just seem to "come to mind" as needed) we can organize these experiences into tables, chairs, up, down, left, right, near, far, now, later, was, is, will be, may be, persons, friends, strangers, love, fear, right, wrong, just, unjust, yes, no. Gradually, we "sense" objective, ordered *reality* which we can "count on" in certain ways. Gradually, the changes we experience are conceived as changes in that objective reality. And as we conceptualize *patterns* in these changes, that objective reality is conceived as increasingly more complex, but also more orderly.

Among the first patterns to be noted by early humans were likely day following night and season following season, over and over again, year after year. Next, perhaps, came recognition of patterns in plant growth, from small seed to full bloom. The aging process in all living things must have been recognized early.

To the extent that we can conceptualize such an ordered reality we can begin to experiment with how it responds to our choices. Gradually we note a new kind of pattern: a pattern to the responses we receive from each kind of choice: a choice to move the hand results in actual hand movement; the choice to walk results in walking. As the child discovers patterns in body movement in response to choices, a sense of control, of power, *power over reality*, becomes part of the panorama of experiences.

The combination of (1) patterns in reality prior to our choices, and (2) patterns in the way reality responds to our choices makes for the history of events taking place in our world. And to the extent that we can pattern our choices themselves, by way of commitments, we can predict what the combination of these various patterns will bring about in "objective reality."

It is clear from the start of our education in the ways of this life that the changes which are brought about are not of our making — except for those choices and commitments which we make from time to time. These are of our making, but even these are in response to prior activities which we do not originate, only respond to. Something (Someone!?) else is the original actor, and remains at all times the main actor. For lack of a better name, we call it *Nature*.

Nature is constantly bringing about the changes we have been noting. Nature is bringing about the plant growth and growth we have noted above; and growth in animal bodies, ours included. Nature is constantly producing things we can eat, or make into edibles; constantly producing things we can make into shelter, and into tools. Nature is clearly the basic producer on this earth. All we do is respond to Nature's basic activities and activity patterns. We respond by way of our choices from among the options for choice which "come to mind." Even when humans participate in producing things, it is Nature's materials (wood, stone, slate, soil, clay, minerals) which are fabricated, and without which nothing physical can be produced.

These basic materials are part of our common heritage on this earth, a heritage which extends to all of our physical environment. We are immersed in our Nature-given common heritage and patterns of change.

It is only as we learn about Nature and its operations that we can bring about those changes which will yield more pleasant and happier results than otherwise would take place. As Francis Bacon said, "If you would control Nature, you must first obey her."

Down through the ages, humans have identified an ever-increasing number of Nature's patterns of change and ways to communicate about them. As noted, conceptualization is important for understanding Nature. It is also important for understanding each other, and for entering into mutually rewarding agreements with each other. By means of good communication we can accomplish together what we couldn't accomplish alone. And, in doing so, we get to know each other as a unique creation of that very special entity called *a person*.

Countless, inter-related concepts and conceptual systems, their ways of ordering our experiences of Nature and Nature's changes, and their various ways of aiding communication among persons have been passed down from generation to generation — not as private property, but as an ever-increasing *common* heritage. The most identifiable have taken the form of knowledge, knowledge about how Nature works, and how it will work differently by inserting carefully chosen and sculptured combinations of choices and commitments into Nature's processes.

We in this present generation are recipients of the present state of this "common heritage" of Nature's raw materials for building, of Nature's processes still ongoing, of reliable *knowledge* about Nature, Nature's materials, processes, changes, and patterns of change, and of cultural subtleties contributed to our generation by past generations.

This knowledge includes the intellectual foundations upon which today's high-tech is built. We in this present generation add to this knowledge, both as individuals, as identifiable groups, and as whole societies.

So, let us never forget that it is Nature that is the basic producer, and that we humans are come-lately partners only. An automated factory, for instance, is as much Nature working as the growing of yonder tree or the wind blowing through its branches. Indeed, to say that a factory is automated is to say that it is operating entirely by the laws of Nature, with no human participation, except for maintenance work. Humans have, of course, had to participate in the building of it, but it could only be built with Nature's materials and with Nature cooperating at every step by means of the reliable operation of Nature's processes and patterns of change.

## A-2: *Principles of Justice for Sharing Nature*

How, then, are the ever-more-valuable products of Nature, supplemented by human effort now and then here and there to be divided among the residents of the earth in a *just* way? How are we to distinguish between that part which is our *common* heritage, that which is private heritage, and that part which is justifiably attributed to private enterprise?

For lack of a better way to divide the goods and services which Nature has been manipulated into producing, we could just conclude that half should go to the Common Heritage Fund for general distribution, and the other half to the appropriate private parties. Without Nature, nothing would get produced. Without humans working with Nature, only the most primitive of our needs and desires would get satisfied. Each is a necessary condition for all but the most primitive productions.

However, Nature must be given the most credit. Humans are not sufficient unto themselves, but Nature evidently is. Indeed, Nature is still capable of producing all humans' most basic needs without any human assistance: air which is simply breathed in (by "natural instinct"), fruit to be simply picked off trees and berries off bushes, and the constant production and development of physical bodies which function "naturally" in ways which do our bidding in such remarkable detail that we tend to identify ourselves as spiritual *persons* with them right up to the later years when, as *persons*, we give directions to our bodies as clearly as ever but they simply don't respond as they once did.

Is it *just*, then, to attribute more of the products of our joint efforts to "private enterprise" than to Our Common Heritage? On the face of it, justice would seem to require attributing at least half of these products to Our Common Heritage for general distribution in some fair way.

There is still another consideration that bears on the question. All the changes that humans have brought about in Nature and Nature's processes are not positive contributions to future generations. Many are quite negative. The earth, its water, and its atmosphere are not as life-friendly as when handed down to us by previous generations. In working with Nature to produce all those high-tech methods and products (many of them ominous, like nuclear weapons and plants) Nature and Nature's creative processes have been severely damaged. The fertility of many soils has been greatly reduced, forests have been almost completely destroyed or reduced to tree farms, and the surface of the earth has become overcrowded. And the polluting human activity continues, almost all of it the result of "private enterprises."

In short, justice requires that those responsible for this destruction be charged for the cost of compensating future generations in some way. So, in the final, overall division of income from future production, justice might call for allotting to private enterprise less than half the total profits from the production of goods and services. We keep these various considerations in mind as we turn to actual calculations in dollars and cents.

## A-3: *Some exploratory calculations*

In this section, we calculate what the distribution of income from leasing our common heritage among the various fifths (upper fifth in income, lowest fifth, etc.) would be like in three different eventualities.

*Eventuality #1:* Assume that 50% of total US income were assigned to a Common Heritage Fund, and this income distributed roughly equally among US residents, rich and poor alike.

*Eventuality #2:* Same, except assume 35% is assigned to the Fund.

*Eventuality #3:* Same, except assume 25% is assigned to the Fund.

We begin by noting some relevant facts. In 1996, the total income in 1996 U.S. dollars is projected to be about $7,000,000,000,000 (seven trillion dollars).[1] Of this total, about 52% is projected to go to the upper 20% in income level, and about 3% to the lowest 20%.[2]

*Investigating Eventuality #1:* We assume, then, that a full 50% of this seven trillion 1996 US dollars is somehow transferred to the Common Heritage Trust Fund. In this eventuality, I estimate that about 32% of the 3.5 trillion dollars (50% of the 7 trillion) would be taken from the highest-

---

1. Projected from Table 692, page 452, of *Statistical Abstracts*, 1995, compiled by the US Department of Commerce.
2. The distribution for each fifth is estimated to be, respectively, about 52%, 24%, 15%, 6%, and 3% of total national income. (From Table 741 of *Statistical Abstracts*. The trends from which these projections are made are given in *The Work of Nations*, page 197, by Robert Reich, pub. by Random House, NY, 1991.

income fifth, 11% from the next highest, 6% from the middle fifth, and 1% from the next to lowest fifth, thus leaving the very lowest fifth untouched. These figures are based on the assumption that at present the upper fifth is getting about 32% of common heritage income, the next fifth about 11%, and so on.

This would make the distribution among quintiles (i.e., fifths), *before any equal dividend distribution back to each of them,* as follows: 20%, 13%, 9%, 5%, 3%. *After* adding to each quintile an equal 1/5 of the 50% to be distributed by the Common Heritage Fund, the final distribution among quintiles would be roughly as follows: 30% to the upper, 23% to the next, then 19%, 15%, and 13%. Those in the highest quintile would still be getting more than twice the lowest, and there would still be hundreds of millions of dollars difference between the lowest individual incomes and the highest. People could still get very rich, but not at the expense of others.

We next estimate what the average Common Heritage Dividend per U.S. resident would be under this eventuality. Dividing the Trust's 3.5 trillion dollars by an estimated U.S. population of 260 million, we get about $13,500 for the average Common Heritage Dividend per capita. Multiplying this by four, we get an estimated $54,000 annual Common Heritage Dividend for a family of four. Added to this would be income from wages, salaries, and investments.

Also, many would choose not to work, to work only part-time, to have only one family member working (like old times!), or to have two or more family members work part-time. Add to this a general atmosphere of fair dealing and no humiliating welfare interviews, and one can imagine an entirely different social and economic climate than exists today.

It might be argued that because of reduced return on investment, the total national income would be reduced. This could be. The rate of growth might, in any case, be slowed. But that would seem to be a desirable outcome, for ecological, psychological, social, and spiritual health. What might also be reduced would be annual *increases* in national income, because of environmental restrictions and restraints on trading with global economies which don't respect human rights. But it seems clear that there exists at this time an economic pie large enough to assure a sizeable slice for everyone. And since our main concern is fairness rather than opportunity to accumulate large fortunes, even assigning 50% of annual income to Our Common Heritage Fund seems a practical possibility.

A truly just political system might judge it fair that larger dividends should go to people living in areas with high cost of living, or to areas where their ancestors have lived for several generations and made a substantial contribution to the technology of the area. It would also likely be judged fair that immigrants from other areas would not immediately get a full dividend from the new area. It might be, for instance, that, for the first year, a new resident would receive only her or his dividend from the *previous* area, and that it would gradually decrease over a twenty-year period as the dividend from the new area increased over the same twenty-year period. Such a practice would discourage immigration for economic reasons only.

A major question would be what dividend should go to children. Whatever the amount, it seems clear that a large amount should be held in trust for education and to provide a capital fund with which to begin the life of an adult human being. Thus, parents should not be rewarded for having offspring. They might be allotted a certain amount to cover costs of parenting, but the rewards of parenting their own children should be sufficient in itself. Thus, if *less* than the average dividend is allotted to children (perhaps to be increased over a twenty-year period), then this would leave something *greater* than the average for the annual dividend for a full adult — perhaps as much as $17,000 as an average in the case of Eventuality #1.

*Investigating Eventuality #2:* In this eventuality we assume that 35% of total national income is assigned to the Fund. I estimate that 25% of the total will come from the fifth (highest income) quintile, 7% from the fourth, and 3% from the middle quintile. After adding back each quintile's 7% share (one fifth of the 35%), we get roughly the following distribution: 34% of total national income to the fifth quintile, 24% to the fourth, 19% to the third, 13% to the second, and 10% to the fifth.

We note that in this eventuality the quintile of greatest income retains a considerably larger percentage of the total: more than three times the lowest and almost twice the middle quintile.

In this case, we would have only 35% of the seven trillion dollar national income to divide among the country's 260 million residents, or about $9,400 per capita per year, making an average of $37,200 per family of four. Again, depending on the amount of dividends to children, this might give the average individual adult as much as $12,000 per year.

*Investigating Eventuality #3:* In this eventuality we assume that only 25% of total national income is assigned to the Fund. I estimate that the fifth quintile would contribute about 18%, the next, about 5%, and the middle, about 2%. The final quintile distribution, then, is estimated to be as follows: 39%, 24%, 18%, 11%, 8%.

In this case we would have only 25% of the seven trillion dollars to divide among the country's residents, or about $6,750 per capita, thus making the average dividend for a family of four about $27,000 for the year.

What, then, are we to say about these eventualities? My intuitive judgment is that the middle eventuality is the one which would turn out to be most just. This is why, in the Preface, I have suggested a figure of $36,000 per year in 1995 dollars for a family of four.

But we do have a way to arrive at an approximate figure by a different, more down-to-earth approach. That is, we have a way to estimate the possible income from at least the land part of our common heritage. The part contributed by knowledge, such as of technology, would, of course, be more difficult to estimate.

We are forced to get national land values in an indirect way, because land is taxed only at local and state levels. But the U.S. Census Bureau does issue approximate figures every five years, based on their surveys.[3] The last figures available at this writing are for 1991, but if we project from the figures given from as far back as 1961 we can estimate that by 1996 the *assessed* value of all U.S. "real property" (land and improvements) to be about $9 trillion in 1996 dollars. The Census Bureau estimates that land values constitute about 40% of this total, or about $3.6 trillion.

However, we can be sure that this figure doesn't include all valuable land. In "company towns," for instance, valuable land is normally grossly undervalued. In many cases companies are given land in return for offered jobs. Also, a very large part of land in western United States is owned by national and state governments, and therefore is not included in the above figure. For these reasons, I believe that if all land in the US were assessed the figure for land would be closer to $5 trillion.

Also, I emphasized that these are "assessed" values because assessed values are normally far below market values. It is true that in California, in response to that notorious "Proposition 13," the two values tend to be much closer than in other states. But, even there, the higher assessments only

---

3. Table C, page XIV in Volume 2 of the 1992 U.S. Chamber of Commerce Bulletin called *Census of Governments*

apply to properties sold after 1978. So, those which remain unsold, or simply traded, aren't covered by Proposition 13.

A researcher in this area has told me that he estimates the market values across the country to average about 3.25 times assessed value. Taking the conservative figure of 3 to 1, and multiplying the $5 trillion by that three, we get an estimated market value of land in 1996, in 1996 dollars, at about $15 trillion.

What, then, could this land be leased for if it were owned by our Common Heritage Trust? I estimate that it would yield about 10% annually, on average — urban land would bring more than this and other land would bring less. The total annual income, then would be about $1.5 trillion. Dividing by 260 million we get an average Common Heritage Dividend from land of $5,800. I assume that our common heritage of technology is generating at least as much as land. Assuming this, we get an estimated Common Heritage Dividend per capita of about $11,600 per year, or about $46,000 for a family of four.

This figure is admittedly very speculative, but it does seem to indicate that the an average of $36,000 per year for a family of four is the right order of magnitude. In any case, the above calculations are the basis for the $36,000 figure given in the Preface.

How close this figure is to the one which would have been actual if Our Common Heritage Fund had been in operation in 1996 is not as important as the following realizations:

*Realization #1:* That income from our common heritage is presently being all but completely monopolized by the most aggressive and acquisitive individuals all over the world, and with the "legal" support of governments which they largely control.

*Realization #2:* That the income which would accrue to all the residents of the world if the financial and other benefits of our common heritage were justly distributed is so substantial that there would be no abject poverty anywhere.

*Realization #3:* That the denial of our common heritage rights is such a severe injustice, with such tragic consequences, that a major effort must be generated to remedy it as quickly as possible.

*Realization #4:* That, until this remedy is accomplished, existing social programs should not only generally be continued, but often increased.

# Index